TROJAN HORSES

TROJAN HORSES

*Deception Operations
in the Second World War*

Martin Young and
Robbie Stamp

THE BODLEY HEAD
LONDON

For Sue Young and Sue Stamp

A CIP cataloguing in publication data
is available from the British Library

ISBN 0 370 31127 2

Copyright © Martin Young and Robbie Stamp 1989

Printed in Great Britain for
The Bodley Head Ltd
31 Bedford Square
London WC1B 3SG
by Mackays of Chatham PLC

First published in Great Britain in 1989

CONTENTS

LIST OF ILLUSTRATIONS
AND CREDITS

1 (*Above*) Dummy mobile cruiser in production[1]
  (*Below*) The completed model ready for battle in North Africa.[1]
2 (*Above*) After sizing, a dummy's turret is given a first coat of paint.[1] (*Below*) Sunshields were used to disguise tanks as three-ton lorries.[1]
3 (*Above and below*) Dummy Sherman tanks positioned in the Wadis, known as 'Simpole Street'. These fake tanks replaced real tanks which were repositioned to take part in the Battle of El Alamein.[1]
4 (*Opposite above*) A dummy twenty-five-pounder gun trailer and guard.[1] (*Opposite below*) The lorry was inflated with a foot pump. (Designed by Messrs R.F.D. Co. Ltd, Godalming.)[1]
5 (*Above*) Also of 'pneumatic construction', this tank was used in many theatres of war. When deflated, it could be packed into a carrying case a little larger than an average cricket bag. (Designed by Messrs Dunlop Rubber Co.)[1]
6 (*Above*) Fake landing craft, the so-called 'Big Bobs', were used as decoys.[1] (*Below*) They formed part of FUSAG, the successful attempt to build a phantom army in south-east England and East Anglia.[2]
7 Wartime posters which neatly illustrate the paradox of successful deception operations.[1]
8 (*Above*) The poster illustrates the way in which information could be pieced together like a jigsaw puzzle.[1]
9 (*Above*) General the Hon. Sir Harold Alexander C-in-C Middle East (*left*), with Lieutenant-General Montgomery, Commander Eighth Army.[1] (*Below*) Alexander before Operation Diadem.[1]

10   (*Above*) Churchill's support for the London Controlling Section was vital to the success of deception operations in the Second World War.[1]

11   (*Opposite above*) General Sir Archibald Wavell, a firm believer in the value of deception, conferring with British staff officers in India in December 1942.[1] (*Oppposite below*) Monty talks to troops, post D-Day.[1]

12   (*Above*) Colonel David Strangeways worked closely with Dudley Clarke in the Middle East and commanded 'R' Force, Monty's tactical deception unit attached to 21 Army Group.

13   (*Above*) Colonel David Hunt, a university don who became involved in Intelligence and deception work.

14   (*Above*) Dr Peter Tooley, the young naval officer who supervised the launching of the Big Bobs during the build-up to D-Day.

15   (*Above*) Terence O'Brien, the Australian pilot who flew on many deception missions for Colonel Peter Fleming in the Far East.

16   (*Above*) General Sir Charles Richardson, the mastermind behind the deception operations prior to the Battle of El Alamein.

[1] Copyright Imperial War Museum.
[2] Copyright Peter Tooley.

LIST OF MAPS

ACKNOWLEDGEMENTS

This project was first suggested to us by Bill Jones and John Chesterman to whom we owe a real debt of thanks. We would also like to acknowledge the tremendous amount of help we have enjoyed from the following people: Henrietta Brunt, who carried out many of our interviews with the men and women involved at the coalface of deception; Dee Brady, who was a most valuable assistant in all the preparation work; Chris Holifield and Derek Johns at the Bodley Head for their helpful and constructive general comments on the original MS and Corinne Hall at the Bodley Head for her studious and detailed editing work on the final text. Thanks also to Colin Stamp for all his careful work on the MS.

Our thanks are due above all to the many men and women, not all of whom appear below, who gave us their time and their memories. In structuring and editing the book some have been lost, but all were interesting in their own right. We thank them for sharing this extraordinary period of their lives with us and thereby with you. We owe a special debt to Nigel West for his invaluable advice at the beginning of our research.

PROLOGUE

This book is full of lies.

There is here an impressive catalogue of lies employed exclusively to protect the truth. We are told the 'lies' by the few men and women still alive who remember how the deception-planners operated. Some of them constructed the deceits, some had the job of carrying them out:

> Who built the seven towers of Thebes?
> The books are filled with the names of Kings.
> Was it Kings who hauled the craggy blocks of stone? . . .
> In the evening when the Chinese wall was finished where did the masons go?
>
> Bertolt Brecht

This book is about the people – the kings *and* the masons of deception. Sadly, there are not many left.

It was, typically, Winston Churchill who placed deception and clandestine operations in their true context. At a conference in Teheran in 1943 he told Stalin, in a phrase that has become understandably famous: 'In wartime, truth is so precious that she should always be attended by a bodyguard of lies.'

This clever conceit of Churchill's is said to have delighted Stalin and in the pages that follow we have tried to produce a testament to the men and women who made up, in every sense of the expression, that bodyguard.

We make no pretence to write a definitive history of deception operations in World War Two. That work has been done by others far more qualified. Charles Cruickshank's *Deception in World War II* is one of the more authoritative works to date. His

1

book draws on official papers in the Public Records Office at Kew and the National Archives of the United States in Washington DC. *Strategic and Operational Deception in the Second World War*, a series of lengthy essays edited by Michael Handel and published more recently has been invaluable. *British Intelligence in the Second World War*, the Official History of Intelligence by Professor Harry Hinsley, although only touching on deception in Volume 3 Part 2, has provided valuable background. Ronald Lewin's *Ultra Goes to War* has done the same. Anthony Cave Brown's best-selling *Bodyguard of Lies*, is remarkably comprehensive. Many of the practitioners have at one stage or another written their story and contributed to our understanding. Dennis Wheatley for example, the author of thrillers and books on the occult, has written *The Deception Planners*. David Mure, who worked in the Middle East, has written *Master of Deception* and *Practice to Deceive*, his tributes to one of the war's most distinguished deceivers, Dudley Clarke. Some of these personal memories are decidedly partisan.

We have also been able to draw on a number of papers, the most useful of which has undoubtedly been Colonel Roger Fleetwood Hesketh's manuscript completed in February 1949, *Fortitude: A History of Strategic Deception in North Western Europe – April, 1943, to May, 1945*. Hesketh's report is still not widely available but we have been able also to draw on other unpublished papers, which are less well known.

A selected bibliography lists these books and some of the papers which we, at least, found most helpful.

This material has been drawn on not simply in an attempt to write another history of deception. What follows is a mosaic. The interviews we conducted are about impressions and feelings as much as the day-to-day business of being a deceiver. The historical material can fill in some of the missing pieces of the mosaic, but inevitably many of them are still missing.

We are still waiting for the 'official' history and we have been since 1980. Michael Howard, until recently Regius Professor of Modern History at Oxford, was charged with the responsibility for writing the official history by the last Labour government in the late 1970s. He has had his manuscript ready since the beginning of the decade. As we complete this manuscript in the early summer of 1989 permission to publish Professor Howard's book from Margaret Thatcher's government has still not been forthcoming. Reticence in this instance is surely absurd. Of course there are some operational matters which should not be made public and no researcher or historian can fail to respect oaths of confidentiality sworn many years ago, and the loyalty of those who have guarded secrets down the years. Nonetheless it is a shame that after fifty years this government does not see fit to free some of those oath takers to share with a wider audience those elements of their own special wartime contribution which cannot today have any conceivable bearing on National Security. Soviet Intelligence would, after all, make short shrift of an army of rubber tanks and wooden landing craft in East Anglia.

For a large part of the fifty years since the start of the Second World War, the story of another kind of war lay hidden. Sir Winston Churchill, writing in 1951, declared that 'it would not be proper even now to describe all methods employed to mislead the enemy'. Accordingly we can read the biographies and autobiographies of the war's famous men, Montgomery, Ismay, Churchill himself, and be hard put to find more than a hint of the complex intelligence war that the Allies waged against Nazi Germany and Japan. There were glimpses, though.

A year before Churchill's warning, and indeed possibly part of its inspiration, Duff Cooper published his novel *Operation Heartbreak*, a fictional account of the most famous popular deception of the war. The real story that lay behind the novel was no less dramatic.

The dead body of an officer of the Royal Marines, Major Martin, was washed ashore in Spain. He had been launched into the water off Huelva at 4.30 in the morning on April 30 1943. In the pocket of his tunic the Spanish authorities found a carefully crafted assortment of papers and letters. There was a letter from his fiancée Pam, one from his tailor and another from his bank manager, all designed to make him as English as could be. Martin's corpse also carried more sensitive material at a time when the Germans were anticipating an assault somewhere in the Mediterranean, but were undecided about where it would come. There were letters from the Vice-Chief of Imperial General Staff, General Nye, to General Alexander and from the Chief of Combined Operations, Lord Mountbatten, to Admiral Cunningham and General Eisenhower, all designed to draw attention away from Sicily and to turn German planners in the direction of the Peloponnese and Sardinia. They were part of a cover plan codenamed Barclay, and the corpse had been diligently researched to look convincing as the notional Major Martin. The Spanish authorities found the corpse and the papers, which were duly passed on to the Germans. There is evidence that the information that the papers contained went all the way to Hitler himself, who believed in the 'papers found on the body of a British courier washed up on the Southern coast of Spain'.[1]

At the time of writing his book *Operation Heartbreak* Duff Cooper was British Ambassador in Paris and a close friend of Churchill's, so this first significant, if thinly disguised, breach of the Official Secrets Act went unpunished. But part of the Establishment felt that a trust had been betrayed.

In 1953 Ewan Montagu wrote *The Man Who Never Was*, his version of the same operation which had been codenamed Mincemeat. Montagu was intimately involved in the conception and execution of the complex plot and in the far from easy task of procuring a suitable corpse. The book was made into a popular film.

The other story which emerged in the early 1950s and which captured the public's imagination was the tale of the substitution of Montgomery by an obscure actor, Clifton James, at the time a soldier in the Pay Corps, who bore a striking resemblance to the famous general.

The plan was that Clifton James should attempt the performance of his life and go on an inspection of troops in Gibraltar a few days before D-Day. The intention was to persuade the Germans that the senior British officer responsible for the planning of the invasion was miles away from the beachheads of Northern Europe at a crucial moment in the run up to D-Day. The plan, developed by Lieutenant-Colonel J. V. B. Jervis Reid, was a small part of Copperhead, a strategic deception plan designed to draw attention away from north-west Europe towards Italy and the South of France.

After the war this piece of play-acting was made into a film *I Was Monty's Double*, starring Clifton James as himself and as Montgomery and Sir John Mills as a Secret Service agent. In the film, after the ruse had been successfully carried out with the right number of near misses, Sir John rescued the hapless 'Monty' from a kidnap attempt by a crack squad of German troops. They had been landed by submarine at the dead of night and had definitely been fooled by the successful substitution.

The film does not stick too closely to the facts and belongs firmly to the *Boy's Own Paper* tradition of spy stories, which characterised for so many years most of the public understanding of the secret war the Allies fought against the Germans.

Geoffrey Barkas's lyrical book about visual deception in the Middle East, *The Camouflage Story*, published in 1952, was another glimpse for anybody beginning to put the jigsaw together. One of the most colourful and partisan of the contributors to the gradually emerging picture was Sefton Delmer in his 1962 book *Black Boomerang*, about black wireless propaganda and the follow up, *The Counterfeit Spy*, 1971.

Big pieces of the jigsaw were still missing, until in 1972 J. C. Masterman, a Vice-Chancellor of Oxford University, and former international hockey and tennis player, opened the flood gates on the 'secret' Second World War, with the publication of *The Double Cross System*. It was an account of the Twenty (XX) Committee on which he sat throughout the war, which controlled a network of double agents. The Committee decided, along with a number of other secret organisations, what information could safely be given to the Germans. As if to foreshadow more recent events, and especially the protracted litigation over Peter Wright's *Spycatcher*, Masterman had his book published initially in the United States by Yale University Press. Here was the first elaborate clue, for those not already in the know, to a network of deception in the Second World War that operated on a scale few had guessed at — a scale that went far beyond the exploits of Clifton James and the fictional Major Martin.

The revelations upset a lot of people, those who felt that an important confidence and trust had been breached and also former members of other branches of the intelligence service who felt that their contribution had been undervalued. The internecine strife that had sometimes threatened to damage operations during the war resurfaced. The trickle of reminiscences swelled.

One of the most significant of these was the publication in 1974 of *The Ultra Secret* by Group Captain F. W. Winterbotham, which revealed for the first time the work done in cryptanalysis at Bletchley Park, the story of the Enigma machine and the Ultra decrypts. What Churchill called his 'most secret source' is a vital complement to the history of deception.

The world in which the deception-planners worked and were able to keep their secrets was very different from today. At the heart of their task lay the need to manage information, huge amounts of it, which needed to be controlled and manipulated delicately and firmly.

Two world wars forced the pace of technology. In terms of armaments the war opens with the famous, if romanticised, image of the Polish Cavalry charging German tanks and finishes with the mushroom clouds over Hiroshima and Nagasaki. A host of other technologies developed rapidly under the stringent necessities of war, among them 'information technology', wireless communications, sonar and radar. But the planners still had no computers. They and their military masters co-ordinated large amounts of complicated and detailed information without databases and satellite communications.

Today's information technology, spy satellites, computer analysis and electronic eavesdropping would have made their job almost impossible. Both the military and the public now have access to far greater sources of information. Now, whenever the military even considers a course of action there is a fair chance that the enemy will already be in a position to analyse their intentions. The public will also expect to be informed, largely through television. We demand the picture, we wish to scrutinise the available data.

All this would have made the job of the deceivers well-nigh impossible. For those of us born since 1945, the only war we have experienced was the Falklands conflict. For those who worked in television it was hard to understand the change in the ground rules, the need for the all-seeing eye of the media to be deliberately and voluntarily blinded by the needs of the state. When Brian Hanrahan, the BBC man posted with the Task Force, told us about the latest Harrier raid on the Falklands he perhaps came closest to defining the change that the war had wrought on the media's inbuilt self-confidence, a confidence bred of at least three decades of increasingly liberal communication.

Why did we want to know about the Harriers? We wanted to know whether 'our boys' had survived or been shot down by the enemy. As a journalist Hanrahan, born not so far away from the immediate post-war era, probably expected as his right a view of the operational orders, a casualty list if such existed, a detailed debriefing from the officer in charge. What he got was a dilemma. He could not reveal the number of Harriers that were operational. He could, in the report he devised, tell us that all the planes and their crews survived: 'I counted them all out and I counted them all in again.' It was a responsible way of telling the story, but it represented a return to a kind of censorship that journalists have not, since the Second World War, had to cope with. His considered sentence was also one of which the clever men who planned the deception operations on such a grand scale during the Second World War would have approved. In this book a world re-emerges that is very different from that of the West in the 1980s.

Fortunately for the inhabitants of the Falklands the world of General Galtieri was undemocratic, repressive and, ultimately, unsustainable. For Winston Churchill the world of Adolf Hitler and the Third Reich was a manifestation of evil. The Allies were not struggling with the rival claims of right-wing rebels and left-wing dictators or vice-versa, they were dealing with a man who had put himself and his powerful military dictatorship outside the law, a man who had already swept through the sovereignty of several nations, a man whose racial policies were evil. So the nation rallied to the cause.

The military heroes and indeed the ordinary servicemen who gave their efforts and, sometimes, their lives to defeat Hitler are well documented elsewhere. This book tries to give credit to those who, with their brains, sought to confuse a powerful enemy and by forcing him to squander his efforts, diverted his purposes, and saved the lives of those colleagues who were in the front line. It also celebrates those who were not entrusted with the 'big picture' but dutifully gave their labour to causes that they sometimes must have suspected were of doubtful value or even, on a bad day, a complete waste of time. But here again a different age, a different view, obtained. Repeatedly, when interviewing the electricians, plasterers and carpenters, the people who were the 'nuts and bolts' of deception, we asked the question, 'Did you not ever think for a moment, "This is a nonsense, why am I wasting my time playing with strange toys that can have no perceptible effect on the enemy?" '

The simple answer is 'No', they did not. When the nation was bent to the task of war, you did as you were told. More than that, both the Ministry of Information and commanding officers were constantly reminding you not to talk loosely about your work. You had to understand the need for unquestioning obedience, exemplified in the slogan: 'Careless Talk Costs Lives.'

Contained in the message of that best known of wartime posters are, paradoxically, the two most important elements of successful deception: the need for utmost security and the simultaneous ability to leak selected information and disinformation to the enemy. In other words deliberately, on occasion, to make your 'talk' careless.

Brigadier Dudley Clarke, commander of the first fully fledged tactical deception force in the Second World War, grasped the significance of that paradox. On the wall behind the desk in his office in a building in Cairo, which had once been a brothel, there was a poster, which was a picture of all the little bits of a jigsaw puzzle jumbled up together and the burden of the message underneath was: don't give the enemy even little bits of information that he can put together. Dudley Clarke's interpretation was that that *was* just the way to achieve a successful deception plan. The trick was not to give the enemy the plan on a plate, but through a multitude of channels to give him glimpses, little bits of truth and falsehood and let him piece it all together.

In the Second World War, particularly after the Americans added their vital economic muscle, war became a question of which protagonist could exert the most pressure of men and materiel on the conflict. Industrial muscle would win in the end.

But another group of military men, some of whom speak in the pages of this book, believed that the application of intelligence, in every sense of the word, could speed the path to victory and save hundreds and thousands of lives along the way. In many of the cases recalled, not a shot was fired in anger. Theirs was a war of the mind. In *The Great War* (Volume One) Winston Churchill summed it up with characteristic grandeur: 'There are many kinds of manoeuvres in war, some only of which take place on the battlefield. There are manoeuvres far to the flank or rear. There are manoeuvres in time, in diplomacy, in mechanics, in psychology; all of which are removed from the battlefield, but react often decisively upon it, and the object of it all is to find easier ways, other than sheer slaughter, of achieving the main purpose.'

Geoffrey Barkas, a camouflage expert and one of Churchill's 'mechanics', echoes this in his book of recollections about visual deception in the Middle East. The Battle of El Alamein had been fought and won. It was a vital turning point, and the first real success that Churchill could announce to an increasingly restive House of Commons. In that historic speech he called it 'The end of the beginning'. Barkas writes that: 'Though none of us was so foolish as to think that it had been won by conjuring tricks with stick, string and canvas, we could at least feel that we had earned our keep. It was good to feel that camouflage had helped to put the fighting men into battle on more favourable terms, and so to purchase victory at a lower price in blood.'[2]

Brigadier Michael Calvert, who tells his tales of deception below, remembers the group of people with whom he trained in a special commando ski battalion at the beginning of the war. Many of them went on to play a significant role, but as young soldiers they gathered together to discuss ways in which the ritualised slaughter of the First World War could be avoided: 'It became like a sort of university in the Renaissance, that was my impression. We were all determined not to fight another 1914–18 War, where your skill appeared to have no bearing on whether you were killed or not. We felt that in the next war we should go for the enemy's guts, his communications, his headquarters and we should start revolutions behind his lines.'[3]

Brigadier Calvert refers to acts of sabotage and subversion, the world of SOE, the commandos, the SAS, the SBS, Force 136, but his words could equally refer to the need to use your brains to out-think the enemy, to creep inside his mind and help him to do some of his own thinking, not too much, just enough.

The battle for the senses was on. The enemy's eyes could be deceived by inflatable tanks or fake airfields; his hearing could be tricked by recorded sounds of revving engines, shouted orders, hammered rivets and muffled oaths; his judgement could be undermined with a tangled web of doctored information and rumour fed through a network of double agents or filtered through the conversation at diplomatic dinner parties in Lisbon and Stockholm, and in pubs the length and breadth of Britain. Dead bodies, dead pigeons, fake maps, fake car accidents, fake orders, fake wireless traffic, fake marriage announcements in newspapers, 'ghost' armies, even to the ludicrous – exploding coal and camel dung. The list is endless.

Stop and think a while about all the ways in which you receive the information which informs your opinions, shapes your judgement and your decisions. Imagine what it is like in time of war, thousands of decisions large and small being made every day: an individual soldier in the half dark deciding which shape to shoot at, a battlefield commander trying to assess the disposition of his enemy: how many? where? who? Intelligence officers piecing evidence together and passing their assessments on; strategic decision makers planning long term, and committing men and material to the battle. Thousands of pieces of information to be gathered, sifted and acted upon.

Imagine again a group of people systematically subverting the various sources of all that information. That is just what the deceivers during the Second World War set out to do in the Allied cause, and in their fight against Germany, they had an unwitting ally, an increasingly paranoid Adolf Hitler. Until early 1944, Hitler routinely played off Admiral Canaris's Military Intelligence organisation, the Abwehr, against the ambitions of Heinrich Himmler's SS Intelligence. As a result of the divisions that he himself created he ensured that the blandishments of ambitious men distorted his own perception of events. There were too many men prepared to tell him only what they thought he wanted to hear, and too many times when his own preconceptions played into the hands of the deceivers.

Truth, in a totalitarian state, is an unreliable commodity.

Two quotations highlight the enigma of truth in wartime. Von

Clausewitz, the military historian, recognised that: 'War is the province of uncertainty: three fourths of those things upon which action in war must be calculated are hidden more or less in the clouds of great uncertainty.'[4]

Deception probes that uncertainty.

In his stimulating book *On the Psychology of Military Incompetence* Norman Dixon claims that: 'War is primarily concerned with two sorts of activity – the delivering of energy and the communication of information.'[5]

Deception feeds off the communication of information.

The application for the first time of deception techniques in every theatre of war was one of the most significant innovations of the Second World War. There were vast inventions of notional armies. There were whole tank divisions which had been blown up with foot-pumps. There were cardboard men to man wooden guns. All of this, from the grand strategic deceptions, through the mass of specific tactical deceptions on the battlefield, to the almost farcical enthusiasms of individual deceivers, was controlled by a handful of clever men, whose style and character will become evident in what follows.

When Neville Chamberlain read his grim message to the British on the BBC at 11.15 a.m. on September 3 1939, Britain was entering into a conflict which has become known as the 'Second World War', but which at the time looked like the latest in a long line of European civil wars. At the beginning of the war it was Britain with her Empire at her back and France who faced Germany. This was not the triumvirate of Britain, America and Russia, which in 1945 marched into Berlin and finished the war. That morning, the support of the two 'Superpowers' looked a very distant prospect.

Rearmament had only started seriously in 1936 and although Britain began late she rearmed relatively quickly. Despite the late surge in activity, Britain's military and political leaders both perceived themselves to be, and were, vulnerable. After the lull of the Phoney War, the Fall of France and the Dunkirk evacuation increased that vulnerability to the point of desperation.

By contrast, the future for Germany looked far from bleak. Hitler summed it all up in an after-dinner conversation recorded by Martin Boorman early in the war: 'We need have no fear for our future. I shall leave behind me not only the most powerful army, but also a Party that will be the most voracious animal in World history.'[6]

Interestingly, Hitler's great period of deception and bluff occurred when he knew himself to be vulnerable, in the 1930s. Hitler and Nazi

Germany had enjoyed a staggering run of success between 1933 and 1939, the march back into the Demilitarised Zone of the Rhineland, the Anschluss, the Sudetenland and the entry into Prague had created an atmosphere of confidence, which belied what Hitler and his generals knew to be major vulnerabilities in the Third Reich. The brutal success of Blitzkrieg heralded a new era. With German tanks storming through Europe, and with the unexpectedly rapid collapse of the French and the humiliation of the British at Dunkirk, Hitler was squaring up to an enemy who he was convinced would be destroyed with blood and iron. The days of cunning and diplomatic brinkmanship had gone.

Michael Handel, Professor of National Security Affairs at the US Army War College in Pennsylvania, has summed up the British position in 1939 and the early days of the war: 'The side which *a priori* recognises its own numerical and material inferiority is anxious to avail itself of all possible courses of action . . . their early defeat in 1940 and the threat of invasion left the British no choice – they had to resort to deception.'[7]

The Germans practised both tactical and strategic deception, but they never developed the systematic application of deception techniques in every theatre of war the way the British did. Nazi ideology and military strategy on the grand scale, increasingly dictated by one man, were predicated on strength. Revealingly, initial American suspicion about the value of 'deception' illustrates the same point about perceived and real weakness and strength. America had muscle, so why bother with these games?

General Sir Archibald Wavell, Commander-in-Chief in the Middle East (1939–41), was probably the first senior British commander in World War Two to use deception effectively. Wavell, who had learned his craft with General Sir Edmund Allenby in the Palestinian Campaigns in the First World War, was convinced of the value of misleading the enemy in any way he could. He himself wrote in a memo to the Chiefs of Staff in 1940 that: 'The elementary principle of all deception is to attract the enemy's attention to what you wish him to see and to distract his attention from what you do not wish him to see. It is by these methods that the skilful conjuror obtains his results.'[8]

Wavell's conjuror was Brigadier Dudley Clarke (also known as Galveston and Colonel Croft Constable), a regular Gunner, and considered by many to be the Father of Deception. Dennis Wheatley, the famous novelist and himself a member of the inner circle of deceivers, describes him as: 'a small man with fair hair and merry blue eyes, an excellent raconteur and great company in a party, whose military knowledge, combined with a fertile imagination and tireless energy, made him the perfect deception-planner.'[9]

A story told of Dudley Clarke is wonderfully indicative of his character and of a sense of values shared by the deception-planners. In response to an offer from Admiral Sir Dudley Pound to head up deception planning back in Europe after his early successes in the Middle East he is said to have replied: 'I am a Staff Officer of Archie Wavell who alone is conducting active operations. You can't pinch another man's butler when he has only been lent you for the night.'[10]

In late 1940 Dudley Clarke, under the command of Wavell, founded 'A' Force, which was the only active and serious deception organisation in operation on the Allied side until late 1942. Cruickshank says that: 'it was a small organisation – three years after its formation it had only 41 officers, 76 NCOs and three units of company strength, specially trained in the operation of visual deception devices.'[11]

Just like the Twenty Committee in Britain (also known as the XX Committee, the Double Cross Committee) 'A' Force also ran, in conjunction with SIME (Security Intelligence Middle East), numerous double agents in the territories where it operated of which maybe the best known was Agent Cheese.

The embryonic 'A' Force's first target was the Italian army before the Battle of Sidi Barrani in summer 1940. Wavell's plans called for a phantom army to pressurise the flanks of Graziani's invasion force, and a phantom army meant all the panoply of deception that Wavell was later to detail in his memorandum to the Chiefs of Staff[12] – visual, aural, even nasal ruses, and fake wireless traffic. In addition to the careful attention that they paid to the physical details of tactical deception, Clarke and Wavell ensured that the full benefit of their considerable effort should not be wasted. They did this by sticking to the golden rules of strategic deception and keeping their plans plausible and secret.

Throughout the Middle East Dudley Clarke and his men used dummy tanks and lorries to confuse enemy reconnaissance planes. They developed the so-called 'sunshield' which covered a tank and made it look like a lorry from above. They developed clever games of bluff and double-bluff as we shall learn from the men who fought the deception war in North Africa. In Libya they produced entire fake army camps, complete with cookhouses and slit trenches.

They would lay up concentrations of dummy tanks interspersed with real tanks. On the night before the engagement the real tanks would withdraw to their genuine point of attack. On one occasion the Germans brought down artillery and mortar fire on a dummy tank division for two hours before they realised they had been fooled.

Two of the major deceptions they perpetrated on Rommel were at the Battle of Alam Halfa and the decisive Battle of El Alamein. In the run up to El Alamein, Dudley Clarke and his men developed an elaborate deception plan codenamed Operation Bertram, involving the concealment of a huge build-up of supplies in the area of the genuine attack in the north and an apparent build-up of stores and materiel in the notional area of attack in the south.

All too often with deception operations it is practically impossible to determine to what extent the enemy was fooled. But in the case of El Alamein, we know from the statements of General von Thoma, the Commander of Panzerarmee Afrika, that he did not detect the increase of activity in the north and was convinced that the build-up was taking place in the south. Even after the genuine attack had happened in the north he still retained two of his armoured divisions in the south for four days. And the British, as Charles Cruickshank notes, were able to put one whole armoured division into the battle that the Germans did not realise they had. He concludes: 'The deceptive measures at El Alamein had the effect of shifting the balance of forces in favour of the British; and in doing so there can be no doubt that they contributed significantly to the Eighth Army's famous victory.'[13]

With the benefit of hindsight, the significance of the El Alamein experience in relation to the build-up for D-Day can hardly be over-estimated. 'A' Force was the inspiration for so much of what followed. Success in the Middle East was crucial in convincing both London and later the Americans that organised deception had real impact.

By the time Wavell's insistence on deception had finally impressed the Chiefs of Staff he was operating in the Far East, but it was largely as a result of his recommendations that Churchill took the significant step of 'institutionalising' deception. The Prime Minister decided to strengthen the London Controlling Section, and invest Colonel Johnny Bevan, its new chief, with responsibility for co-ordinating deception in all theatres of war.

What made Churchill's decision so dramatic was the degree to which deception was to be co-ordinated. Individual commanders have practised deception since military operations first began. Indeed it was essentially in this spirit that Wavell, Clarke and 'A' Force performed their work in the Middle East. What they had both recognised was that as other theatres of war gradually opened up there was going to be an increasing need to ensure that operations and deception were not constantly tripping over each other's toes and that what one commander sought to persuade the enemy to do was not flatly contradicted by another commander on another side of the world. It was thus the co-ordination that was new, and its introduction marks a decisive turn in modern military history.

Michael Handel[14] has pointed out that the world's ancient epics, the Bible, the Iliad, and the Odyssey, Gilgamesh and the Maha-bharata, Greek, Roman, Indian and Chinese histories 'abound with examples' of imaginative and cunning commanders. He has also pointed out however, that 'In medieval Europe, the inter-related influences of Christianity and chivalry caused the resort to deception to be considered a dishonourable and unfashionable course of action.' This influence lasted right up until the First World War, and in some circles beyond.

The cryptographic successes of Admiral 'Blinker' Hall and his colleagues in the Admiralty's Room 40 had not been developed between the wars. It was only in 1938 that a mobilisation of similar talent began in earnest. It was in the best traditions of British amateurism and brought the likes of Ian Fleming, the creator of James Bond, into the intelligence fold. Stockbroking firms, Oxford and Cambridge colleges, top law firms, gently passed the word. Ten years earlier the American Secretary of State Henry Stimson had made his famous comment that 'Gentlemen do not read each other's mail'. On the eve of war in 1939 such a sentiment had been consigned to another age. Churchill most certainly *did* read other gentlemen's mail. Indeed his enjoyment and support for all forms of intelligence and the world of derring-do is one of the key components in the success of the deceptions of the Second World War.[15]

By the end of the war Stimson's world, built on centuries of good chivalric intent, had been left even further behind.

At the end of the war in his report to the Combined Chiefs of Staff on the operations of the Allied Expeditionary Force, General Eisenhower remarked that: 'Lack of infantry was the most important cause of the [German] army's defeat in Normandy, and his failure to remedy this weakness was due primarily to the success of the Allied threats to the Pas de Calais . . . I cannot over-emphasise the decisive value of this most successful threat, which paid enormous dividends, both at the time of the assault and during the operations of the two succeeding months.'[16]

These 'enormous dividends' were the culmination of five years of trial and error and the fruits of the combined efforts of a large number of people with a fascinating mix of talents, from a bewildering range of backgrounds. The inner sanctum of deception, however, drew on a certain kind of man and woman who, although by no means exclusively aristocratic, did share certain assumptions about the right way of doing things which bonded them together and enabled them to work together to enormous good effect.

Indeed it appears that from 1943 until the end of the war German Intelligence consistently over-estimated the size of the Allied Forces by about 100 per cent and, equally consistently, had those troops in the wrong place.

By the end of the war, the network that operated deception had become quite substantial. Individual organisations remained fairly small, but, taken together, they constituted a fair number. The list and the acronyms that follow are typically military: 'A' Force in the Mediterranean, 'D' Division and, towards the end of the war, 'D' Force in the Far East, 'R' Force under the 21st Army Group in the UK, the Twenty Committee and its support, B.1A, the section of MI5 that controlled the double agents, those affiliated to SHAEF Ops B, those involved with Ultra and Enigma at Bletchley Park in Bedfordshire who provided the essential flow of information without which the work of all these organisations would not have been nearly as effective as it was and, finally, at the centre of the web the London Controlling Section.

Clearly, deception in the Middle East won its spurs earlier than its counterpart in Europe. Indeed it was a visit to England by Dudley Clarke in October 1941 at Wavell's urging that persuaded the Chiefs of Staff to create a body in London to liaise with 'A' Force. It would study the range of possibilities available for organised deception in the European theatre. Colonel Oliver Stanley was appointed Controlling Officer for Deception and in April 1941 he and his deception-planning function were transferred to the Prime Minister's Joint Planning Staff (JPS). Colonel John Henry Bevan took over from Oliver Stanley, in June 1942; the deception-planning function was reorganised and renamed the London Controlling Section (LCS). Bevan determinedly set about rescuing the organisation from the 'semi-somnolent seclusion' with which Dennis Wheatley, a founder member of Stanley's deception organisation, characterised its early months. 'It was upon his taking over that the section gradually began to move from a position of near impotence to one of . . . influence and power.'[17] Bevan started the long climb towards the most successful and surely the most crucial deception of the Second World

War, Bodyguard, the cover plan for Neptune, the Allied invasion of northern France.

In the minutes of the Chief of Staff to Colonel Johnny Bevan, dated October 11 1944, the LCS received the following accolade:

> The COS wish me [Major General Hollis] to place on record their warm appreciation of the outstanding contribution which the LCS and its subsidiary sections in the operational theatres ('A' Force, 'D' Division) have made to the success of the major operations which have been carried out during the last two years. In their view the record of the success of the cover and deception plans had been unique.
>
> The COS went as far as to record the opinion that, in one instance, the cover and deception plan had made a decisive contribution to the success of a major operation, namely Operation Overlord.[18]

Dennis Wheatley describes Johnny Bevan, old Etonian, head of a much respected stockbroking firm, as 'a rather frail looking man of medium build with sleepy pale blue eyes and thin fair hair, which turned grey from the strain of the remarkable work he accomplished in the three years following his appointment on June 1st 1942.'[19]

His colleagues were an interesting mixture and typical of that blend of the amateur and the professional that so characterised the make-up of the intelligence community in wartime Britain. It was a mix which infuriated some professionals at the time and has gone on infuriating some of the die-hards to this day, especially those most obsessed with the security lapses of the 1950s, 1960s and 1970s, who see conspiracies and Soviet plots wherever they look.

Bevan's second in command was Colonel Sir Ronald Evelyn Leslie Wingate, educated at Bradfield and Balliol, who started his career as an assistant Commissioner in India, and whose subsequent list of appointments reads like a guide to the British Empire. Together Bevan and Wingate had direct access to an important network of decision makers, military and political, who could smooth the path of their deception plans. Many vitally important conversations were held after luncheon or dinner in the clubs and restaurants whose membership these men shared.

A team grew up around these two men, which included Dennis Wheatley, a soap manufacturer, a financier and ship owner, a tea importer, a scientist, a banker diplomat, and army, navy and air attachés. Lady Jane Bethell, who as Lady Jane Pleydell-Bouverie was

Colonel Bevan's secretary towards the end of the war, describes in her interview below what it was like to work in Storey's Gate, the centre of deception operations in the Second World War. Here, deep below Whitehall, this intriguing assortment of men met and planned a host of schemes, some successful, others never to see the light of day.

LCS had been charged by Churchill with the responsibility for co-ordinating deception in all theatres of war, so their tentacles spread far and wide. They found their way into the Pentagon through Lieutenant-Colonel William Baumer, into Cairo through Dudley Clarke and into the Far East through the dashing Colonel Peter Fleming, later husband of Celia Johnson, who became famous for her role opposite Trevor Howard in the film *Brief Encounter*. He was also, appropriately enough, the brother of Ian Fleming. Links also existed with another list of military acronyms: COSSAC (Chief of Staff Supreme Allied Commander), the headquarters of the COS for the planning of the invasion of Europe, which became SHAEF (Supreme Headquarters Allied Expeditionary Force). The committee responsible for Deception was the Committee of Special Means (CSM) or Ops B. This involved two more high powered figures in the world of deception, Roger Fleetwood Hesketh and Noel Wild, the former a 'charming witty man, with a fine intellect and one of the best cellars in England'[20] and the latter an immaculately turned out Cavalry Officer and former member of 'A' Force, who came back to England to work with planners at SHAEF.

The important link into B.1A was T.A.R. Robertson, the universally popular and extremely able head of the section which ran the double agents. If some form of psychological pressure was what a deception plan required then the LCS had a direct line into the Political Warfare Executive. This was the home of, among others, Tony Crosland and Richard Crossman, the future Labour Ministers, and Sefton Delmer, the ebullient broadcaster of black propaganda designed to disturb Germans at home and abroad with a subtle concoction of falsehoods. There was liaison too with MI6 and with the intelligence departments of all three services.

To co-ordinate policy with the Americans, Bevan was able to go directly to the Joint Security Council, which corresponded roughly to the LCS and which, like the LCS, reported directly to the Joint Planning Staff and their own US Chiefs of Staff. The US planning and implementing agencies which carried out deception plans were OWI, Office of War Information, the Political Warfare Agency, and the OSS, Office of Strategic Services, the forerunner of the CIA, a secret intelligence and special operations service.

17

Cave Brown has remarked in his book, *Bodyguard of Lies*, that the 'structure of the LCS was such that a stone cast at Storey's Gate rippled in ever widening circles' – political, financial, civilian, diplomatic, scientific, military until it became, according to the historian of OKW (Oberkommando der Wehrmacht, the German Supreme Command), Helmut Greine, 'waves of confusing deceptions'.[21]

It is important always to bear in mind – and this was stressed over and over again in our interviews – that neither intelligence nor deception are ends in themselves. Their value is in direct proportion to their contribution to the success or failure of operations, to the fight that has to be fought at some stage. With this in mind, the direct link that the LCS had through General Sir Hastings Ismay, the Prime Minister's Chief of Staff and Military Secretary, to Winston himself, to the War Cabinet and to the Chiefs of Staff was of the utmost significance. Without access to planning and to deliberations at the highest level deception would have remained at the tactical battlefield level throughout the war. As Wavell had recognised early in the war, there had to be a body whose responsibility was essentially strategic and not executive. It was there to promote the case for co-ordinated deception and to oversee its complexities.

Ronald Lewin, the military historian, summed up their task: 'To distract Hitler and his High Command from the real intentions of the Allies by fatally infecting them with grand delusions and to convince them of a threat where none in fact existed.'[22]

In a letter from Neil Gordon Clark, one of the members of the LCS, written to David Mure in 1980 he remembers that: 'It is difficult at this late date to recapture the atmosphere of those days, the sense of urgency, the sudden problems and much sheer hard work. I do recall that when I first presented the outline Bodyguard to ISSB (Inter Services Security Board) they flatly refused to believe that 'it would be possible to deceive the enemy over the Normandy landings, which in their view, at that time, must become obvious.' He went on to quote the minutes cited[23] above from Hollis to Bevan about the decisive contribution of deception to the success of Overlord.

Ronald Lewin's book *Ultra Goes to War* is, apart from the lengthy and exhaustively detailed official history of intelligence by Professor Harry Hinsley, one of the most important books on Ultra to have been published so far. Enigma and Ultra and their Japanese equivalents, Purple and Magic, were the most significant means of facilitating deception available to the Allies. These crucial sources of information, which Churchill called his 'golden goose', gave access to a significant proportion of the enemy's plans and assessments at the very time that those plans were under consideration.

Lewin has written that: 'Put in the simplest possible terms the operation called Ultra involved intercepting enemy signals that had been mechanically enciphered, rendering them intelligible, and then distributing their translated texts by secure means to appropriate headquarters.'[24] One of these secure headquarters was the London Controlling Section where, for this most secret source, only Bevan and Wingate were in the know.

The work from which the deception-planners and so many others benefited so greatly was all done at a modest country house in Bedfordshire called Bletchley Park. As the war went on it was hedged in by a sprawl of Nissen huts, inside which some of the country's most able minds, boffins and eccentrics of the kind so beloved by the English, laboured alongside a host of signallers and cipher clerks. They relied on the teams of ordinary women from the Navy and the RAF who operated the machinery. This not inconsiderable establishment made critical interceptions which were distributed via the Special Liaison Units. These units covered all the theatres of war and were the special responsibility of Group Captain F. W. Winterbotham. Neither they nor the nerve centre at Bletchley *ever* suffered a leak.

Lewin recounts the story of a woman who had been vouchsafed the Ultra secret as a member of Field Marshal Alexander's headquarters in Italy. Years later, in the early 1960s, she suffered a brain haemorrhage, from which she recovered. Her main memory was how, in all her pain and confusion, her overriding fear was that in her delirium she might give away the secret of Ultra. She was one among many who guarded this vital weapon in the Allied cause with a dedication and loyalty which to this generation seems almost incredible.[25] Throughout the war and for many years afterwards, indeed up until the present day, stories abound of husbands and wives, brothers and sisters, though both involved in some aspect of security work, never knew what the other was doing.

For the deception-planners such secrecy and rigid security was just as essential and it enabled Ultra to provide the vital component in constructing deception cover plans, in helping the deceivers to reinforce existing German perceptions, in allaying suspicions when they arose, and in pressing home the advantage. It gave the LCS their own thermostat, helping them to turn the heat up or down in their complex war.

The other organisation closely involved in deception, which benefited considerably from the Ultra decrypts, was the Twenty Committee. The difficult question of precisely what kind of information could be safely passed to the Germans through B.1A and its network of agents could not be decided either by Tar Robertson of MI5 and his other case officers on their own or by Bevan and the LCS. A separate committee was needed which could make the appropriate assessments about the degree of truth and falsehood required to maintain the credibility of the agents. As a result, almost every Wednesday afternoon throughout the war the XX (Double Cross) Committee met to decide on what items of information should be passed by 'most secret channels' to the enemy. The first meeting took place in Wormwood Scrubs, the prison at Shepherds Bush, on January 2 1941 and included representatives from the LCS, MI5, Robertson and Masterman, the three Directors of Naval, Air and Military Intelligence, the War Office, PWE, and representatives of the Home Forces and the civil authorities. As the re-entry into Europe came closer the Wednesday afternoon meetings were joined by members of COSSAC and later of SHAEF.

The LCS and B.1A under the guidance of the XX Committee, and occasionally more senior authorities, began the careful task of building up the credibility of certain agents in the eyes of their German Controllers. Finally, as D-Day approached, the vitally important misinformation with which they wished to influence German decisions would be swallowed whole. This German spy network was kept under tight control so that, when the time came, no unsuspected hostile source would intervene and jeopardise the entire operation. Such a possibility was a constant fear throughout the war and it increased as D-Day approached and the XX Committee worried that Britain was about to be flooded with a whole new batch of agents.

J. C. Masterman, Chairman of the Committee, defined its goals as they appeared at the beginning of the war:

1 To control the enemy system, or as much of it as we could get our hands on.
2 To catch fresh spies when they appeared.
3 To gain knowledge of the personalities and methods of the German Secret Service.
4 To obtain information about the code and cypher work of the German services.
5 To get evidence of enemy plans and intentions from the questions asked by them.
6 To influence enemy plans by the answers sent to the enemy.
7 To deceive the enemy about our plans and intentions.[26]

It was only as the war dragged on that the last two aims gradually grew in importance, but Handel[27] has pointed out that the Double-Cross System, developed in the Middle East by 'A' Force in co-ordination with SIME as well as the one in England, had by the end of the war become the best means of communicating false information to the Germans.

It now seems quite incredible that the British succeeded in picking up every German agent sent to Britain, especially when they so signally failed to pick up Soviet penetration of their own Secret Services at precisely the same time. Nonetheless, they did. Some they 'turned' successfully – others they locked up later to imitate their radio 'signatures' in false messages to their German controllers. They knew that this deception was working because, through Ultra, they would read that such-and-such an agent was 'a good Abwehr source'. It was clear that the Germans still believed the double agent was free and working for the Axis and that they trusted his information.

Masterman's book[28] lists thirty-nine agents, who were by no means uniformly valuable and many of whom were wound up at various stages during the war. The most significant of the agents were probably those codenamed Garbo, Brutus, Treasure and Tricycle but there were others who made significant contributions at important moments. Two of them, codenamed Mutt and Jeff, tell their story below.

As the picture begins to emerge of the network of organisations which grew up to co-ordinate and effect the cover plans in Europe and North Africa and as we build towards D-Day itself, it is important to remember what was going on at the same time in the Far East. Colonel Peter Fleming faced problems in trying to construct the stories and stratagems that would mislead the Japanese. These throw an interesting light on the nature of deception in all the theatres of the war.

By Fleming's own admission deception operations in the Far East never came close to achieving the sophistication of those overseen by his parent organisation, the LCS, and by 'A' Force first in Africa and later in the Mediterranean.

Dennis Wheatley again provides us with a colourful pen portrait of Peter Fleming: 'Unlike many authors of travel books, who turn out to be pale, bespectacled little men, his bronzed, tight-skinned face always gave the impression that he had only just returned from an arduous journey across the Mongolian desert or up some little known tributary of the Amazon.'

When Wavell was moved from his North African command and took up his position in the Far East, he took with him his belief in the value of deception and presided over the creation of 'D' Division, a small deception staff affiliated to the LCS with Peter Fleming as the commanding officer. Fleming stayed in close touch with both Bevan and Clarke throughout the war and was responsible for a staff with an official muster of 30 officers, 32 other ranks and 9 secretaries, which in reality never reached that number owing to a shortage of qualified personnel. 'D' Division offices operated all over Asia in Kandy, Delhi, Calcutta, Rangoon and even in Chunking in China.

The scale of strategic deception in SEAC (South East Asian Command) was always limited. In a secret supplement to Mountbatten's Report to the Combined Chiefs of Staff written in 1948, the section written about 'D' Division, most likely by Fleming himself, gives a number of clues about the complicated set of circumstances that needs to obtain for deception to function effectively on a grand scale.

The first reason that Fleming gives for the limitations placed upon him 'was a chronic uncertainty as to what operations SEAC was in fact going to be able to carry out'. This uncertainty inevitably trickled down to deception-planning and contrasts with the situation in Europe, where the planners were usually able to work with a clear strategic objective. Interestingly, their major failures, like the abortive Operation Cockade, which was designed to make the Germans believe in an invasion of northern France in 1943 when the likelihood of such an invasion was extremely small, were largely the result of muddled strategic thinking.

There was always a danger in too great an enthusiasm for deception for its own sake. It could never be a substitute at the strategic level for military plans that made sense and that the enemy were already predisposed to believe. Peter Fleming observed that: 'It is impossible, or at least highly dangerous, to tell a lie until you know what the truth is going to be.'

The second mitigating circumstance that Fleming cites may sound like special pleading but it does raise the important issue of the nature of the enemy's intelligence service. How thorough was it? What kind of credibility did it have with battlefield commanders and with the strategic decision makers? Were there rival groups, fighting among themselves and subsequently prejudicing the value of the information that they passed on?

We have already suggested that rivalry between the Abwehr and the SS led to distortions in Germany's intelligence-gathering operations. Nevertheless, despite their gullibility as far as the agents they believed they ran were concerned, the Services were on the whole well organised and crucially they were, despite their shortcomings, influential.

The Japanese were well prepared to 'swallow the most outrageous and implausible fabrications' but their intelligence service was inefficient and apparently relatively ineffectual. Japanese officers, whose contempt for their prisoners of war had such cruel consequences, were unwilling to modify their own ideas in response to assessments of threats from an enemy whom they had come to despise. Another 'weakness' in the Japanese capacity to respond with suitable vigour to the scheming of Fleming and his team was a logistical one – their increasing inability to respond to any threats, real or imaginary, owing to their chronic shortage of shipping and other transport difficulties. If deception plans are going to work, the enemy has to have a pretty efficient system for getting it wrong.

Lastly, the means for sifting intelligence material effectively were lacking so that ill-trained commanders and staff at all levels had considerable difficulty in distinguishing between a mass of conflicting scares. As a result, a carefully laid deception plan was simply swallowed up in a mass of what the military today call 'noise'.

When Mountbatten took over as Supreme Allied Commander South-East Asia he had meagre resources at his disposal. But, despite all the problems that Fleming faced, documents captured in November 1943 proved that Japanese Imperial HQ assessed the strength of Allied forces in SEAC and India Command at slightly over 51 divisions, which was a considerable overestimate. Some of this was straightforward self-delusion but some of it can be put down to 'D' Division's attempts to build up a fake order of battle. Of the importance of this Dudley Clarke was in no doubt. In a paper entitled 'Some Personal Reflections on the Practice of Deception in the Mediterranean Theatre from 1941 to 1945' he wrote:

> I cannot overstress the importance of building up a false order of battle. This must be the first task of all deception staff ... It is a dull, hard, slogging business but it gets its reward from time to time in the shape of captured documents ... However unspectacular, this grinding job will in fact provide the base for all deception plans. As the general can only influence the battle by the use of his reserves, so the deception staff can only implement its planning by the employment of its notional forces.[29]

Despite the success of Fleming in this regard on the grand scale, he writes with some exasperation that at a more local level:

> In 'D' Division's experience the Japanese were virtually incapable of assimilating any order of battle Intelligence, which dealt with identifications below a divisional level. They could not, for instance, be relied on to identify a division from one of its component brigades, even when they knew its composition; and it was a waste of time to give them information about battalions in regiments since, although they were glad to get it, they were unable to make any deduction from it.

On the tactical level there was often scant reward for ingenuity and hard work too. 'D' Division's own version of Mincemeat, described later by Terence O'Brien, was not the success that Montagu enjoyed with Major Martin in the Mediterranean. They were not well rewarded for their body snatching efforts, another example of a project too advanced for the 'bungling Japanese'.

There were many forms of tactical deception available to the operational groups like 'A' Force and, in the run up to D-Day, to 'R' Force in Europe, fake wireless traffic, sonic deception, dummies and the full panoply of camouflage devices. In the Far East the most useful of all was considered to be airborne deception equipment. This consisted of Paragons, which were dummy paratroops, Pintails, Very light signals, Parafexes, which were rifle fire and grenade simulators, and Aquaskits and Aquatails, aquatic Very light signals. In the confusing terrain of the jungle, this meant that a single Liberator aircraft could put down equipment which would simulate a fight on the scale of a platoon battle lasting from one to six hours. The organised tactical HQ responsible for these disturbances was established relatively late in the war. 'D' Force was headquartered in Barasat near Calcutta; after 'A' Force and 'R' Force had been largely forgotten during the drive to Berlin, it was probably the last of the deception organisations founded during the war using the techniques of the tactical deceivers. Two men, Brigadier Michael Calvert and Terence O'Brien, who both operated in different places in the Far East during the war with Japan, fill out the details of a number of the operations with which 'D' Division were involved later in the book.

There is a sense in which the organisation for what was to be the biggest military invasion in history really began on December 7 1941, when the Japanese attacked the American Navy in Pearl Harbor. As Albert Seaton argues in his book *The Fall of Fortress Europe*[30] there was never really any doubt that, once Hitler was fighting on all sides of his Third Reich, and once the immense resources of the United States and the manpower of the Russians had been added to the Allied cause, it could only be a matter of time before a Second Front opened in Europe, before the Allies came back across the Channel.

Certainly, but where and when? The questions were simple enough, but the Germans singularly failed to find the answers. Every effort was made to keep Hitler and his generals spinning in indecision as they looked around their enormous frontiers, trying to gauge where and when the Allies would come ashore.

To support Operation Torch,[31] the North African landings in November 1942, several feints were suggested by Bevan and his LCS. The most significant of these were probably Operations Overthrow and Solo, suggesting threats to the Pas de Calais and to Norway respectively. Such German activity as there was on the Western Front, like the strengthening of the Atlantic Wall, is difficult to credit to the deception plans. But the lesson was beginning to be learned that, if you were going to fool the enemy with a false operation, then you had to commit sufficient resources to the bluff.

After the 1943 Conference at Casablanca, at which the Allies determined to invade Sicily in Operation Husky, the most elaborate deception cover-plan yet conceived was built up side by side with the true invasion plan. In the course of planning Operation Barclay, Dudley Clarke and his small team constructed so many false threats of possible invasion that they were able to show that the Germans had sent important divisions to reinforce the Balkans, and divided their reserves equally between Sardinia, Corsica and Sicily. It was also clear that the Germans thought Greece might be the intended target of the invasion. Even here there were many other circumstances contributing to the success of Husky. Cruickshank points out a few of them: the Allies had complete air superiority, the beach defences were very thin. Many of the mines had not been armed and the Italians put up feeble opposition.[32]

The success of deception operations could never be guaranteed. Despite their increasing experience, in 1943 the deception-planners, as has already been noted, suffered the failure of Operation Cockade and its three components, Tindall, Wadham and Starkey. They were all designed to make the Germans believe that a cross-Channel invasion was a real possibility throughout 1943. The humiliation of Cockade was not for want of trying on the part of the deception-planners. They were responding to a brief from the highest level, a brief prompted as much as anything by the Allies' wish to try to do something to convince Stalin that they were serious about a Western

Front. They wanted to show that they would do what they could to draw troops from the Eastern Front, even if a genuine invasion was out of the question for that year.

The Germans simply did not fall for it. When 'Bomber' Harris had been called on during the planning stage to divert precious aircraft from his offensive against Germany, he had sent a stiff telegram to the planners, dismissing the operation as 'at best a piece of harmless play acting'. Unfortunately he had been right. It was hardly a good omen for the immense task that now faced them.

Operation Bodyguard was the crucial deception. Yet the story, the lie, was extremely simple. The main Allied invasion would be launched against the Pas de Calais six weeks after the landings in Normandy, which themselves would be merely a feint. Five years of experience went into the elegant simplicity of the story and into the means by which the enemy should be made to act upon it.

It was at the Casablanca Conference in January 1943 that the decision had been taken to invade France in 1944. At the Teheran Conference in November the Combined Chiefs Of Staff ordered that a general strategic plan for 1944 should be prepared. The Russians also agreed that they would set in motion plans for a simulated attack on northern Finland, the details of which Johnny Bevan was to help them with some two months later.

Professor Hinsley has shown that by January 1944 the evidence about the German defensive preparations 'and the increase in the strength of their army in France had put it beyond doubt that they expected the main effort of the Western Allies in 1944 to be a cross Channel invasion; and this evidence had been reinforced by decrypts disclosing their response to General Eisenhower's appointment as Supreme Allied Commander and their decision to appoint Rommel to a command in the West.'[33]

The Bodyguard plan as originally conceived would have to be modified. It had been intended to convince the Germans firstly that the Allies believed that they required 50 Divisions for a cross Channel invasion, and that because of the sheer logistical difficulties of assembling such a large force the invasion could not take place until late summer. Secondly they were to believe that, as a result of this delay, the Allies would concentrate their *Schwerpunkt* against the Balkans, something which Hitler had always believed was likely. Lastly they had wanted the Germans to believe that they intended to bomb Germany into submission and that the heavy demand that this made on manpower and resources was a further reason for their inability to stage a cross Channel invasion at an early stage.

Mounting evidence from Ultra forced SHAEF's deception staff to sit down with Johnny Bevan and MI5 and write a new and more elaborate version of the original COSSAC plan for concentrating enemy attention on the Pas de Calais. The original plan had been written in September 1943. The new plan, codenamed Fortitude, was approved on February 23 1944. It had two parts: a threat to the Pas de Calais and to Scandinavia. In the Mediterranean plan Zeppelin sought to 'exaggerate the amount of Allied assault shipping in the area and to convince the Germans that, although the Allies were considering a landing in the south of France, they might not carry it out because of their large intentions in the Balkans'.[34]

At all stages of the planning the German predisposition to believe that the Pas de Calais was the most likely point for an invasion was essential to Fortitude. Despite the shortness of the crossing, the proximity to the Ruhr and the likelihood that a successful Allied invasion from there would outflank all enemy forces to the south, the Allies had chosen the Caen–Cotentin area for their re-entry into Europe. A vast range of information had informed their choice. It was the result of three years of exhaustive surveys of every available beach from Holland to the Bay of Biscay examining everything from tides to the composition of the sand to the nature of the beach exits.

Once the place had been chosen, the next problem was going to be getting the British, Canadian and American troops ashore with minimum casualties and then keeping them ashore. Hitler had more than enough troops at his disposal in northern France to throw the Allies back into the sea. Fortitude was there to prevent that kind of disaster and although the story was simple enough, its logistical requirements were formidable.

In December 1943 Lieutenant Colonel David Strangeways came back to Britain from the Italian theatre to take control of Deception and Camouflage within 21 Army Group, which came under Montgomery. In February 1944 Strangeways' command was designated 'R' Force and the British equivalent of 'A' Force was born.

Prior to that point in the United Kingdom, the 'Q' and 'K' sites, the dummy airfields whose function was to confuse enemy aircraft, had made their contribution to the Battle of Britain: they are described in interviews with men who made their visual magic work. There had also been Colonel Turner's Department, responsible for camouflage, which had, among its many deceptive creations, built false cities on the Yorkshire Moors. It was David Strangeways however who was to pull together all the lessons of the previous five years in tactical deception and put them at the service of the strategic plan, which he himself also helped to formulate.

'R' Force created two phantom armies: one on the south coast of England, apparently threatening the Pas de Calais, another in Scotland threatening to invade Norway. First United States Army Group, FUSAG, was an enormous deception, involving masses of dummy vehicles, tanks and landing craft half-hidden in the southern ports facing Calais. A network of false wireless traffic simulated everything that a modern army would need to say between its separate units in the build-up to a great invasion. FUSAG even had its own real-life General. General Patton, who was temporarily out of the real war, was made the Commander of the notional army. He was photographed in his Staff Car on the way to parades of divisions that did not exist. His presence in such a 'crucial' role, one which the Germans fully expected him to fill, lent considerable weight to the deception.

All coastal territory in the south of England and in parts of Scotland became the subject of rigid security. No-one was to know which divisions were real and which were fake. Given the virtual impossibility of blanket security, it is astonishing that nobody saw through the Fortitude South deception.

Captured German records for the vital months leading up to D-Day make it quite plain that the military assessment changed from a belief that there was a build-up of forces opposite Normandy to the conviction that the enemy would attack through the Pas de Calais. That went hand in hand with a similarly mistaken belief that the Allies would attack many weeks later than June 6. Even after D-Day, the double agents worked hard to convince their German controllers that the main invasion was yet to come. This was a vital twist in the tail, which had emerged relatively late in the planning process. Agent 'Brutus' told his controller in Paris, on June 8 1944, that he had seen evidence of Patton's First Army Group preparing to embark at east coast and south-east English ports 'with my own eyes'.

Double-agent 'Garbo' backed this up on June 8 with a very long transmission to his Controller, Kuhlenthal, purporting to come from his network of correspondents and spies throughout Britain — his 'orchestra'. Roger Hesketh quotes this vital message at some length. Garbo's message went into great detail about the mass of men and materiel that was still apparently ready to invade Calais. The message, which arrived at 2230 hours, took a formidable amount of time to transmit and contained the following passage:

After personal consultation 8th June with my agents Jonny (sic) Dick and Dorick, whose reports were sent today, I am of the opinion, in view of the strong troop concentrations in South East and eastern England which are not taking part in the present operations, that these operations are a diversionary manoeuvre designed to draw off enemy reserves in order to make a decisive attack in another place. In view of the continued air attacks on the concentration area mentioned . . . it may very probably take place in the Pas de Calais area, particularly since in such an attack the proximity of air bases will facilitate the operation by providing continued strong air support.[35]

Hesketh noted that the message was seen and signed by Hitler himself. Immediately on receipt of this message the 116th Panzer Division, which had been stationed north west of Paris, was moved to the Somme, and the first SS Panzer Division was moved from Turnhout to Ghent – that is, both converged on the Pas de Calais[36]. That loss of armour and troops from the beachheads was fatal for the Germans.

This was the real grace of the plan. Not only had it deceived the enemy about the place of the landing but it had also convinced them that, when it did occur, it was no more than a diversionary tactic, albeit on a considerable scale. Any doubts that individual German commanders may have had were overridden in the consensus that the real attack had not yet begun.

Even so, as General Morgan, one of the planners of Neptune, remarked in a paraphrase of the Duke of Wellington after the Battle of Waterloo, it was 'going to be a close run thing, a damned close run thing – the closest run thing you ever saw in your life'.

On June 10 1944, the deception-planners met at their head-quarters in London's Storey's Gate. Ronald Wingate has described the atmosphere as 'heavy with tension and pipe and cigarette smoke, combined with a faint aroma of good whisky'. He goes on to paint a vivid and no doubt rather romantic picture of those moments when the deceivers were waiting to know if their bait had been swallowed, or if they themselves had been outwitted:

It was a frightful moment – there were those big red blobs on the war map moving towards Normandy all the time. Were all the bridges out over the Seine? Had the Germans built underwater bridges? . . . Had Garbo overplayed his hand? That was the sort of thing that was being discussed. Then the news came through via

Ultra Hitler had cancelled Case Three. [His plans to move troops and Panzer armour to the beachheads of Normandy.] We'd won, and what an astonishing moment that was! We knew then that we'd won – there might be heavy battles, but we'd won. There was nobody more astonished than Bevan, for I don't think he thought that we'd really pull it off. Brooke's attitude was the oddest. He said if Hitler was such a bloody fool why had it taken us so long to beat him? Then he stalked off. The Prime Minister came in with Stewart Menzies [the Head of MI6] and the PM said this was the crowning achievement of the long and glorious history of the British Secret Service – or something like that.[37]

This is the world we now enter, a world that may seem rather like a cross between a Gentlemen's Club and the High Table of an Oxbridge College.

Deception does not break down into neatly defined areas, but we have tried, for the purposes of definition, to place our speakers in several categories: the men who provided the brains, the men who made the nuts and bolts of deception work, the talented amateurs so beloved of the British and, finally the men of action who fought the deception war on the enemy's territory.

It is, though, all lies, all stories constructed to deceive. It is as if the ageing general settles back after dinner and reconstructs the battle with the condiment set. Except that the pepper is not quite what it seems to be and the salt merely a figment of his imagination. Occasionally in the pages that follow the general may forget what he did with the mustard altogether. But this is not definitive history, not the official war record. It is the recollections of men and women who fought with their brains fifty years ago to outwit an enemy of immense strength and frightening determination.

It is also, sadly, the last time that many of them will have the opportunity to roll back the tablecloth and make their deceptive dispositions on the mahogany board.

Part One

THE BRAINS

It is now half a century since the events of the Second World War. The men who shaped the events of that war, the generals, the statesmen and the planners, are largely gone. Only those who were extremely young to hold positions of such power or those whose natural resilience has allowed them longevity still survive. These are the kind of men we are about to meet, the brains behind operational and strategic deception. Men like Canon David Strangeways, who wrote the 'stories', the overall deception plans, for some of the major theatres of war; Sir David Hunt, the intelligence colonel who put deception into operation on the ground; General Charles Richardson who learned to deceive in North Africa and the historian Michael Foot who planned some of the diversionary and deceptive operations for the morning of D-Day itself.

CHAPTER 1

THE CANON'S TALE

Canon David Strangeways

David Strangeways is now a retired Canon of the Church of England. During the war, many years before he was ordained, he planned and executed deception operations in the Middle East, North Africa, Sicily and Italy. Most important of all, Colonel Strangeways was one of the people who wrote and executed the deception plan for D-Day, 1944.

As for so many other people, David Strangeways' experience of Dunkirk was seminal. Fears about the French ability to resist the Germans had been growing throughout the Phoney War but few had expected that France would collapse so quickly. Strangeways was one of those who experienced at first hand the weakness and vulnerability that, as Michael Handel[1] has pointed out, was one of the most important spurs to the development of deception by the British.

An old Thames sailing barge and a typical streak of initiative brought one of Britain's best strategic brains home from Dunkirk. David Strangeways was a major in the Duke of Wellington's Regiment when the call came to evacuate the army from the beaches. His regiment fell back to guard the perimeter of the town while the evacuation went ahead. In due course, they moved to their own appointed embarkation point. But the promised boats were nowhere to be seen. David Strangeways, who talks disarmingly about being under 'light shelling', did not intend to expose himself or his men to a long wait on the beach. Some distance offshore he spotted two old Thames sailing barges, riding at anchor and apparently unattended. He, another officer and 22 of his men plunged into the sea and swam to the barges. 'I can't imagine how we clambered up the side, but we were young and fit and we managed it.' A group of gunners made it to the other barge. Although the young Strangeways was an accomplished sailor he had never sailed a lumbering Thames barge before. But he got her going, pointed her in what he assumed was the general direction of England and set out on what he calls a broad 'soldier's reach'. Down below he searched in vain for a chart but in the end he brought the barge and his men home safely to Dover with the help of a page torn from an old atlas.

'That night my wife, Eleanor and I sat down to dinner at the Savoy.'

No one could accuse this young officer of not having seen action. In the years that followed Dunkirk, he was to transfer that practical sense of what works on a battlefield to the world of tactical and strategic deception. Today he is one of the few surviving members of the group which was involved at a very senior level in planning the major deceptions of the Second World War.

He had always wanted to be a soldier. The rule in his family was uncompromising, Cambridge first, then the army. So he went to Trinity Hall, Cambridge, and then to the army as a university candidate, receiving his commission in 1933. In the Duke of Wellington's Regiment he saw service in Malta before being mobilised in the summer of 1939. Dunkirk in May 1940 was a rude awakening from the Phoney War.

His first foray into the complex and inventive world of the deceivers came when he was summoned to Whitehall in August 1942, where he was briefed for a special task. Colonel Bevan had recently taken over from Colonel Stanley as the man in charge of the London Controlling Section, which was now moving from its rather passive role under Stanley towards a much more active part in military operations. The first major task confronting Bevan and his colleagues at Storey's Gate was to devise cover plans for Operation Torch, the Anglo American invasion of North Africa planned for that November. Gibraltar was a vital staging post for the invasion, and despite all Dudley Clarke's best endeavours in the eastern Mediterranean it was very difficult to hide the build-up of Tank Landing Craft, boxed fighter aircraft, spares, stores and personnel, which were piling up in advance of D-Day for Torch. The cooperation of the Governors of Gibraltar and Malta was considered by Bevan to be essential and so he asked the Director of Military Intelligence (DMI) for an officer who could be trusted with the task of briefing them fully about organised deception. Strangeways was the chosen officer. He was to go to Gibraltar and Malta to meet Generals Mason-MacFarlane and Gort and to brief them in turn on the cover plans for Operation Torch. Subsequently he was to fly to Cairo with 'most secret' dispatches for General Sir Harold Alexander, newly appointed Commander-in-Chief in the Middle East. The dispatches contained plans for the first invasion of North Africa. On the last leg of the journey he went by flying boat and Wellington bomber, the so-called 'Wimpy', and it was as he says 'a somewhat dicey journey as our pilot made an approach for landing on an enemy airfield'.

During his briefing he had made a good impression on the small staff at the London Controlling Section, and many years later Dennis Wheatley remembered that, 'He was a regular officer and so beautifully turned out that, even in battledress, he looked as if he had stepped straight out of a bandbox . . . a small good-looking man, with a brisk, efficient manner and a very quick mind.'[2]

Wheatley also remembers enlisting Strangeways in an endeavour to 'pull a fast one' over the enemy by planting a misleading letter in an autographed copy of his most recently published book, which Strangeways was to carry in his suitcase. The letter and the book were destined for Henry Hopkinson, a personal friend of Wheatley's, who was in Cairo as a Foreign Office adviser to the Minister of State. Wheatley knew that the hotels in Cairo were insecure and that Strangeways' luggage was almost certain to be searched, so the letter contained misleading information about the British build-up in Gibraltar. It would almost certainly be passed on to the Abwehr.[3]

It was in Cairo that Strangeways first met Dudley Clarke, who was then a brigadier and in command of 'A' Force, the unit 'whose main purpose was to devise deception plans and to execute them on the battlefield'.[4] Dudley Clarke, already well versed in the components of deception, recognised the young officer as a potentially useful ally.

'A' Force had been established on December 18 1940 under the Middle East Command in Cairo. It had grown out of the success of operations against the Italians like those before the Battle of Sidi Barrani, when a phantom army had been created to threaten Graziani's invasion force. The deception had been established by the extensive use of camouflage, fake wireless traffic and the development of a double-cross system in co-operation with Security Intelligence Middle East (SIME).[5]

David Strangeways remembers: 'Shortly after I came back from Cairo, I was promoted to Lieutenant-Colonel and told that I was being posted to Teheran. I have to admit that I was less than overjoyed at the prospect.'

To his relief, the posting to Persia never became a reality. When

Eisenhower became Supreme Allied Commander in January 1943 Alexander was appointed his deputy and commander of the 18th Army Group. Alexander set up headquarters in Constantine and it was here that Strangeways was given command of Tactical HQ, 'A' Force, working to Brigadier Dudley Clarke, and from then on under General Alexander.

David Strangeways believes that Dudley Clarke was truly the father of deception in the Second World War and that it was he who, with slender resources, proved to the people who mattered just how much could be achieved. It was in many ways a lucky historical accident that had brought together Wavell and Dudley Clarke, and then pitted them first against the relatively ineffective Italians and then, only once they had gained that vital experience, against the efficient Germans and the ability of Rommel. With their early success in the Middle East, Wavell and Clarke gave deception the reputation it needed to be taken seriously by other more sceptical commanders. By the time that Strangeways came into the picture in Egypt, deception's credentials were well established. He takes up the story.

'Dudley Clarke was, of course, a total character. He lived in his own world, independently. He was a charming man, thought a great deal, and dealt easily at the highest levels. He was, to me, the originator of everything, without him we wouldn't have started, I don't think. I certainly wouldn't. He had the capacity to leave people alone. The only time he tried to interfere was when I went on an actual operation. He said I was very naughty and I wasn't meant to go on operations. But I believe you *are* meant to go on operations. If you've got troops under you, you must be seen with them. I'm very sorry but to me that's essential. So if my troops were up front I would go once a day up front. You can't ask men to do what you feel you're too precious to do yourself. Everybody is replaceable.'

An ironic incident, itself the consequence of a deception plan, bears out Strangeways' belief in the importance of maintaining a first-hand sense of what goes on in the battlefield. At one point during the North African Campaign in early 1943 Strangeways was so successful in deceiving the Germans that his tiny force, pretending to be an enormous one, was nearly overrun by the enemy.

'In North Africa in 1943 the object was to draw down whatever we could draw from opposite the 1st Army. There was already an Italian division in the area. So far as I can remember I had about a hundred sappers, a battery of Bofors anti-aircraft guns, my jeep and that's about all. And then we were alarmed to hear that an entire

German division had moved down opposite us. In one sense this was very encouraging, but somewhat alarming.

'Of course you always had this strange contradiction within you. You couldn't tell the men why you were there, that the object of the exercise was for the enemy reconnaissance aircraft to spot you and photograph you. You had to have anti-aircraft fire to make yourself look important and threatening, but of course you were hoping like hell that at least one of the recce aircraft would get clear and back to base with his false information.

'Well, we got out of our dilemma of the advancing German division by carrying on much as before and kept our fingers crossed that they wouldn't patrol in strength or with armour while we were still there. As soon as the battle commenced up north, we withdrew. We were just lucky, that's all.'

The deception-planners had grown in strength and confidence during the North African Campaign. David Strangeways has a particular affection for the deceptions he carried out in North Africa. He admired their simplicity: 'We had so few resources. And it was such a clean battle out there.'[6]

Victory at El Alamein had come after almost two weeks of fighting in late October and early November 1942 and by the time of the push to Tunis in May of the following year Strangeways had gained considerable experience. 'It was all go, and Alex and Dudley Clarke between them had given me one task after another.' Tunis and Bizerta fell on May 7 1943. By May 13 von Arnim, who had taken over from Rommel in March, surrendered along with about 125,000 Germans and almost as many Italians. Almost one million German and Italian troops were dead or captured.

Strangeways' enthusiasm for being involved in the front line was to be rewarded by a DSO (Distinguished Service Order) for his quick thinking and bravery during the first hours of the rush to Tunis. 'The collapse of the Germans was imminent and I was given the task of forming a force to get into Tunis as quickly as possible in order to seize intelligence targets. I had my own little HQ and then added a number of Field Security Sections, Military Police, a troop of Scout Cars and a Signals Unit, plus a detachment of the French Garde Mobile and most valuable of all, the American Consul, who became my political adviser.'

As Dennis Wheatley relates, Strangeways dashed ahead in an armoured car, was the first man into Tunis, shot his way into the German HQ, blew open the safe and seized all the secret documents before they could be destroyed.[7] Even if Wheatley has, in Strangeways' eyes, gilded the lily somewhat, the operation was a success and much later on during the war, Strangeways was asked to do similar jobs in Rouen and Brussels. The important element in all this was his determination that front-line soldiering, far from being incompatible with his involvement in deception, was instead an essential part of it.

With Tunis in Allied hands, following the German and Italian surrender on May 13, the time had come to regroup in North Africa where the planning for the invasion of Sicily was under way. After considerable wrangling between the British and the Americans, the Casablanca Conference in January 1943 had concluded that the Allies' next objective must be the capture of Sicily. Codenamed Husky, the invasion plan was a huge undertaking involving 160,000 men and 3000 ships. The deception plan to accompany the landings was called Barclay and the famous Operation Mincemeat, with its floating corpse,[8] was only one of a range of schemes designed to persuade the Germans that the Allies would attack Greece a fortnight after the attack on Sicily. Beyond that they wanted to persuade the enemy that attacks on Corsica, Sardinia and the South of France would follow a week after that.

Both the Sicilian Campaign (July 10–August 17 1943), and subsequent British landings at Taranto and American landings at Salerno (September 9), on mainland Italy, involved Strangeways and his tactical deception force.

'We landed at Salerno on about D plus 4 or 5, I think, and went to Bari on the east coast to join Alex's HQ. It was unfortunate there that my cover was blown because of a clerical error from London. I got a citation for my work in the North African Campaign. It was published in the press of course and so from that moment on I had to be called Culford instead of Strangeways. This caused even more confusion because when I arrived at the American HQ on the west side, I introduced myself as David Strangeways, obviously, and they weren't expecting anybody by that name at all. They were expecting a Colonel Culford. It certainly wasn't me who'd given myself that flipping name, they did that from London.

'I did various operations which were reasonably successful as we slowly worked our way up through Italy. Just the usual stuff, you know, battle taking place so you had to persuade the enemy to reinforce the wrong side, writing "the stories", and the important thing about those stories, their essence, was that they had to be simple, clear and convincing. My "stories" were never more than a few lines long. Essentially my job here was tactical. The tactics often appear the same, but they weren't because you couldn't use the same story again. You had to vary things or otherwise you'd get a "signature", something which one of their intelligence people, who was doing his job properly, might come to recognise.'

Before there was any danger of that happening, Strangeways handed over Tactical HQ 'A' Force and left the Italian theatre. He returned to England in December 1943 to 'get cracking with the invasion'. He was based at St Paul's School, at the big Victorian red-brick buildings in Baron's Court in London, where Montgomery, Commander-in-Chief 21 Army Group, had his headquarters for planning the Allied return to north-west Europe.

On November 29 the Overlord directive was issued and when, in December, Montgomery had been appointed, it had become his responsibility to oversee the planning and execution of the cover plan for Overlord. He was to liaise fully with the Naval and Air Commanders-in-Chief and it was their joint responsibility, clearly established on February 23 1944, to direct the threat towards the Pas de Calais and to conceal the state of readiness of the forces under their command so as to indicate a target invasion date of 45 days after D-Day. Back in December Montgomery had announced his intention of establishing at 21 Army Group a small, self-supporting, mobile headquarters whose duty would be to plan and implement deception matters in collaboration with the other bodies responsible for deception such as the LCS. The staff branch was called G(R) and the work on the ground was to be carried out by 'R' Force. The scale of the strategic deception, in which 'R' Force was to play a crucial tactical part, was vast. Experience gained in the Middle East, and lessons learned from the fumbled deceptions in north-west Europe during 1943, were all now being brought to bear on the planning for the re-invasion of Europe.

In January 1944, according to Professor Harry Hinsley: 'SHAEF's deception staff began to draw up in conjunction with the LCS and MI5 a more elaborate version of the original COSSAC plan for concentrating German attention on the Pas de Calais. The new plan codenamed Fortitude was approved on February 23. Simulating a threat both to Scandinavia (Fortitude North) and to the Pas de Calais (Fortitude South), it was also divided into two chronological parts.'[9] The first step was to convince the Germans that the main cross-Channel invasion would take place only after attacks had been made in Norway in conjunction with the Russians. The intention here was to make the Germans believe that the Allies intended to take advantage of any weakening of Germany that might result from

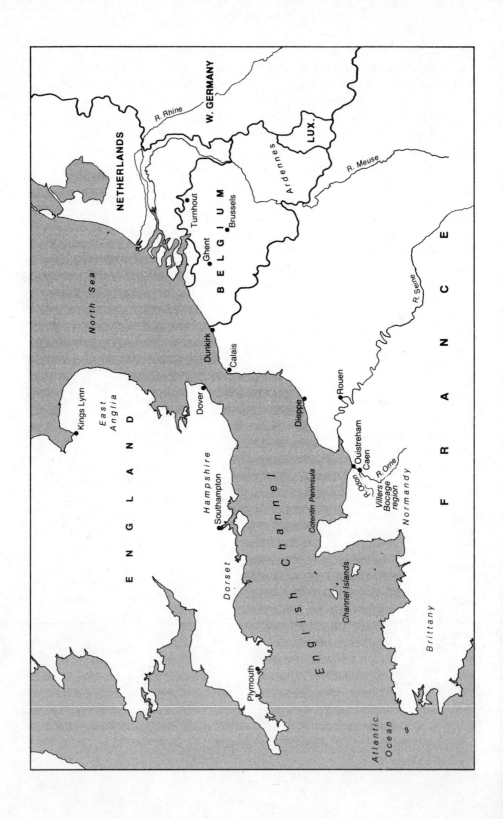

these attacks. The second step was simple and elegant. The landings in Normandy would be built up as a diversionary attack, while the main attack would come with six assault divisions across the Pas de Calais, who would consolidate a bridgehead with 50 divisions aimed at Antwerp and Brussels.

To bolster the lie required the creation of notional armies, the most important of which was undoubtedly FUSAG (First United States Army Group), under the apparent command of General Patton. To convince the Germans of the threat posed by FUSAG, information about its whereabouts and its intentions had to be channelled through a variety of means. 'Special Means' were the double agents run by the Twenty Committee, 'the stuff on the ground' was the responsibility of 21 Army Group, and 'R' Force in particular was commanded by Colonel David Strangeways.

'I was never recorded as a force commander – we called it "R" Force because it sounds like "recce". I resisted the natural temptation to call it "S" Force. We had a badge, a little black shield with a white "R" on it. And you'll find it on the order of battle of divisional signs even to this day. "R" Force had a number of strings to its bow. It consisted of three Light Scout Car Companies[10] and a Light Scout Car Field Park Company. After a series of training exercises in April we decided that the companies should be merged. These were our sonic deceivers, vehicles which carried enormous loudspeakers which could reproduce any battle noise that you'd recorded previously, tanks moving, small-arms fire, heavy artillery, whatever you like.'

The RE (Camouflage) units were called Special Field Companies and officers and senior NCOs as well as being trained sappers gained further valuable experience at the Camouflage Development and Training Centre at Farnham in Surrey. Training for the units themselves was augmented by night-lighting decoy work at Richmond Hill under the auspices of Colonel Sir John Turner of the Air Ministry, who had been involved since the earliest days of the war, when he had been responsible for the creation of dummy airfields during the Battle of Britain, known as Q and K sites.[11]

'We had problems with the camouflage staff, which I inherited, when I took over command of "R" Force in December 1943 – they'd built up a huge empire. But they didn't understand the military aspect of these things. They could do a little project beautifully, far better than any of us could think of doing. But they couldn't do the big sweep. You've got to know what battle is all about. That's why my time at Staff College and my two Brigade Majorships served me as an immensely useful background. Because I was an operations officer, not an intelligence officer. I had never been in Intelligence so I looked at it from the battle point of view.[12]

'A number of difficulties arose. The idea of this large camouflage staff was that they should conceal the troops. But I slashed their numbers by 50 per cent which caused great consternation. I had broken somebody's empire. What I did want was a very small select group which could help when I thought that we needed extra concealment or any kind of special measures. I was very lucky in the end. I had a super team which included men of the calibre of Basil Spence, the architect, who redesigned Coventry Cathedral after the war, and John Hutton, the artist. I kept them on my staff G(R) at 21 Army Group and sent them out where they were needed. A whole string of officers, though, is a waste of time.

'During January and February 1944 a Royal Signals wireless deception unit was formed by the War Office. It was called 5 wireless group, which had the capability of representing a corps and of course fantastic communications. They were wire recorders, not tape recorders, in those days. You could plug in the wire, and then from one source it would give the impression of a brigade network talking together.[13] I had a field HQ which had a G1, a lieutenant-colonel, and a number of officers who operated as scriptwriters. The idea was that you told them what was happening. They then wrote the script and the actual signallers and officers of the brigade you were representing would read the script sitting round a table with their mikes. That would be recorded on a wire and it would be the same noise as if they were all stationed in their various vehicles all over the country. Now that was all prepared. Nothing to do with me. I received the benefit of other people's work. That was "R" Force.'

Once the Overlord Directive for the invasion of Europe had been issued in November and Montgomery's responsibility for the planning and execution of the cover plan had been established, it was important that there should be proper liaison with the Naval and Air Commanders-in-Chief, Cunningham and Portal respectively. At the level at which Strangeways worked this co-ordination was essential.

'What one had to do was to study the aerial reconnaissance by the RAF and the actual interdiction bombing by the RAF. So I made all that into a map and that revealed, inevitably, exactly where we were planning to invade. So this is where the RAF were tremendous. I had to ask would they please mind, for every recce they did in the real area, Normandy, would they please do one and a half or two in "my" area, the Pas de Calais. I used to call it "my area" because it made it clear where it was. "Their area" and "my area". I requested that any interdiction bombing must lay stress on the Pas de Calais, as though they were intent on cutting off communications there, although they could also cut the other lines of communication elsewhere as well. And they played ball magnificently. And this is when you get down to the real nitty gritty. The good commanders get the form in one.

'Likewise with the Navy, it's a costly thing to send a chap on an exercise that really hasn't got any significance at all. And he may not come back with his ship. But, just as with the RAF, their recce raids for beaches had also to go on in "my" area. So one had to watch what the Navy were doing, what the Air Force were doing.

'It was the same thing with the dummy landing craft.[14] That project had to be boosted up and made to look real. I used to go and inspect it. I'd put on an alarm and see what happened. The chaps who had been manning these craft had been there for weeks. They'd come out, blinking, wondering what was happening. But all that needed covering with anti-aircraft. It all needed boosting up. There had to be more determination that this was real. Hundreds of lives were going to depend on whether we succeeded or not. On one recce of the Eastern Area I saw that the number of dummy aircraft, though well backed by our notional forces, lacked something essential. Enemy air recces would have shown that there were not enough "hards" to embark a force of the size that the number of landing craft suggested. 21 Army Group organised a recce through the Chief Engineer at once and the hards were to be prepared. I sent my rep along. Fortunately he was quite a character. He had been with me in North Africa. On his return to Headquarters late at night I asked him how things had gone and when the hards would be completed. He reported that the area Chief Engineer had more or less decided that it could not be done at all and was about to pack it in when he had intervened. "Sir, speaking as probably the biggest muck shifter in England, if you can't do it, I can." He was a close colleague, Chandos, Earl Temple of Stowe, and in peacetime his firm built roads. He was a tall, lanky, somewhat stooping Cavalry officer, with a very quiet voice, and I can just imagine the effect he had. The hards were duly completed in time by the Royal Engineers.'

There were further important aspects of the running of 'R' Force both at the planning stage for D-Day and afterwards at the beginning of July when the majority of 'R' Force had landed and established a Tactical Headquarters in Normandy. Prominent among these was Ultra. David Strangeways was aware both of its value and of its limitations.[15]

'It's important in deception to know what the other fellow's thinking, what he's swallowing. Philip Curtis[16] was allowed to be an Ultra reader for me. I hadn't got time to read it all. It gave us a hell of an advantage. But to get from the field, say, an actual staff officer's map, captured when his position was overrun, now that was something rather special. Later on, when we were in the bridgehead in Normandy, just after Operation Goodwood, Monty's big armoured push on Caen, which we had supported with a cover plan, we captured one map showing our imaginary division right where we had placed it. That wasn't me or Ultra or Philip, that was all those chaps doing their wireless work, doing their bits and pieces, backing you up. Before we left for Normandy, there were other elements to our wireless work. When we had first started thinking about Overlord, it had been taken almost for granted that the assault would have to take place in almost total wireless silence. When we thought about it a bit more, we realised that this was not such a good idea, as a radio silence would be bound to alert the enemy that something was up. Operation Quaker was the plan designed to achieve surprise by ensuring that the build-up to D-Day was a period of almost constant wireless activity. It was also intended to cover the final moves of the assault corps on their way to their embarkation points and would try to limit the damage in the event of a serious delay.

'So one had all of that going and, of course, the ramifications were infinite. At the same time I had to prepare for our landing and what we did after that. So I'd exercise my little HQ and make sure that they ran smoothly as a team. I had an integrated American staff with me before D-Day. On March 26 First US Army Group formed an American cover and deception staff, which was called Special Plans Branch. My immediate colleagues, Bill Harris and Ralph Ingersoll, were excellent chaps, but I was not always happy with some aspects of the way the Americans operated. The Americans did not understand the loose, autonomous way of working that we had developed. Each signal in their camp had to go out under the name and signature of the executive of the commanding general. To them it was impertinent for a staff officer like myself to send a signal off his own bat.

'With the Americans everything went up to the top, was vetted, and then sent. You got the attitude that every member of staff was subordinate through this extraordinary chain of command. Which in war is a hell of a waste of time and it's wrong. If somebody's in charge of the cooks then let him get on with the cooks until it's proved that he's not up to the job. The point is you've got to give him the chance to prove his competence, you've got to trust him, you haven't got time for all this reference upwards. If you make a nonsense, fine, the boss can sack you.

'Look, let me give you a specific example: back in North Africa we had learned the need to keep the chain of command short and decision-making as fast and painless as possible, when we were thinking up deception plans. We had an interesting Staff problem, which in the end we resolved quickly sitting under a tree. It had been decided that the 8th Army were to send one of their divisions to join the 1st Army. I was in on it because it was something in which I wanted to introduce an element of deception. So I was one of the officers and Peter de Havilland, who was the Staff Officer concerned with the actual issue of orders, was another.

'And the only sensible place to sit was under this nice fir tree. I suppose that it took us no time at all. I would make one objection, then someone would say something else about the bridges not being strong enough or some such thing, and then Peter de Havilland would act as chairman, as the boss. After no time at all, he wrote the order which was contained on one side of a message pad. We added a further note: Strangeways coming over to see you – and that was that.

'Now, two years before, there'd have been a meeting of many officers sitting round a table, masses of orders produced. But by then, all the 8th Army wanted was an order to move so and so to so and so at such and such a time. That's the way we did things then. The Americans would have made a great song and dance over the whole thing with masses of orders. Not necessary. Just a few people with their heads screwed on correctly.'

As with so many of the officers involved in deception-planning it was this early, vital experience in North Africa that taught them how to ensure that operations and deception went hand in hand. They had learned that the planning required must not be encumbered by unnecessary red tape.

'I was in the final conference for D-Day when the decision was made to go. The moment that decision was taken I had to go jumping into action and there was no sleep that night. The next morning there was the conference of course, and there was a great photograph on the steps outside, which still exists, and there's a curious little chap at the back somewhere. I think it must be me.

'Making the decision to go was one hell of a weight off our minds. But we still didn't know, as we set out on D-Day, whether or not Fortitude South had worked. It wasn't until the next day that we knew it was working. Each day I learned from Ultra whether or not Fortitude South was *continuing* to work. It went on for 15 or 16 days. I just thought, Crumbs! This is unbelievable! There was 15 Panzer still stuck up \there in the Pas de Calais. Of course you couldn't say anything about it, so a lot of it was carried in my head.

'Every morning I went to work – I had a small Nissen hut with my tiny staff in it – and that's where everything started from. You have to go on in faith, you've done your plan, go on to the next one. You didn't have time to worry after D-Day, you're too busy, you're waiting to take the remainder of the chaps over. I had already been over for 24 hours by myself. You're thinking ahead, you're learning by listening, not interrupting what the senior BGS and staff are talking about, what their problems are, whether any calamities are happening, what can be done, you're totally involved and yet totally separate. It's a curious feeling and the more successful you are the less you can say anything. And the only people who know precisely what you're up to are the Chief of Staff and the Commander-in-Chief, and to some extent the BGS1.

'When we finally got to the other side, "R" Force really set up shop. We opened for business, using our wireless units, our camouflage units and all the tactical skills we had picked up since the early days in the Middle East.'

The first important deception with which 'R' Force was involved was carried out on June 12 and 13. Called Accumulator, it was designed to draw enemy forces from the First US Army by posing a threat to the area near Granville on the south-west coast of the Cherbourg Peninsula. Its effects were hard to judge. Operation Raindrop is a better example of the kind of work that 'R' Force was now engaged in. It too took place on June 12 with the object of drawing the enemy attention to the east of Caen before an attack by 51 (H) Division west of Caen. With the use of fake wireless traffic one brigade of 51 Division was shown coming under the command of 6 Airborne Division to strengthen the left flank, while the remaining two brigades made as if to attack from the east. The operation as a whole was judged a success and 51 (H) Division achieved complete tactical surprise. This kind of small-scale tactical deception began to form the bulk of 'R' Force work and with codewords in increasingly short supply they made their way through a succession of operations, with names such as Trousers, Hallucinate, and Harley Street, gradually towards the Rhine.[17]

'It was the Rhine Crossing that was my last "do". After that it became pointless because the enemy hadn't got the facility to react to it.' All these years after the Rhine Crossing David Strangeways has no doubt about how to organise deception: 'You must start with a background in the ways and organisation of battle. This isn't a job for an intelligence officer. It's not paper work, it's a feel for the field. I was concerned with tactical deception, in other words, where the troops were. Johnny Bevan at the LCS did what I call strategic deception, and he was superb at it. He dealt with all my requests and I never had any complaints ever, either in our relationship or in connection with what he did.

'In the early days of my involvement with tactical deception back in North Africa there was a man in 8th Army, who'd done a lot of work using canvas and also sound. I think his name was Davenport, a very nice, intelligent officer – he helped me a lot. He thought and thought well. So we got a little force together and I was able to use it in North Africa to put up these fake canvas tanks and things. They were very primitive, but they were an indication of what *could* be done. They weren't there to represent a particular tank. They were something or other that might be a tank – might not be. But they fitted in with the wireless deception side, they fitted in with the ack-ack protection side, so everything was fine.

'I suppose I could put it this way. Suppose you lived in this house and every morning at eight o'clock the postman came or the milkman drove past, and you were sitting here one day and you heard the van go by with the milkman in and you heard the steps of the postman and somebody said to you the next day: "Did you see the postman on such and such a day?" "No, but he came," you'd reply. You'd be perfectly honest. You'd heard the familiar sounds that you always hear. That's all you need to do, reproduce the sounds of the postman. That idea can be transferred across – at any level you like. Indicate that something's happened. Indicate something that's related to that something. It's got to be an indication – you don't want to be too clear. Because what's going to happen when they realise they were wrong? They're going to start searching through their air photographs. If you're too accurate, if your story is backed up to the hilt, you'll bust the next operation.

'I had a monitoring set in my vehicle and I had all the frequencies of our own side, and I'd listen in to units as I was travelling around – get the form – and you'd often get a particular line on a particular regiment. They were all bickering about casualty returns or something – then you would use that, your scriptwriters would use that in a script and then their "Y" service would think, "By Jove, same chap again!" It's a little touch. A bit like fly-fishing, I suppose.'

Echoing Dudley Clarke, Strangeways believes in the 'softly-softly' approach. 'You don't take a great big silver salver and give it to him on that. He's got to make the story up himself. Then if the story goes wrong he blames himself, not you.

'You always have to ask yourself first, "What do I want the enemy to do?" Then you compose a story that you want him to work out for himself. It need only be four lines of text. But he must, through various sources, piece it together for himself. Everything you do is directed, inexorably, to bolstering that story, that false idea in his mind. Every means: spies, aerial reconnaissance, troop movements, bombardment, ship movements, it doesn't matter. It all must conform to the central story.'

CHAPTER 2

THE NEIGHBOUR'S TALE
Philip Curtis

Philip Curtis was the man who read the Top Secret Ultra files for Colonel David Strangeways. He was given the job because of a geographical accident.

'My family lived next door to the Strangeways family and David, on his way back from the desert in late 1943, called in at Algiers where my brother was in hospital. He had been wounded in the North African Campaign. They were both in the Duke of Wellington's Regiment. He had asked my brother what I was doing and learned that I was serving as the Intelligence Officer in the second Northants Yeomanry. David, who was coming back to London to form the staff for a field force, wanted an intelligence officer, knew my background and what I was like. He knew I was reliable and could keep a secret. So he whisked me away from my regiment, which at that time was stationed up in Yorkshire.

' "R" Force was the field force which David had been brought back to command and it was his job to put into practice the tactical deception that was planned by the Staff branch, G (R) at 21 Army Group, which was in turn part of the wider strategic deception plans co-ordinated by the LCS. "R" Force was in its earliest stages but I joined David Strangeways just before Christmas 1943 at St Paul's School, which was Monty's HQ. "R" Force itself had signals, engineers, armoured cars, and over the coming months, the full force necessary to carry out the ambitious plans for Fortitude South was gathered together. The only thing that was centrally located in London was the Staff side, which consisted of David Strangeways, his G2 and a G3 Ops. The other part that was involved was the camouflage department, which was based in and around London.

'As far as David Strangeways was concerned, the way it was run at 21 Army Group was that G was General Staff, G Ops was simply operations, and was kept totally separate from "R" Force itself. The Deception Staff I always thought of as G (R). I don't know why they chose R, perhaps there wasn't an R. It was just to make it separate. It probably had top-secret above it, and all that. One of the keys to understanding this whole set-up is that David had access right to the top. If he wanted he could go straight to the Chief of Staff, Freddie de Guingand, and he and Freddie would get together and sort things out. David would only do that if he was having a full-scale row with BGS Ops about something. David was really on a par with all the commanders. He knew that he had to co-ordinate what he wanted to do very closely with them but sometimes if there was something specific that he wanted to do, which they were not overkeen on, then his ability to go straight to Freddie became very important. Equally he recognised that he needed to keep abreast of what BGS Ops were intending.

'David was a man of enormous intelligence and he was fully aware that it would have been much more difficult to have an authoritative deception plan if you didn't know what the enemy were doing. In this instance he relied on someone like Bill Williams, who was Monty's most trusted intelligence officer, and in full receipt of Ultra. His appreciation of the situation had a considerable impact on David's thinking.

'I know that this all sounds a little complicated but what it boils down to is that David was not directly under either Operations or Intelligence, but he recognised that he must know what both were doing before he could make his plans. I think that David himself would have said that he was under the Chief of Staff.

'From my point of view, since I was the "R" Force Intelligence Officer, I had far more to do with Bill Williams. My responsibility at that time was to acquaint myself with the overall plan and to make sure that the people under David's command were put in the picture. I did no direct intelligence work myself. It was mostly a matter of absorbing great quantities of paper and digesting it. A lot of it would have been Ultra material and after D-Day, it was only because we knew what the enemy were doing that we knew whether they were, or were not, falling for the main strategy.

'We also had relationships with SOE because they were the agents we used in other forms of deception and we needed to know what other deceptions were happening so that we could co-ordinate them all. On the Secret Service side, we had our liaison with MI6. Occasionally we used to go to Broadway to see Lina – she was Kim Philby's secretary. There were also connections with the XX Committee and the section of MI5 that ran the double agents. All this liaison work was leading up to the big day.

'I vividly remember the last planning meeting before D-Day. They were all major-generals and admirals from the Combined Services. I was very junior but I went along with David Strangeways. It was highly restricted, only people given the Top Secret designation: Bigots. About all we knew before D-Day was that we wanted them to believe the invasion was coming from Kent, when, of course, it was not. During Operation Fortitude I had to liaise with the Americans. They brought a force over very similar to "R" Force. David Strangeways was responsible for training the Deception Unit. I was liaising with MI6, the Navy, the Air Force and so on because, of course, Fortitude was all sorts of deception from all sides. I suppose because I was trained as an intelligence officer I did recognise the German divisions and battle plans, "that's a Panzer division, you don't want to get involved with them." You did know a bit more than the average soldier. Looking back at it from this distance one wonders what the hell use one was really.

'I've always wanted to know what the Germans actually made of it all. You know, you put these messages out, but were they picked up, what did they make of it, did they make of it what we wanted them to? Certainly with 1st Army Group and Patton I think they genuinely believed in that. But Rommel never thought the Allies would land anywhere but in Normandy and he was completely overruled by von Rundstedt, who was totally under the influence of Hitler. Although Hitler did waver in the end, I honestly think if it hadn't been for von Rundstedt the whole of the deception plan would have fallen flat on its face.

'The fact that they also had that awful storm on D-Day itself lulled them into a false sense of security. That probably added 12 hours to their reaction time. Once the landing happened it was about 24 hours before they moved. Those 24 hours were vital.

'Once we got into Normandy, David virtually took command, with all the field commanders being miles away. "R" Force was involved in quite a few tactical deceptions and on a number of occasions, when the need arose, "R" Force came out to fight too, but gradually the need for tactical deception withered away. Certainly after the big set-piece battles had all been fought and there was neither the time nor the need to devise cover plans I think the great value of "R" Force then was that we would rush ahead and capture all the maps and bits of intelligence. We were generally searching for German documents to find out whether we'd been doing any good or not. The fighting troops never had the chance to do that, they were too busy chasing the enemy. All the way to Caen and on to Brussels, we were always looking for enemy plans and in particular any reaction to what "R" Force had been doing. It gave us a very good excuse to go swanning.'

CHAPTER 3

THE INTELLIGENCE COLONEL'S TALE

Sir David Hunt

Sir David Hunt's career as a Colonel, General Staff Intelligence, is a fine example of the mobilisation of talent that occurred on a massive scale during the Second World War. He was subsequently a Private Secretary to both Clement Attlee and Winston Churchill. He wrote Harold Macmillan's famous 'winds of change' speech, and went on to the highest levels of the Diplomatic Service. Much later on, during his retirement, he won the title as the BBC *Mastermind* Champion of Champions.

The description which follows of his day-to-day work gives an insight into the level of detail required by the deception-planners and how deception relates to the other means of fighting a battle. 'Without good intelligence properly used, one can never hope to plan and execute a good military operation, let alone a good deception operation.'[1]

Sir David Hunt's story begins with his initiation into the world of intelligence.

'I originally enlisted and was commissioned in the Infantry, but during the course of the campaign in Greece it was discovered that I spoke Greek, German and Italian and so I was speedily put on to the Intelligence Staff. At that time in the Middle East we had to recruit all our intelligence from our own resources. The advantage of that was that those concerned in Intelligence had been in Operations and knew precisely what the relationship between the two was.

'Having arrived in the Middle East in June 1940, I was seconded to Intelligence when the Greek Campaign opened in the winter of 1940–41. I was then sent immediately to the Western Desert and, apart from a couple of brief gaps, I stayed there the whole time until we reached Tunisia. By that time they'd made me a lieutenant-colonel, which was going a bit far, I thought, but still . . .'

David Hunt served under both Wavell and Alexander and his career took him from the North African desert to Sicily and Italy. The desert was the testing ground for so much of what followed.

'If there had been such a thing as a typical day, I suppose it would have gone something like this: get up really rather early and look at the first reports from all of the units under command. The first thing I always did was to ascertain the operational situation, find out how we were doing at the front. A lot of people treat intelligence as though it were some sort of mystical secret. Military intelligence at any rate is not a mystical secret, anybody can pick it up. It's quite easy. The essential thing is that the intelligence officer should have sufficient experience of operations as well. It was my practice first of all to find out what our own troops were doing. Then I would look at the reports that were coming in from the proper intelligence sources. I was Chief of GSI (A), that means intelligence regarding the enemy operations, so by the time the reports reached me they had already been pretty well sorted out.

'The bread-and-butter work of intelligence had four main components: prisoner-of-war interrogation; the study of captured documents; aerial reconnaissance by the RAF, and wireless interception. As far as aerial reconnaissance was concerned the RAF boys would bring pictures and reports to the tent I used to work in. It was attached to the side of a lorry. End of the day you just packed it up and stowed it in the lorry. I'd pore over the pictures, puffing a pipe as I did in those days, and I'd ask myself, what do all these bits of evidence show?

'I'd also make a point of going out to a corps or division headquarters somewhere, because often you'd find information there that they hadn't thought worth sending to you which was, in fact, of vital importance. I had been at the game longer than them and so I'd see more in certain information than they could.

'Another part of an intelligence officer's day was dealing with the interception of enemy radio and during the Second World War this was on two levels. One level, very important in operations, was what we called "Y", which was the code letter for tactical interception of either plain language or of messages sent in a fairly simple code. The "Y" stations were one of the greatest successes in the Middle East. We started them with the Greek Campaign in 1940–41 and by the time we got to Tunisia in May 1943, they were really going strong.

(*Above*) Dummy mobile cruiser in production.

(*Below*) The completed model ready for battle in North Africa.

(*Above*) After sizing, a dummy's turret is given a first coat of paint.
(*Below*) Sunshields were used to disguise tanks as three-ton lorries.

(*Above and below*) Dummy Sherman tanks positioned in the Wadis, known as 'Simpole Street'. These fake tanks replaced real tanks which were repositioned to take part in the Battle of El Alamein.

(*Above*) A dummy twenty-five-pounder gun trailer and guard.

(*Below*) The lorry was inflated with a foot pump. (Designed by Messrs R.F.D. Co. Ltd, Godalming.)

'In May 1943 I was given more or less *carte blanche* to form an intelligence staff in Tunisia. Alexander's headquarters in Tunisia was very small for an army HQ. We nearly all knew each other, because we'd come from the Middle East. We were joined by some Americans when we reached Tunisia, but otherwise we knew the men and the troops involved. One of the first things I insisted on was a "Y" section which was 101, Special Signals Unit attached to us. This was immensely valuable. Frankly "Ultra" intelligence, which was the other major level of interception, though it was tremendous and we couldn't have done without it, wasn't relevant to the events of a typical day. Ultra would give you the enemy's strategic plans, what they were thinking and planning, but what you really wanted to know, operationally, was what was going to happen in the next six hours in your particular sector. That's why it was vital to have "Y". If something is going to happen quite soon, then it's likely to be sent out in a simple code. You mustn't forget that the Germans weren't nearly as well disciplined as we sometimes tend to think and they'd transmit quite a lot of plain language messages.'

These reflections are endorsed by Bill Williams, another 'militarised intellectual'[2], who served on both Alexander's and then Montgomery's intelligence staffs. In a paper written from the 'point of view of a British consumer' in October 1945, Williams recognised that the material provided by Ultra was 'dangerously valuable not only because we might lose it but also because it seemed the answer to an intelligence officer's prayer . . . The information purveyed was so remarkable that it tended, particularly if one were tired or busy, to engulf not only all other sources but that very common sense which forms the basis of intelligence . . . yet it must be quite clear that Ultra and only Ultra put intelligence on the map.'

David Hunt illustrates the value of 'Y' and its relationship with Ultra with a down-to-earth example: 'I remember one very interesting incident that amused me. It was known from Ultra in March 1943 that Field Marshal Erwin Rommel was to be withdrawn from Africa, mainly to preserve his reputation because he certainly mustn't be taken prisoner. He had been commanding, briefly, the Enemy Army Group Africa. This was known through Ultra, but it wasn't telegraphed to us in the field, because it was reckoned that we didn't really need to know. Shows what a lot of nonsense this is about "getting into the mind of the enemy commander". Secondly, they thought this would be hot stuff and people would be liable to gossip about it. Montgomery was notoriously "leaky". He caused the most ghastly anxiety at the time of Alam Halfa in August 1942 by giving a great deal away to war correspondents. He told them he thoroughly anticipated all of Rommel's movements. He knew exactly where and when he was going to attack, and Monty made it sound as if this was his own intuition.

'Anyway, this particular Ultra news was not given to us. I found it out myself almost immediately afterwards because there was a splendid bit of plain language conversation between two troops of a German Army reconnaissance unit. One said to the other: "Are you going to be in Spax tonight for the party?" And the answer comes back, "What party?" "The party for the Army Group Commander's birthday." This was around the end of March, March 20, and I knew damn well that Rommel's birthday was November because he had been away celebrating his birthday in November 1941, which is why we had chosen that date for attacking Tobruk before he could.

'The Germans were always going away on leave. Rommel was *always* absent. Throughout the war we never attacked Rommel without finding that he was off on leave. Knowing then that November was his birthday that was clear evidence that General Jurgen von Arnim had taken over as Army Group Commander. That shows you the value of "Y", particularly in plain language transmissions. Now I come to Ultra. We had an SLU attached to us, a Special Liaison Unit.'

The SLUs were 'the voice of Station X' at Bletchley.[3] Without them the full value of Ultra would have been almost impossible to exploit. Lewin has described how Group Captain 'Fred' Winterbotham's system for distributing and ensuring the security of Ultra gradually spread to all theatres of war, except where the Navy was concerned. The Senior Service went its own way from the beginning. 'The existence of the SLUs was covert and shrouded'[4] from most eyes but Hunt recalls the sergeants and officers who made up the SLUs: 'They were mainly dressed in RAF uniform and they could therefore just be passed off as part of co-operation between Army and Air Force. They lived in a tent some distance removed from the rest of our headquarters in the woods of Tunisia. Of course we were all very dispersed because in the early days in Tunisia the Germans had air superiority, so we had a minimum of 200 yards between each officer. The SLU would be even further removed. We didn't want the Ultra boys and the whole lot of us being knocked out by one bomb.

'The SLU chaps sat there with high-powered RAF wireless equipment and received telegrams in code that they had to decipher with one-time pads, which made a lot of work for them. They used to receive the gist of the main enemy signals, courtesy of Ultra. The

one-time pad is covered with groups of numbers, five-figure groups
of numbers. You have a cipher book, rather like the kind of thing the
Foreign Office would use. For example, the FO had a single group
for: "Immediately on receipt of this telegram you should request an
interview with the Minister of Foreign Affairs and inform him that:"
So you take your cipher book, you look up the group and then you
add to it a number which you've taken off the one-time pad. When
you've used it once you throw it away. This totally defeats efforts to
decipher the code. It is very difficult and only works if you have very
highly trained cipher clerks. You couldn't use it as a General Army
cipher.

'As far as I know, the Germans never used the one-time-pad
system. For a start they were so proud of Enigma. So the Ultra
information came to us in a totally indecipherable form. Then an
officer from the SLU would come to me, about four times a day,
show me a copy of the telegram – I wasn't allowed to keep it, but
I could take it to show Alexander. Then I had to give it back and it
would be destroyed. We could use the same links that SLU provided
to send back enciphered material on the same subject.

'I first became involved in Ultra in Greece in the spring of 1941.
I was attached to the Air Force headquarters in Greece because, as
I said, I spoke Greek and various other languages. I was shown
everything. The Greek Campaign was the outstanding example of
Ultra as a real help. We got everything, right through the campaign,
the movement of enemy air and army units. When the Germans
postponed the H-Hour on D-Day by half an hour, we got that even
before their commanders on the ground heard about it.'

Developing his thoughts, Sir David Hunt moves on to describe
how the work of an intelligence officer meshes with the work of
the deception-planners and how the day-to-day analytical nature
of 'I', the gathering and sifting of information, fed the demands
of deception. It was the understanding of their own work and of
the pitfalls involved in trying to assess the relative values of large
amounts of often contradictory information that enabled Hunt and
his colleagues to work closely with the deception-planners. After all,
much of their work was aimed at the German counterparts of people
like David Hunt and Bill Williams, although there were few people of
that calibre working for the Abwehr in North Africa.

'There was a special branch called "A" Force which was concerned with deception. They were, in fact, a bit cagey, bless their
hearts. I didn't mind. I was brought into it, of course, and told
what the cover plan was. Operational Staff, down to about G1

level, to Lieutenant-Colonel, were told the real plan and the cover plan on all occasions. We could put forward suggestions because of our extensive knowledge of what the enemy were up to, where they were, what their strength was and who particularly was involved.

'In Tunisia, the man in charge on the spot was David Strangeways, a very clever fellow. We worked hand in glove. If Strangeways had to construct the deception he had to know where the chaps he was trying to fool were, and also what they were thinking, what they were expecting. As soon as the operation was under way he needed minute-by-minute feedback from the other side about what was going on. We were very close, besides which we were great friends.

'Strangeways wrote the story of the cover plan. If you like, I was the man who painted the picture. It worked like this: we would all be at a meeting and Operations would say what they would like the cover plan to effect – never ask what the enemy is to think, he is always liable to change his mind, it was what we would like to *see happen* that mattered. I'd pipe up and say "the enemy's dispositions are such and such." I might be able to say that the enemy seem to believe that we intend to attack shortly on such and such an axis. By sharing that kind of information we would produce a credible cover plan.

'Once Strangeways and his colleagues at "A" Force had produced their cover plan, they'd have to get it through the Chief of Staff. At the meetings, the real question would be: "How can we get the Germans out of the way while we do this?" And then it would be up to "A" Force to put together the plan. But as they went along they would keep in close touch with intelligence. Dudley Clarke, David Strangeways and the whole of "A" Force were brilliant, it was astonishing how often the tricks worked. But they did work and they've got to have the credit for it.

'One of the other vital parts of successful deception is the use of double agents. It didn't always work, of course. It *did* though with the Germans because they had been led to believe that the way intelligence works is through the use of agents. They thought it was all done by spies. Whereas in fact we all know that spies are no good at all. I don't think they produced anything of any value what-soever during the Tunisian Campaign or later on during the Italian Campaign. I never relied on or used any agent information except to conceal information I had really obtained from Ultra. If I already knew something from Ultra and some spy said something that could be twisted into it then I would put it in my intelligence summary very cheerfully. Trouble was a former colleague of mine at Magdalen once looked through it and remarked: "Well, it's very good, but I'm not sure the evidence is good enough to back it up." Of course, on the face of it, it wasn't.

'In the Mediterranean we did indeed get hold of a number of enemy agents and turn them round. Once they were working for us as double agents they were of the most immense value. That, paradoxically, is when spies come into their own. I remember a good example of how to use a double agent in Sicily. We had a double agent, a French lieutenant-colonel. He was a patriotic Frenchman but the Germans thought he was one of their agents. One day someone from "A" Force came rushing over from Sicily to tell us what the Germans were asking of their so-called agent. "We're having a dreadful time with this agent, because we can't think what to give him – it's got to be something really quite serious, not just chickenfeed." They went on to say that they were thinking of sending him, notionally of course, to Sicily. "What would you suggest he could send back from here that would be true and safe?"

'I said, I tell you what, this very morning most surprisingly we had a German reconnaissance aircraft over Syracuse harbour so why not send an absolutely accurate account of every ship that's in Syracuse harbour? They'll be gone before long, and the Germans have got a photograph of them already. That's the way to use double agents, lots of truth and then the big lie.

'If you have an enemy who is convinced that intelligence is all a matter of spying and if you can get hold of his spies and turn them round this is one of the most powerful weapons of deception. This is exemplified by Overlord and Fortitude but that is getting a little ahead of ourselves, so let me tell you about one of our more elaborate ruses, which took place without double agents much earlier in the war in North Africa. We called it the "Going Ruse".

'Before the Battle of Alam Halfa, the Chief of Staff at 8th Army, Freddie de Guingand, consulted with "Spud" Murphy, his G1, and Bill Williams, his G2. The Alam Halfa position, which gave flank protection to our main line, had originally been fortified and defended by Auchinleck. It was on the basis of this two-fronted position that we planned to fight our next defensive battle. We felt fairly sure that the enemy would come round our southern flank, which was the standard, old-fashioned tactic in the desert.

'But Freddie de Guingand said, "Suppose he goes wide of this ridge and keeps on going round the bottom of the 'L' created by our two fronts? He can then have a free ride into Alexandria." Naturally, he wanted to dissuade the Germans and Italians from doing this. Hence

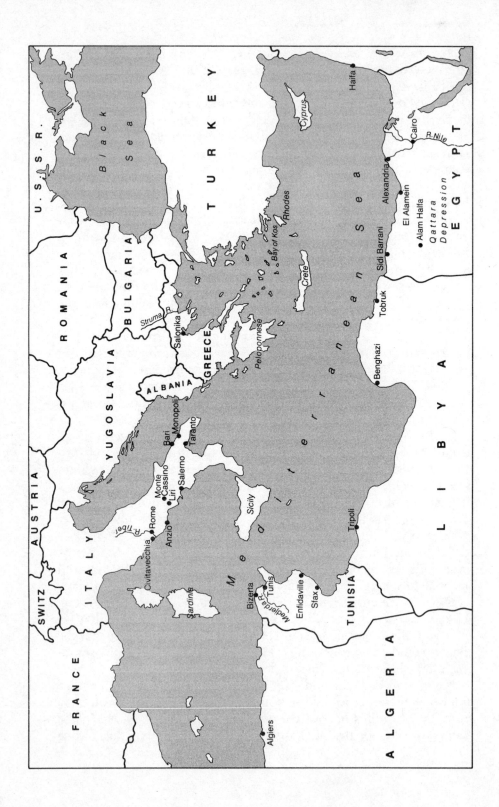

the deception. Throughout the desert campaigns we had much the best maps of the whole desert, especially of Egypt, thanks to our long connection with that country. A special sort of map was issued to formations fighting in the desert which was drawn in four colours showing whether it was easy going or hard going across the desert. One colour said: impassable, another one was very slow, another not too bad. The best was only about 10 miles in the hour.

'The deception was this: in circumstances of great secrecy we printed a false "going" map, which showed that there was a wide strip of good going leading straight on to Alam Halfa. From the position which we thought they'd reach having gone round our flank, south of Alam Halfa, the map showed good going all the way up to Alam Halfa. And it indicated bad going, very heavy sand, shown further east, which was the line we didn't want them to take. The point was to discourage them from going too far eastwards. Three copies of this map were printed. One was handed over to the 11th Hussars, who were an armoured car reconnaissance regiment, it was folded as though it had been in use, smears of oil put on it. A patrol was sent out, fully briefed of course, and drew enemy fire as they carried out a recce on the southern flank. They faked a breakdown of one of the vehicles, the crew baled out and, I believe, were rescued by the others. The patrol raced away, leaving the enemy to search the armoured car and find the false "going" map. There were other interesting bits of paper left around, and they of course were true. The vital thing about deception is that you must give four or five truths for every one lie or you're sunk.

'As a matter of fact, in the Battle of Alam Halfa, the German-Italian Army followed exactly the course which we had forecast and not long before Alam Halfa we had a sketch of the plan on Ultra. In the battle they did advance direct from the south against the Alam Halfa ridge, and were seen off. The ridge had been prepared with tanks and guns dug in. They did get stuck in some fairly bad going but that was an incidental benefit to us.

'The question is: had they been fooled by the false "going" map or was there some other reason? Ever since the war the Germans have maintained that they took the route they did because they were short of petrol and hadn't got enough for the wide sweep which the British feared.'

There is a considerable debate about the success of the 'going' map ruse. Handel[5] points out that a number of distinguished commentators have significantly different views. On the one hand, Major-General Sir Francis de Guingand, Field Marshal Alexander (who also participated in the deception) and Winston Churchill all felt that to a significant extent the ' "going" map ruse' was a success. On the other hand, more recently Professor Harry Hinsley and Correlli Barnett have questioned its importance. The unresolved debate clearly demonstrates the difficulty of determining the success of any individual tactical deception. But David Hunt has his own well-informed view on this: 'Now it's true that they were short of petrol, which is the explanation of Rommel's action preferred by Hinsley and others, but here I think I can claim to be a good historical source. The Commander of the Afrika Korps, Lieutenant-General Wilhelm von Thoma, was an admirable Bavarian aristocrat from the Cavalry. He was captured when the Germans discovered that their line was penetrated and that they were going to have to retreat. The story of his capture is quite an amusing saga. Von Thoma was at Rommel's headquarters and he pointed out a line of armoured vehicles moving eastwards somewhere to the south of them. He said: "My God, that's a British armoured force and they've got right through." "Nonsense," said Rommel, "nothing of the sort, that's the Italian Ariete Armoured Division." Von Thoma said, "I bet it isn't." Rommel said, "I bet it is."

'Von Thoma went off to take a look and was taken prisoner. That night he dined austerely in Montgomery's mess. Next day he was brought back to Cairo where I was living in the suburb of Maadi and I had him to lunch. The flat was on the second floor of a kind of two-up, two-down house with a nice garden. Lunch was a pretty grand affair with a steaming lentil soup, swimming in grease and liable to take the skin off your tongue, probably some fresh lamb and then a crème caramel. We lived pretty well in that billet in Maadi. Anyway, at lunch I raised the question very tentatively about the Battle of Alam Halfa. Now he hadn't been there, he was on the Russian front, but he knew all about it.

'He said, "The fact is we Germans knew nothing about the desert – you British with your long colonial experience, you know all about the desert. The Italians were no good either. Couldn't even produce decent maps of the place. The only maps we had which were any good at all were the British maps we captured. We used to copy them." "Oh, really," I said, "you found them useful, did you?" "Yes, we found them particularly useful just before the Battle of Alam Halfa, because we were intending to move much further east. Just in time we captured from one of your armoured cars a map which showed very bad going there. So we didn't go that way, we concentrated on Alam Halfa instead. We didn't succeed, but still it would have been much worse if we had got stuck in the sand, going the other way round."

'I was very pleased this confirmation had come out. I didn't, of course, undeceive him. Later on I learned from someone who'd looked up the Combined Services Direct Interrogation Centre records that in England, when he was in a bugged prisoner-of-war camp, he'd confided to another prisoner that he thought the Germans had been fooled by that "going" map. I'm bound to say that I think he realised it because people kept coming back to it and asking him questions about it. When he was talking to me however, he had no suspicions and fortunately the topic came up quite naturally.

'The whole "going ruse" was an 8th Army affair, but I knew all about it because it would have been useful if I could have picked up something on enemy wireless traffic that might indicate whether they had swallowed it or not.

'Tunisia, in May 1943, the final battle, was unquestionably an outstandingly good example of deception. It was very remarkable really, when you come to think of it, because it was quite a small front. By the time 8th Army had lurched forward as far as the Enfidaville position, it was a small front and the Germans ought to have been able, if they'd known what they were doing, to find out absolutely everything about us. Of course, the Germans had the wrong ideas about intelligence all along. They didn't really take enough trouble over the interrogation of prisoners, or over the scrutiny of captured documents. And in addition, by this stage of the North African Campaign they had precious little aerial reconnaissance.'

David Hunt's dismissive view of German Intelligence, at least as it operated in North Africa, is endorsed by an even more damning assessment from Brigadier Raymond Maunsell, Head of Security Intelligence, Middle East: 'The Abwehr was a thoroughly corrupt organisation, careless, dilettante and foreign to exact administration which is essential to good intelligence work. And, after all, Admiral Canaris and Colonel Oster were "traitors" and, in any case, the whole organisation was permeated with the "pins-in-the-map" syndrome.'[6]

As far as Tunisia was concerned the Germans failed to discover where the main attack was going to be, although they ought to have done. David Hunt continues: 'It was the natural access down the Medjerda River, which had been used by all armies since Scipio. First of all they got the idea that the 8th Army was going to deliver the final blow, because it was the most experienced. They were massing heavily on the 8th Army front. But we intended to attack on the 1st Army front. On the 1st Army front we fooled them by a very elaborate piece of deception, which included a lot of bogus wireless traffic and a number of dummy tanks.

'The wireless traffic was important because one of the things the Germans were very good at was direction-finding. They also listened like hell. They were good at radio monitoring. The deception people sent a large number of wireless sets to a certain area of the front, where they would open up and start passing messages like fury, back to Army Group Headquarters, on to other units and so on. These messages in cipher sounded authentic but were totally false, nonetheless they read as though they came from a corps headquarters. In other words they put out on the air the amount of traffic that a corps headquarters would normally generate. The Germans quickly located them and drew the inference that we were taking a great deal of interest in that particular sector.

'In Tunisia we did a sort of triple bluff. We had a lot of dummy tanks and then, all of a sudden, we concealed them so that the enemy was looking for them. Then we would reveal them again, pushed out of the woods a bit. The effect was that when we made the thrust direct up the main road by the most obvious route, on to Tunis, the enemy were absolutely convinced and had got all their reserves and counter-attack forces over to the south-east of our line of attack. We were attacking north-east and they were stuck out on the right of our thrust.

'Just before the final attack we got them so excited that they did what they thought was a spoiling attack on this area that they assumed to be very strongly held. It was a bit awkward really, because it was rather weakly held. They nearly overran a divisional HQ there. But we managed to fight them off. Thank goodness they didn't get anywhere near the dummy tanks or the game would have been up. The striking fact was that on the day before the attack, D–1, the German commander brought round from his front opposite 8th Army his last squadron of Tiger tanks and two batteries of the "famous 88", the heavy anti-tank gun, and put them in this sector on the right, where they were left behind. I remember being very pleased with that and telling Alex that the deception was plainly going to work.'

Once the Germans had been chased out of North Africa, the Allies turned their attention to the Mediterranean theatre. David Hunt was subsequently involved with many of the deception plans, as the Allies painfully and slowly fought their way up through Sicily and Italy.

'A very important piece of background to every deception operation in the Mediterranean was the fact that we had thoroughly convinced the Germans that we had very much larger forces in the area than we really had. This had been achieved as a result of a patient build-up of persuasion over the years mainly by "A" Force, Middle East, aimed at creating the fake "order of battle" on which Dudley Clarke placed such importance.[7] Whenever you brought a "notional" division in you always had, for example, somebody in the right kind of vehicle driving around with imaginary insignia. "A" Force had compiled an order of battle for us which gave something like 23 more divisions in Africa than we actually had.'

A classic example of the significance of the fake order of battle was Operation Barclay, the cover plan for the invasion of Sicily, codenamed Operation Husky, in 1943. The aim of Barclay was to divert enemy reinforcements away from Sicily and towards Sardinia on the one hand and the Peloponnese on the other.

'The Germans, you see, in their logical way, said this is far too large a build-up for nothing more than the conquest of Sicily, or for that matter the advance from Sicily into the Italian peninsula. This must be destined for some much bigger project. Therefore they were prepared to believe that we were ready to invade the Balkans. At its most successful deception trades on the enemy's own preconceptions. Hitler always feared an Allied thrust up through the Balkans. They were rich in copper, chrome, and bauxite, and Romania provided much-needed oil for the Reich. But we were not going to invade the Balkans, not because the Americans didn't want to get involved in the Balkans – although they were paranoid about the place – not because they didn't want fine, upstanding American boys involved. No, the reason was that you can't carry out effective amphibious landings without good air cover. So, if we were going to invade the Balkans, we would first have to invade Crete, to ensure we had air cover. That might take us the whole winter of 1943–1944. Then we would have to land in the Peloponnese, which is pretty beastly. There were very good reasons against a Balkan adventure. So the German idea that this is what we must logically be intending to do was totally wrong.'

After the successful conquest of Sicily in August 1943 the next target was mainland Europe which, it was decided, would be attacked through Italy. In Italy King Victor Emanuel, at the request of the Fascist Great Council, had deposed Mussolini on July 25 and assumed supreme command of Italian forces in the field. The new Premier, Marshal Badoglio, sued for peace in secret with the Allies and an armistice was announced on September 8. Germany's reaction was swift. Hitler seized northern and central Italy, rescued Mussolini in order to install him as the puppet head of a Fascist republic and disarmed Italian occupation forces in Greece and Yugoslavia, many of whom were put into POW camps.

The Allied invasion began on September 9 1943, at Salerno and Taranto, and the Germans retreated to a line that stretched across the peninsula north of Naples. The battle through Italy was long and hard. The Allies took nine months to reach Rome. General Mark Clark's 5th Army in the west and the British 8th Army in the east were frustrated by Field Marshal Albert Kesselring's defensive Gustav line. The breakthrough was finally achieved when Alexander launched Operation Diadem on May 11 1944. It had come about as a result of Alexander's secret transfer of the 8th Army to his western flank. Ronald Lewin has described it as 'one of the most beautifully orchestrated offensives of the whole war'[8] and that 'next to Normandy's D-Day, Diadem was deception's consummation'. As a result of the success of Diadem Alexander broke through the Gustav line at the bitterly contested Battle of Monte Cassino and his divisions poured up the Liri Valley towards Anzio, Rome and the north.

David Hunt remembers some of the aspects of Operation Dunton, the cover plan for Diadem that gave him great satisfaction at the time: 'In that "Dunton" operation there was a terrific amount of physical deception. We built a hessian screen a mile and a half long to conceal the movement of troops below Monte Cassino. All movements were made by night and dozens of dummy tanks were left behind in their place. All the tracks leading down to the crossing of the River Rapido were made at night and covered by brushwood during the day. That was a negative way of deceiving the enemy but we also tried positive ways. We tried to convince the enemy that we were going to make an amphibious landing. He was not to know, thank goodness, that this would have been impossible, since all our landing craft were at that time lining up on the northern side of the English Channel. We were playing yet again on a German perception, misplaced but working powerfully on their strategic thinking, in this instance that we had more shipping available than we did, so we decided to try to simulate a landing at Citavecchia. This was also pretty cheeky since we'd already tried a similar deception at the same place at the time of Anzio. But if we had had landing craft and troops to put in them, Citavecchia would have been a good place to land since it would have put us on the other side of the Tiber. The Canadian Corps and the American 36th Division were nominated to carry out the notional landing there. The reason for this was that the two Canadian divisions and the 36th American would all be in reserve at the start of the offensive and therefore there was no chance of them losing prisoners to the enemy and thus blowing the gaff. So Canadian signallers were sent down to the Naples/Palermo area, passed lots of wireless traffic and splashed about in boats for the sake of the aerial reconnaissance.'

Lewin describes how the bait was swallowed: 'Hitler called an investiture at Obersalzburg at the end of April which was to be followed by a senior officers' indoctrination course.' A number of senior German officers were called away from the Italian front to attend and 'several were still on leave when Diadem broke on May 11'. Von Senger of the 90th Panzer Grenadier Division had 'told his corps to be ready from 24 May onwards'.[9] The deception-planners of 'A' Force had used every conceivable device to suggest that the 8th Army could not possibly be ready to attack until mid June, whereas, in fact, the attack was scheduled for May 11. David Hunt takes up the story:

'The beauty of Operation Dunton, from the point of view of the historian and the intelligence officer, is that we were very rapidly able to prove how successful the deception had been because we overran 14th Army Headquarters and captured the whole of their situation maps in the first week of the engagement.

'The Germans also contributed to their own downfall, because we used to put chinagraph on our maps and rub it out when the situation altered, but they used to draw on the map itself and file all the maps. As a result there was a map for every day, in fact the whole intelligence series of maps for the first 10 days. When we looked at the maps it was clear that they had simply fallen for every one of our deceptions.'

The enemy had disposed his forces exactly as the deception-planners wanted him to do. The perfect series of situation maps captured from the Germans revealed what David Hunt calls 'the fog of war' on the German side. The most significant map was dated May 12, the day after Diadem began. It showed that even then the Germans had no idea what was about to hit them.

Sir David Hunt's final comment on their success: 'When we finally did attack the German commander was away on leave. I tell you, they were always away on leave.'

CHAPTER 4

THE GENERAL'S TALE
General Charles Richardson

General Richardson's father was also a soldier. There was never any doubt that his son would be a sapper.

'My father told me, if you get tired of the Army, or much more likely the Army gets tired of you, then at least you'll have learnt something you can fall back on.'

After an Honours Degree at Clare College, Cambridge, Charles Richardson soon found himself in India, working as a Royal Engineer officer throughout the sub-continent, notably in the Hindu Kush and the North-West Frontier. In 1938, after seven years, he was clearly close to being obsessed with India and realised he had better return to England to pursue his army career back at home. He became assistant adjutant at Chatham, in charge of mobilisation among other things.

'It was terribly depressing really, because one knew that the cupboard was bare, and that these mobilisation plans were getting further and further removed from reality.'

Early in September 1939 Captain Richardson went to France as adjutant to a Territorial group of engineer companies. He fought through France and Belgium, where he found that the Belgian Army had large quantities of heavy artillery, heavy horses and very heavy guns: 'They were often quite immobile on those paved lanes, so all hell was let loose when we arrived, and the chaos continued throughout that particular operation.' Like David Strangeways and many hundreds of other officers, and thousands of men at that time, he was driven back to the beaches of Dunkirk:

'I got back to England in a naval sloop. We were all very wet to begin with. We had to wade out up to our necks to get on board. The Navy were marvellous of course. They told us all to strip off and go and sit on top of the casings of the boilers to dry off.'

Back in Britain he took up a command defending 120 miles of the English coast from a headquarters at Crewkerne. His division was not overendowed with men and material: 'I knew we had six boxes of small-arms ammunition, eight French 75-millimetre guns, which had been found in some depot, with about three shells per gun. So again, in August and September 1940, this was a pretty depressing kind of time.'

It was at this stage that Charles Richardson experienced precisely that weakness which others have identified as the spur to the development of deception – the need to use something other than sheer force of arms to defeat an enemy who appears overwhelmingly stronger. Emerging from this 'pretty depressing kind of time', he was soon posted to teach at the Staff College at Haifa in the Middle East. From there, after a year in the Special Operations Executive in Cairo, he found himself in North Africa: 'By the time I'd packed my bags and said goodbye to the lovely ladies of SOE – an unbelievable organisation providing many comic incidents – the 8th Army was a hundred miles nearer Alexandria and moving much too rapidly eastwards. I joined them at midnight and I was sent off to a place called Alamein, which I hadn't heard of. There I met the Corps Commander whose plan I had to obtain, and we had a terribly depressing breakfast where he mooned around saying "we need about 25 divisions to hold this place and we've only got eight." '

In June 1941 Claude Auchinleck had succeeded Wavell as C-in-C Middle East. He forced Rommel to retreat beyond Tobruk, but in January 1942 Benghazi was captured by the Germans. Building momentum, they continued their offensive in May and had taken Tobruk by mid June. Auchinleck took direct command of the 8th Army and by the end of the month had managed to hold the El Alamein corridor, but was unable to go on the offensive. Shortly after that he was relieved of his command.

'Churchill came out, Auchinleck was sacked and soon we had Monty out there. I served Monty for three years and you couldn't ask for a better commander to serve anywhere.'

He served well enough to become a brigadier at the age of 34, young even by the standards of wartime service.

'It was the Monty "hot-breath" that wafted me on to such heights. There had been a time though, before Alamein, of low morale. We used to meet in Auchinleck's caravan every night, about five of us, so I saw it all at very close quarters. It seemed that there wasn't a light at the end of the tunnel anywhere. I was told by the then Chief of Staff to get out a plan to withdraw the 8th Army to Khartoum. But then Monty arrived, with his plan for Alamein as well as a plan for Alam Halfa. I was a bit of an odd-job man in Plans, so I was rather surprised when Freddie de Guingand said, "Charles, get out a deception plan for Alamein." I was given Monty's outline plan, which was desperately obvious really, concentrating the main thrust on the coastal road on the right. This was dictated by the fact that there were some very dominant features there in a desert which was rather short of dominant features. I pondered on this: obviously what one had to do was to try to persuade Rommel that the main thrust was going to be in the south, where there were miles and miles of rather nondescript country ending in the Qattara Depression, which was ground which could hardly be penetrated by wheeled traffic at all as the "going" was much too soft. The first thing was to persuade Rommel that the main thrust was in the south. I thought this might appeal to him because he was an expert in turning flanks. One thought that if he attributed to Monty his own sort of thinking – the wish to avoid frontal attacks – he might be led into believing our tactical deception. The second thing, of course, was to persuade him that the day of our attack was not going to be October 23 but later. I considered how much later one could conceivably convince the enemy it would happen. The preparations for that battle were vast: it was the biggest operation in the Second World War up to that time. I came to the conclusion that we could hope to stall the enemy's thinking by about ten days.

'But then, the question of how to do it? The first thing was as far as possible to conceal all these vast activities on the northern, coast-road sector. One had to conceal the preparations in the forward area such as dumps of petrol and ammunition, and "spoof" assembly areas at the back. This was to conceal the true nature of the proposed attack. Then for the time factor, the thing that immediately sprung to my mind, being a sapper, was a pipeline for water. Water had played a big part already, and pipelines had been detected by enemy Tactical Reconnaissance. Misleading the enemy over pipelines could be done very easily. Our camouflage people did this by taking empty petrol tins, bashing them out and laying them by night to look from the air like a pipeline gradually snaking its way through the desert. The clever thing about the fake pipeline, codenamed "Diamond", was that the enemy watching the progress of the work by air photography could be led to judge how long it would take to complete. The intention was to make it look as if it could not be ready until at least ten days after D-Day.

'I took the plan to Freddie de Guingand who approved it and put it up to Montgomery who also said yes. Monty was remarkable really in the way that he immediately accepted and exploited anything, however unconventional, that he reckoned was good. I don't think he would have developed this deception plan himself, although his major outline plan was always worked out by him personally. Freddie de Guingand, of course, had been Director of Military Intelligence in GHQ, Cairo, and therefore was soaked in MI6 and MI5 and Dudley Clarke's exploits.'

Lieutenant-Colonel Richardson met Brigadier Dudley Clarke of 'A' Force from time to time. He found him great fun, with a ready sense of humour, but he never had to worry about the interweaving of 'A' Force's plans with his own.

'Dudley Clarke took a lot of interest in what I was doing, but I regarded his stuff as being so stratospheric and secret that I thought it was probably best to keep out of it. He played his cards very close to his chest: he was so pleasant to meet that he could get away with that. Nobody could poke into what he was doing, because he'd retort by telling funny stories about something quite different. One of my major concerns was that the plan should remain secure, so I said to Freddie, "This is going to be a major piece of organisation and it only needs some fool in Headquarters or some infantryman somewhere to make a mistake and sabotage the whole thing. We must instil very tight discipline throughout the whole operation." It needs strong discipline to get British soldiers to dig false trenches when they're tired already. All these tiresome things that had to be done, putting covers on vehicles, arranging stacks of hay to try to make them look as if they were lorries, concealing vast quantities of petrol and ammunition, involved not just the camouflage units but also at times practically every formation in the whole army.

'Monty believed that it didn't matter how young you were: if you'd got a job to do you had to be given absolute authority to carry it out. So, at my request, Freddie got him to write a letter to the Corps Commanders, and Monty said to me, "You go off with this and see the Corps Commanders personally, explain the whole thing to them and how important it is," which I did. Then it became Monty's plan with all the weight that that attached to it.'

Despite the endorsement of his plan by Montgomery, Charles Richardson remained only too aware of the inherent risks of deception-planning: 'The thing that worried me all along was this:

the object of a deception plan is to get the enemy to arrange his concentrations of force and his reserves on a wrong basis. Hardly any battles of any sort take place where a commander on either side can afford to be strong everywhere. He has to take risks somewhere. If the deception succeeds, then it would conceivably increase the chances of success by say 20 to 30 per cent. But if it fails, if it is "rumbled", it would decrease the chance of success by as much as seventy per cent. In a way, you're on a hiding to nothing. This is what worried me a lot. Bear in mind that I'd never really done anything like this before. I was pretty sceptical about a lot of this deception, dummy tanks and so on, partly because the Luftwaffe had been very powerful in the past and air photography was very good, and some forward patrols would inevitably get captured: so I felt it was extremely difficult to carry through our deception without it being detected. To some extent I had regarded these dummy tanks in Auchinleck's time as a pathetic last resort of British Arms facing total disaster.'

Nonetheless, Charles Richardson's plan was successful. He thought up the major outline of the plan quite quickly in his tent. Then he consulted with the camouflage experts: 'One particular idea they came forward with was to do with petrol dumps. The vast quantities of petrol required in the forward area came up in rectangular tins about two feet by ten inches square. They suggested that these tins should be brought up at night and formed into something that looked from the air like a fire trench, instead of just laying them on the ground as a dump. The forward area was, of course, full of fire trenches, so this idea blended in well, and fooled the enemy's photographic reconnaissance.'

After Charles Richardson had thought of the idea of Diamond, the dummy pipeline, his camouflage expert, Major Tony Ayrton, embellished it with water tanks at intervals and dummy dumps and the deception began to take on a life of its own over a period of about six weeks before the Battle of El Alamein.

'The thing which must be emphasised in all this is the RAF. For something like ten days before the attack the Luftwaffe's Tactical Reconnaissance couldn't operate over our battle area at all. The RAF had established such air superiority that the Germans just couldn't afford the losses. Up to that time, when they ceased to be able to function, I used to get the German Tactical Reconnaissance report through "Y", tactical wireless intelligence rather than Ultra, in my tent every morning. I was absolutely amazed that it said "No Change". Day after day it said "No Change". And I knew that all these vast preparations were going on behind, such as the making of tracks and the assembly of three armoured divisions, enormous activity which the Luftwaffe just was not picking up.'

It was a strange time for Charles Richardson, some of which is reflected in his letters to his mother:

'I'm writing from Alexandria where I have come for six hours relaxation as my work [his deception-planning] is finished. In a few days we shall see the results. It has all been very interesting and I could not ask for a more congenial master than Freddie de Guingand, who is the Chief of Staff. Having been instructors at the Haifa Staff College together, although he is eight years older than me, we can talk together absolutely frankly and argue about plots for this and that.

'I'm afraid I have neglected you very much but I have been working in "predestinate grooves" and it is difficult to think of anything else:

> There was once a man who said Damn,
> It was borne upon me that I am,
> An engine that moves,
> In predestinate grooves,
> I'm not even a bus but a tram.

'And that was the feeling!'

The 'predestinate grooves' were, however, deceptive plans considerably wider in scope than anything attempted up until that date. The overall deception plan for Alamein was codenamed Bertram and it consisted of a number of subsidiary plans: Diamond, which Charles Richardson has described in some detail, and plans Brian, Munassib, Martello, Murrayfield and Meltingpot. Brian was a dummy petrol, food and ammunition dump placed well to the rear in the south as part of the attempt to persuade Rommel that the main attack would come in the south. Meanwhile the genuine ammunition dump at Imayid in the north of the British front line, which the enemy had already located, was enlarged and camouflaged with hessian and sand in the hope that the enlargement would go unnoticed. Murrayfield and Meltingpot were genuine armoured formations, which were moved under cover of darkness during the nights of October 20–22 to the concentration areas in the north in preparation for the assault on October 23. They were replaced with dummy formations. Once in their genuine forward positions they were hidden by sunshields, which made them invisible from the air, plan Martello. The supporting 25-pounder guns were also hidden under dummy lorries, and the result was a so-called 'cannibal', and there were 360 of them. Munassib was a double bluff, consisting of dummy artillery positioned at the southern end of the British front line. Once the dummies had been recognised as such during the battle proper they were replaced by genuine artillery and used to mount a subsidiary attack. Montgomery himself is on record as saying that the deception plan was successful. 'The co-ordinating brain behind this part of the plan was Charles Richardson, a very able officer in the Planning Staff of Eighth Army HQ . . . The whole plan was given the codename Bertram and those responsible for it deserve the highest praise: for it succeeded.'[1] General Richardson himself only found out very recently that Ultra traffic had established clearly that the enemy had been fooled. Rommel was away when the battle started, and it was several days before their reserves were moved up to the northern sector of the battle.

'I think one caveat about deception is that it's inadvisable to try a deception plan except before a real set-piece battle, when you've got time to prepare and you've got resources to do it. Alamein and Normandy I would say are two classic cases when it should be possible to produce a deception plan which could pay a dividend. After Alamein, I really couldn't believe that the Germans could be so stupid as far as intelligence work was concerned. But then some of their commanders were very rigid and this tended to create a mentality that could not react effectively to the unexpected.'

CHAPTER 5

THE HISTORIAN'S TALE
M. R. D. Foot

Michael Foot, renowned for his books on military history was also involved personally in the action of the Second World War. He managed to plan what he describes modestly as 'one or two unimportant corners of a grand scheme', which were, in fact, deceptive airborne operations in the small hours of D-Day.

M. R. D. Foot comes from a military family with, as he says, 'one very distinguished admiral in our recent ancestry'. As a boy he naturally assumed that he would join the Royal Navy as soon as his education was complete. But his military father pointed out that the Navy would 'axe' him as soon as he was forty. Michael Foot became a soldier instead: 'I was a territorial army officer throughout the war. During the first half of the war I had a dull time in Anti-Aircraft Command but later, by accident, I was posted as Intelligence Officer to Combined Operations where I had a very interesting eighteen months.'

During that time Michael Foot saw action in Operation Forfar, a series of small raids on the Channel and North Sea coast, mainly on the cliffs of eastern Normandy. In one of the raids Major Foot was allowed to take part but specifically forbidden to go ashore. He knew too much about intelligence matters for the Army to risk him being captured. The closest he came to the coast of France was in 1943 when he came within a mile of it. Michael Foot and his Combined Ops team were told that the objective of Forfar was to secure German prisoners. But he now knows that the real objective was to keep the Germans' attention focussed on the Channel and the North Sea while the plans for the invasion of Sicily were finalised. His mission was just three or four days before the Sicily invasion on July 10.

Since neither he nor his men knew that the raids were designed as diversionary tactics rather than serious operations, there was bound to be disillusionment. 'I waited out at sea while the raiding party went ashore. They returned very angry with me because there wasn't anybody there at the point they'd attacked. I said, "How do you know there was nobody there?" The fellow said, "Well, after throwing stones at the pill-box for twenty minutes and getting no reply, we went in and there wasn't anybody there – they weren't even asleep. No doubt they'd all gone to the flicks." '

Yet, far from avoiding danger on this particular trip, the raiding party actually brought danger home with them in the shape of a new German anti-tank mine. MI10 was the department responsible for investigating enemy equipment and weapons. Once he was back in England, Michael Foot took his enemy booty to their offices: 'They took one look at the mine and the senior officer present bellowed "Clear the room!" I said, very casually, "Look, it's made safe. There's a nail through the fuse exactly as you recommended." He yelled again: "Clear the room!" So we cleared the room and one brave boy went back in. He came back out a few minutes later and said: "It's all right now, sir."

'I discovered that it was a new type of terror mine which I hadn't met before. If you turned it upside down, it went off. Completely by chance I had carried it vertically and I hadn't turned it upside down, so it hadn't gone off. Just as well, really.'

Michael Foot enjoyed his time as an intelligence officer with Combined Operations and had risen to the rank of major. But a more important job awaited him.

'I was asked: "Would you mind dropping a rank and going to the SAS as their intelligence officer?" I said, "Will it get me any closer to the Germans?" They said yes. So I said, "Of course" and in the spring of 1944 I became the Intelligence Officer to the Special Air Services Brigade, which at that time was an International Brigade of four parachute regiments, two British and two French, and a Belgian Independent Company. As the Brigade Intelligence Officer my job was to keep the various units of the SAS informed about where the enemy forces in Western Europe were, how they were organised, where they were distributed and where their vulnerable points were. I worked all this out partly from my contacts and experience from the eighteen months in Combined Operations and partly from routine handouts like the "Martian" reports put out once a week by John Austin at SHAEF. Once a week, Major Austin, an Oxford don in peacetime, who was on Eisenhower's Intelligence Assessment

Staff, summarised all the important intelligence material about the Wehrmacht that he had received. Austin was cleared for Ultra but no one junior to him, like me, would have known this. When Austin used Ultra material in his "Martian" reports, which was rarely as far as I could tell, the only indication that there was this source, which I knew nothing about, was the standard formula: "Most secret sources indicate . . ." I may not have been cleared for Ultra, and there were very few who had been, including some very senior Cabinet Ministers, but I was "Bigoted". Bigot was the SHAEF codeword which was used on documents containing information about Neptune and a Bigot was somebody who had received the special security clearance necessary to read these documents.'

The International SAS Brigade was to have a vital role in the assault on D-Day and Michael Foot was to be one of the leading architects of Operation Titanic, 'one of the small corners of the grand scheme'.

'My instructions came, as far as I remember, through intelligence channels and not through operational channels. I was told that we were to take a small part in a piece of deception. On the night of D–1 to D-Day itself, SAS was to mount a very few, very small special operations which were to be grouped together under a single codename. This time at least we knew it was deception from the start. I chose the codeword Titanic, because I thought it sounded momentous, as if it must be a really massive operation, reasoning that the Germans, unlike the British, wouldn't associate the name with the great disaster of the *Titanic* liner. The object of Titanic was to deflect enemy reserves while the main beaches were being approached by the main landing force. It was to consist of putting down four small parties, each consisting, as far as I remember, of an officer, an NCO and two privates.

'There was a curious conflict while I was doing the groundwork for Titanic. I went to visit Paddy Mayne, who commanded one of the SAS regiments, and asked him to provide help with Operation Titanic. He flatly refused. I pointed out that what I was politely asking was, in fact, an order. Mayne said he wouldn't touch the operation. He went on to say that when the regiment was very young in North Africa they had been instructed to carry out a raid on an Italian airfield. Everybody was briefed for it and then suddenly it was cancelled. The regiment was allowed 48 hours' leave in Cairo. They returned two days later, heavily hung-over and bleary-eyed, to discover that the operation had been revived. The raid was on for that very night. He was still very angry about what had happened. "When we got there the bloody Italians were waiting for us and very few of us came back. I swore to myself then, I will never have anything to do with intelligence-based operations again. So, now, will you get out of my office."

'Years later I discovered the truth about what had gone wrong with that raid. It had been mentioned to the American Military Attaché in Cairo, who had sent a report to the American President that this operation was about to happen. He thought apparently that it would "entertain" the President. He had sent his message in a cipher that the Germans could, and did, easily decode. The Germans told the Italians and they simply laid in wait for the SAS.'

Stories like that about thoughtless lapses of security have given Michael Foot very clear views about how deception operations should properly be planned.

'The control must come from someone very senior indeed, some-one at the Commander-in-Chief's elbow. It is vital that as few people as possible know the secret. Let me give you an example from a different theatre of war. Terence O'Brien, who flew missions in Burma, says that when the deception people wanted him to do anything Peter Fleming, the head of deception in the Far East, who worked at Mountbatten's elbow, flew himself on to O'Brien's airfield, told O'Brien what he wanted done, and made sure that O'Brien took no notes. There was nothing on paper whatsoever. When the theatre of war became bigger and more complicated it became much more difficult for the deception-planners back in Britain to keep their plans to themselves. By the time the War in Europe was at its height, the SAS people had to clear their deception plans with SHAEF, 21st Army Group, 2nd Army, Airborne Corps, SOE, SIS, and with MI5. Those are the seven agencies that I can remember today. There may have been eight or nine.

'Back at the operational level, Mayne's refusal to help left me with a problem. I solved it by going to see another SAS comman-der, Colonel Franks, and asking him for his help. We had shared the experience of our first parachute drop together. Franks agreed to an SAS involvement in Operation Titanic and it began to take shape. Each party was to be accompanied by dummy parachutists or Paragons. When the dummies hit the ground they were designed to detonate battle simulators. The party was also to be armed with Very pistols and gramophones. The gramophones would play, over and over again, recordings of snatches of soldiers' conversations interspersed with bursts of small-arms fire. Canisters of chemicals which simulated the smells of battle were also dropped. The object of all this disturbance was to give the impression that there was a major airborne landing in process, which had encountered trouble in the drop zone.'

The dummy paratroopers were also to be dropped through a 'Window' screen, which would lead the German radar stations to believe that something serious was happening. Just two weeks before D-Day two plain vans arrived at Fairford in Gloucester carrying the supplies for Titanic. The dummy parachutists were just small anonymous parcels, the gramophones equally anonymous small black boxes. The parachutists had to be inflated just before they were dropped. This was an unwelcome job for the parachute 'dispatcher', dozens of dummies to inflate before he could happily toss them out of the aircraft.

There were four Titanic operations planned. Titanic I involved the simulation of an airborne division north of the Seine, with the object of retaining forces at Yvetot, 30 miles west of Dieppe. Titanic II was a diversion simulating the dropping of a parachute brigade on the coast east of Caen, with the object of delaying local reserves east of the river moving to the west. In the end, this diversion was ruled out because the skies were simply too full. Titanic III was intended to persuade the Germans that a parachute brigade was landing south-west of Caen, in an attempt to draw counter-attack troops away from the real landing of 6 Airborne Division. Titanic IV was originally designed to draw the attention of the enemy at St Lo to the west by pretending that an airborne division had landed in the Marigny area. When the Allies altered the attack plan for the First US Army Airborne Division, it was requested that the Marigny area be changed for the Cap de la Hague area. Enemy flak made this impossible and the original plan was reverted to, only this time the intention of the simulation was widened to include causing confusion in the enemy's rear areas and delaying the movement of reserves into the Cotentin peninsula.

Michael Foot remembers that the men were to fly from Fairford in Gloucestershire. 'Fairford, apart from being an important operational airfield, was also an SAS secure transit camp, surrounded by barbed wire. Soldiers about to embark on top-secret missions were literally imprisoned there. They were shut in, there were no telephones in or out, no post, nothing. By the time the SAS were at this point they had said all their farewells and they were, effectively, already away at war. This was where their final, detailed briefing took place.'

As his SAS teams flew out in their Stirlings, Halifaxes and Hudsons with their strange cargoes, Michael Foot was at Fairford to see them off. It was a very fine summer night, not far away from midsummer's day. The first Titanic party leapt from their plane above the Cherbourg Peninsula shortly after midnight. As each of the four men in each team landed, surrounded by hordes of dummy parachutists and Very lights going off, their first job was to switch on the battery-driven gramophones.

'They made quite a din, the rifle shots could be heard a mile away. The teams banged away with their Very pistols too. Their instructions were to hang about as long as they judged it safe, and then to lie up somewhere and only when they judged the time to be right begin their march towards the beachhead, picking their way through the enemy lines which SAS were trained to do. They were very good at it. Once they had got safely inside the British lines without being shot at by an over-excited sentry, their instructions were to make their way to the Battalion Intelligence Officer and say: "Please feed me back to SAS." By that time, there was a small SAS presence at the bridgehead.

'Titanic I at Yvetot certainly gave the German commandant of Le Havre a nasty fright. We know now that he sent a "Most Immediate" telegram to Berlin direct with copies to all the intermediate authorities he could think of. It was three in the morning, there had been a major parachute landing, he was cut off from Rouen and what on earth was he to do? More important, Titanic IV landed near Marigny at the base of the Cherbourg Peninsula and remember the intention here was to draw troops from St Lo. The four men who dropped there on the night of D–1 had a disproportionate effect on the fate of the landing. Here too they gave the local German Divisional Commander a horrid shock. He woke up his Reserve Brigade and marched them off at half past three in the morning, to search the woods south of Isigny and clear them of enemy parachutists. The German division had just finished a major anti-parachute exercise, as far as I recall, so they'd obviously been taking the parachute threat seriously. These people knew that as soon as you heard of a parachute drop you went after them and cleared them out quickly, because if you don't clean them up quickly they get to be a bloody nuisance. This important German force spent the morning of D-Day scouring the woods south of Isigny and finding nobody there, except a few American parachutists who'd been dropped off course. If they hadn't been off on this fool's errand they'd doubtless have spent the morning on Omaha beach and turned it into a major disaster. God knows Omaha beach was bad enough as it was, but with an extra German force on the spot it would have been very nasty indeed.'

It was going to be many days, even weeks before Michael Foot could expect to see his Titanic teams again. In the meantime, the best he could do was thoroughly to debrief the pilots who had flown the SAS to their dropping points. He worked carefully with the pilots of the planes, going through the aircraft's log and comparing positions with the photographs of the areas where the SAS soldiers were supposed to be dropped. The following morning he was driven from Fairford on the Oxford/Gloucestershire border back to Brigade Headquarters. He knew he would be able to tell the SAS Brigadier that Titanic had gone in successfully, but he knew nothing else about the progress of that or any other operation. He hoped to find out at HQ where a host of other exhausted, excited young officers looked for the latest news.

'The whole of the Brigade Staff were in a high state of elation and excitement, except for the brigadier who'd seen it all before. There was no news. Not one of our wireless sets had come up with a thing. Not one. And there were a few, a pitiably few, extremely brief bulletins which we collected from the BBC, and that was it. The brigadier said this is what battles are like. We shan't hear anything for several days. He'd been in France in 1940, at the sharp end, so he knew all about that. He'd been on the North-West Frontier before that, so he knew all about irregular battles as well.'

When did Michael Foot actually know for sure that Operation Titanic had been a complete operational success? The strictly administered wartime code of need-to-know meant it was over thirty years later when the relevant documents were released to the Public Record Office that Michael Foot, despite being the organiser of Titanic, discovered precisely what effects his parachutists had had on the Germans. Only once the secrets of Ultra were revealed in the early 1970s was a means for rigorously assessing the impact of deception operations made available. The work of historians of the stature of Ronald Lewin and Sir Harry Hinsley has made it possible to piece together the response of individual German commanders to the deceptions of D-Day.

'I had little indication at the time what had happened. Bear in mind how much else there was going on. Even by SAS standards Titanic was a small operation. Just eight chaps. We had about 200 deployed in the first couple of days of the invasion, and about 1000 deployed by the end of the month and the whole Brigade, a little over 2000 men, by the end of the second month.'

It is clear that Michael Foot was most frustrated by the fact that his high security status prevented him from taking much active part in operations. He was in fact one of the last of the SAS Brigade to be allowed into post-invasion France. In the end, he was only permitted to go after he had complained that even the SAS Brigadier himself had been over to France and returned. If they could risk the top man, surely they could risk the Intelligence Officer? In the event, he was given a specific 'search and destroy' mission. He remembers his 'narrow squeak' in France very vividly: 'After I complained to the Brigadier that my not going to France was absurd, he said, "Oh, all right then, listen, there's a very, very nasty man in the Sicherheitsdienst, would you mind going over there and disposing of him? I went and I was taken prisoner by the battalion with which my target had been working up to the morning of the day before. I got very close to him and had a very lucky squeak. Because this Nazi, who would otherwise have taken great delight in torturing me, had spotted early on that the Germans had lost the war and so he ran away. He scarpered. We never found him. He's the only man left alive whom I would willingly knock down if I met him. Very, very nasty piece of work. It still makes my flesh creep when I remember what he did with those whom he could catch. His specific role was being bloody to captured SAS, and he was very good at it.'

As both an active intelligence officer throughout the latter years of the war and a distinguished historian, Michael Foot is in a particularly good position now, nearly half a century later, to deliver a verdict on the efficacy of Allied deception plans in the Second World War: 'I place the role of deception in helping to win the war very high indeed. By far the most important operation, of course, was Fortitude South. Titanic was a very small spin-off. We do appear to have convinced Hitler personally and the bulk of the German High Command, who were at his elbow, that the Normandy landing was a feint and that the main crunch was coming where the German General Staff had said all along it would come, on the beaches south of Boulogne, from where the Allies could make a short run into the Ruhr. It wasn't until after the end of June that any troops made a determined move towards the Normandy bridgehead and that was quite extraordinary. That is solely due to deception and saved hundreds of thousands of lives, Germans as well as Allies.

'I think that a great deal of the blame for the Germans' failure to detect the British deception must lie with Hitler himself. Rommel, almost alone among the High Command, continued to insist that landings in Normandy were quite likely. But the prevailing mood among the other, perhaps less brave, generals was *Es ist der Führers Wunsch*" – It is Hitler's wish. His belief was that the

Allies would come in south of Boulogne. Once that bloody-minded man had become convinced of something he wasn't prepared to be shifted. The nature of the German High Command was that Hitler ran everything, and ran it, on purpose, with a lot of internecine strife and competition. There was never that clear chain of command which was such a notable feature of the Allied fighting forces.

'Every bit as important though was the extraordinary gift of Ultra, the Allies' ability to read the German signals traffic encoded on the Enigma machine and cracked by the boffins at Bletchley early in the war. It was all relatively easy for us if we could read the Enigma key in which the enemy's directives went out. But from time to time they changed that key and we couldn't always read the new one. Most of the stuff went out by Enigma, which had three wheels of coding at the start, when we first cracked it, but had five wheels by 1944. Latterly some of it went out by *Geheimschreiber*, which had ten wheels, which in cipher terms is much more than twice as bad. We just managed to crack *Geheimschreiber* in time. But we spent most of the war terrified that the Germans were going to go over to the system we used, a system which ironically they had invented, the one-time cipher pad.[2] If they'd gone over to the one-time pad we'd have been sunk. I've often thought that we maintained our huge intelligence circuits on the Continent, most of them run for us by our continental allies in exile, as an insurance policy against disaster at Bletchley, against the day when they suddenly announced that they could no longer read the enemy's secret traffic.'

The fear that the Germans would change the Enigma system and that Ultra would dry up reveals the fragility of systems in wartime for gathering information. The need to gather huge amounts of accurate information on which to base both genuine and deceptive operations grew steadily throughout the war.

'You needed everything from information about the enemy's dispositions down to the most simple, easily ascertainable facts like who was the Mayor of each small French town, who ran the electricity, the gas, the telephone exchange, these things suddenly mattered when you were throwing millions of troops ashore in an attempt to take over an entire country.'

These observations of Michael Foot provoke some interesting reflections on the question of the importance of information and the way in which it was managed during the planning of both genuine and deceptive operations. It was the ability to continue to gather the kind of information that Foot describes above which was the essential complement to Ultra in providing an encyclopaedia of knowledge about mainland Europe, without which neither Neptune nor Bodyguard could have succeeded. On the one hand, there was a comprehensive information-gathering capacity and on the other hand the Allies had the ability through visual deception, wireless traffic and the carefully built-up network of enemy agents to disseminate false information; false information, whose effect you could only judge because Ultra and an efficient intelligence service allowed you to do so. This virtuous circle was the *sine qua non* of large-scale, strategic deception.

Part Two

THE FOREMEN

While the intellectual elite in the various deception headquarters created their fantasies and built their networks of lies, it was left to the ordinary soldier, sailor and airman to carry out their often baffling orders.

The next two parts of this book are devoted to the men and women who, always unquestioningly, helped to weave the fabric of falsehood. Few of the commanders are left alive, but we have managed to interview some who can give first-hand accounts of how the plans hatched in Cairo or Storey's Gate were actually carried out on the ground. These men, the 'foremen' who worked with the nuts and bolts of deception, often took great personal risks to put into operation manoeuvres that they knew were designed to attract enemy retaliation in the form of bombs and mortar fire. They practically welcomed such retaliation since it was only when it had been aroused that they could be sure that their elaborate deceptions had worked.

One of the most important of these deceptions revolved around what could be achieved by false sounds.

Throughout the war, from the North African desert to the Normandy landings, the Allies were refining their techniques of sonic deception. The fake sounds of battle, movements of tanks, building of bridges, could all contribute to the enemy's confusion, particularly at night or under smoke-screens. Sonic deception was particularly effective when, as happened so often later in the war, the Germans or Italians had inadequate reconnaissance and lack of airpower.

(Above) Also of 'pneumatic construction', this tank was used in many theatres of war. When deflated, it could be packed into a carrying case a little larger than an average cricket bag. (Designed by Messrs Dunlop Rubber Co.)

(Above) Fake landing craft, the so-called 'Big Bobs', were used as decoys.

(Below) They formed part of FUSAG, the successful attempt to build a phantom army in south-east England and East Anglia.

Be careful
what you say
+ where you
say it!

ARELESS TALK
COSTS LIVES

TITTLE TATTLE
LOST THE BATTLE

Wartime posters which neatly illustrate the paradox of successful deception operations.

BEWARE

JE WANTS TO KNOW YOUR UNIT'S NAME.
VHERE YOU'RE GOING. WHENCE YOU CAME.
VEN ALONE OR IN A CROWD
EVER MENTION THESE OUT LOUD.

You never know
who's
listening!

CARELESS TALK
COSTS LIVES

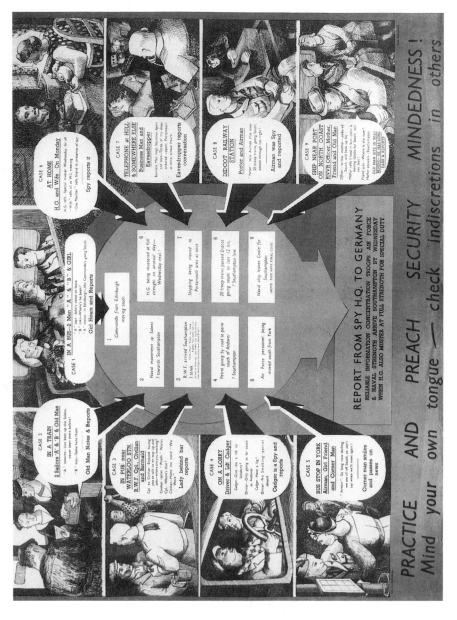

(*Above*) The poster illustrates the way in which information could be pieced together like a jigsaw puzzle.

CHAPTER 6

THE SOUND MEN'S TALES

Lieutenant-Colonel Derek Curtis, Fred Willcox
and Colin Dennison

Lieutenant-Colonel Curtis was commissioned in 1937, spent 'two happy years' at St Catharine's College, Cambridge, studying at the Army's expense. He graduated just before the war. On mobilisation he was posted to 7 Field Company, RE, in 4th Division. He fought in France and Belgium, was wounded near Dunkirk and invalided back to Britain. It's a familiar tale, which continues with the typical anti-invasion duties that followed the evacuation from Dunkirk. He was eventually posted to 9th Armoured Division and then one day his conventional army career was suddenly suspended, when at an interview in London he was asked to join a secret organisation which was being formed in Scotland.

'Any sort of unusual opportunity is exciting, but at the time I'd really got no idea what it was going to lead to.'

It led to Laggan House near Ballantrae, a Total Top Secret classification, and a place in the Sonic Deception team, which was training there. Sonic deception had already been tried with some success in the Western Desert at El Alamein. General Georg Stumme had taken over from Rommel, when he had gone back to Germany in considerable ill health on October 23. It was exactly a month before Lightfoot, the plan to drive the Axis out of Africa, was due to begin. Stumme was fooled into reacting to a non-existent amphibious landing behind German lines between El Daba and Sidi Abd el Rahman. An essential part of the deception had been the use of battle sounds played over amplifiers carried on Motor Torpedo Boats, which had been brought close into the beach. Now the War Office wanted to develop the idea for use in future operations. The scene for this development back in

Britain was a fine Scottish baronial mansion. The establishment at Laggan was called the Light Scout Car Training Centre and was commanded by Colonel Disney Barlow.

'Disney Barlow believed that if you were going to practise sonic deception you had to get it absolutely right. The Germans were quite sophisticated about monitoring wireless output and other sounds. The fear was that if you executed a deception scheme that was less than totally convincing, you could do more harm than good. You might give the game away.

'Behind Laggan there was quite a lot of open moorland, so we used to set up modest tactical situations there. We'd space the vehicles out and they'd run a given programme and we'd have a few monitors at nearby vantage points listening to our output. They'd be the ones who told us whether it was convincing or not. It was usually fairly successful – they could hear tanks moving, but they were sometimes not sure which way they were going. But when it came to bridging operations it was quite difficult to work out what sort of sounds would reproduce the real thing. In fact we discovered that the most convincing sound was that of the man knocking the pins into the Bailey Bridge. It was very distinctive. A certain amount of clanging was also rather effective, when people dropped bits and pieces. The men who recorded all these sounds went out on various exercises to get their tape and on occasion I think they also staged bridging exercises just to get a recording.

'The main sounds projected were vehicle movements, particularly the sound of tracked vehicles, since it was always assumed that the enemy would be trying to guess where the armoured thrust was coming from.

'It was considered terribly important not just to broadcast any old tank sound, but to provide programmes of identifiable tank types, like Churchills or Shermans. Most experienced soldiers could spot the difference. So they went to great lengths to simulate the exact sound.

'There was all this concentration about fidelity of sonic reproduction and it was a big thing in the film business at the time – you know, MGM would say they had better quality sound on their films than Warner Brothers, or whatever. They kept adding gadgets to cut out the background noise and all that business. But we were dependent on getting the equipment from America, because I don't think it was being made in the UK at that time. It wasn't considered to be a wartime requirement.

'The Americans supplied the equipment. Basically it comprised the sound track of a 35mm film being scanned by the soundhead of a normal cinema projector and broadcast through controllable revolving loudspeakers raised above the vehicle. This was the most effective way of reproducing sound at that time. The amplifying and broadcasting equipment could also be used with a microphone. From time to time it was used for broadcast speech, like calls to surrender.'

The search for high-fidelity sound actually led to a rift between the Middle East deception force and London: 'I did know something about it at the time but I've since seen certain signals that went between the Middle East and London. Apparently the War Office in London told the Middle East Command that they were not to use what London considered the rather rudimentary sonic devices which they would have liked to use. The Chiefs of Staff wanted to wait until the very high-fidelity equipment came on stream and they didn't want the Middle East giving the game away. The Middle East, on the other hand, were signalling London, suggesting that London was missing the boat.'

The signals that Derek Curtis refers to can be found in the Public Records Office at Kew. They make interesting reading and throw extra light on the development of sonic deception and also on the different priorities of those deceivers refining their techniques in Britain and those deceivers who were working away at the front. Lieutenant-Colonel Geoffrey Barkas, a film set designer,[1] was one of Dudley Clarke's main camouflage experts. In a 'Most Secret' paper[2] Barkas had some pithy things to say about sonic deception. On the technical side for example he felt that echoing his experience gained in the film industry, 'Bombardment tracks', for example, were usually rather 'silly . . . They tend to sound like . . . empty tins being thrown into a dustbin.' Barkas laid great stress on the psychological aspect of sonic deception: 'I see it as a purely emotional attack on the nerves. A sense of tension or fear is often built up in the minds of a cinema audience by arbitrary and illogical use of sound accompanying a picture . . . Sounds by themselves are very frightening at night if they are associated with ideas that have caused the listener acute apprehension or suspense. In such circumstances the average listener does not stop to work out whether the noises are strictly logical or accurate. His hair just naturally stands on end. I know that mine does within the limited scope still remaining to me . . . It would be a most unusual enemy sentry or local commander who listened carefully and then said, "All right, boys, go back to bed. That noise is a General Grant and I know for sure that there are no General Grants within 50 miles." '

Barkas was in little doubt that the UK was in danger of getting bogged down in a 'search for technical perfection . . . my experience leads me to believe that they will not attain this perfection and that even if they did it would not do them much good. This feeling is borne out by their signal which says that they can send us no tracks because "they have no tracks suitable for ME". Suitable tracks could be made equally well in Tooting or Timbuctoo . . . The danger for ME is that over-anxiety for high fidelity may find them still experimenting at the end of the war without having cracked off.'

Despite a minute written by Dudley Clarke himself on September 5 that he was in agreement with much of what Barkas had to say, Clarke was writing in April 1943 that there was still little prospect of being able to include sonic deception in his immediate plans owing to a lack of equipment emerging from Britain.[3]

Derek Curtis points out that unfortunately the first shipment of equipment from the USA to Scotland had been lost at sea and that this might, in part, have accounted for the delay. 'If we had had a Light Scout Car Company equipped in 1942 and shipped out to North Africa at the end of that year, it might have done quite a lot of good work in the Mediterranean theatre.'

Derek Curtis's commander, Disney Barlow, seems to have been in agreement with one aspect of the foregoing and that was on the psychological effect that noises in the dark might have on an already nervous enemy.

'When the Japanese invaded Malaya they were reported to have caused some disruption using loudhailers to broadcast frightening noises in the jungle. These "terror noises" had two aims, to keep opposing troops awake and to lower their morale. This sort of activity was considered to be particularly effective in the unfamiliar and claustrophobic environment of the tropical jungle and could possibly be used in other situations also. Certain ideas were put forward, for example that you might play church bells ringing sonorous, mournful notes regularly throughout the night or other appropriately emotive, eerie or terrifying sounds. But I don't think these ideas were ever put into practice in the Second World War.

'We did do at least one exercise when we played bells on the Scottish moors to see what it sounded like. It really did sound most eerie!'

As the plans for the invasion of Normandy progressed, the time was rapidly approaching when all the careful work done in Scotland would be put to the test. Although 'A' Force had been restrained from using sonic deception on the scale that they might have liked in North

Africa, they had been using it to good effect from the invasion of Sicily onwards. Now it was the turn of Derek Curtis and his men. They were not the only group to use sonic deception from D-Day onwards,[4] but they did have a significant role to play.

At the beginning of 1944 Nos 1 & 3 Light Scout Car Companies were moved from Scotland to the London area. They were billeted in a dilapidated old farmhouse near Epping and earmarked to be part of 'R' Force which was being set up at that time by Colonel David Strangeways of HQ, 21 Army Group. He decided to merge the two Light Scout Car Companies into one and give the then Major Curtis command of the new, larger unit.

Two troops of Light Scout Cars were standing by to go across to France on D-Day itself. Each troop consisted of only a handful of people with four operational vehicles and one command vehicle. Derek Curtis is in no doubt that this was the right approach. 'It is essential to keep the effort devoted to deception operations as small as necessary to achieve the object. You don't want to put a lot of resources into deception. If you're going to put aside a lot of resources then they might as well be used for "a real Do". A deception plan ought to distract the enemy effort considerably more than it does your own.' As the pressure built up in the weeks leading up to D-Day, more and more units passed through the 'inner sanctum' of the coastline concentration area, where security was rigid. Curtis's two troops of Light Scout Cars were, as we have heard, standing by to cross to France. The remainder of the unit did not move into the concentration area until late on D-Day itself and was temporarily accommodated on Southampton Common.

'We were kept hanging around at Southampton for a couple of days before we were allocated shipping space. On D+2 we embarked on an American LST. I was the senior army officer on board so I reported to the American captain on the bridge. The vessel slipped down a crowded Southampton Water to an anchorage off Cowes where a picket boat came off with sailing instructions. There were only about two paragraphs and the captain said: "Gee! I guess if we were sailing from Newport News we'd have had ten pages!" He was tickled that he was taking part in the greatest invasion in military history with just two paragraphs of instructions.

'Anyway, we sailed in the late evening from Cowes and I'd not long turned in when there was an awful running of feet on the deck and shouting and then a great bump. I went to find out what was going on and saw a long streak of white paint on the side of the LST. We'd scraped a hospital ship returning from the beachhead.

When I asked the captain about it he said: "I guess we got into the wrong channel." Channels had been swept through the minefields, one was an up channel and one was a down. He was going up the down channel. He looked at me and said: "I guess we could have done with another page of instructions!" '

As a result the sonic deceivers arrived at the wrong part of the coast and had to be diverted to the correct beach. But they were quickly off the beach and into a field where they stripped the Scout Cars of their waterproofing. From there they moved off to another field just outside Colombey-sur Seulles where they were to remain in a bivouac until the end of August.

The first major operation with the whole Light Scout Car Company was Operation Hostage, in late June. It was a deception operation planned to divert enemy attention and reserves from the real sector in which Operation Epsom was to take place. Epsom was the first major British offensive that Montgomery launched after the beachheads of the Normandy landings had been secured. It was intended to strike powerfully inland beyond the crossings of the Odon and Orne rivers. The opening attack east of Caen was due on June 23. On June 25, the main offensive south-west of the city would follow.

'The role of "R" Force was to give the impression that it was the main attack that was to go in east of Caen, whereas in fact it was to be delivered several miles to the west. In the few days beforehand there had been dummy wireless traffic indicating that 7 Armoured Division was concentrating in the general area of St Aubin d'Arquenay, north of Caen. Co-ordinated with this radio traffic the camouflage company of "R" Force (179 Camouflage Coy RE) erected dummy tanks and other equipment in the area just behind Periers sur le Dan. On these fields many gliders had landed on D-Day itself and the whole area was strewn with abandoned aircraft. As night fell we came down to Beuville and I reported to 185 Brigade of 3 Division. We started a programme of sound, indicating tanks moving in the valley and then eastward towards Benouville and the Orne bridges to suggest that 7 Armoured Division was moving into the Ranville bridgehead. Several passes were made along the route and then more noises in the Ranville area as if the tanks were sorting themselves out and forming up. We would vary the sound a bit, suggesting that some vehicles were getting off the road and finding positions for themselves.

'Well, that programme was greeted with some quite useful responses. First of all there was mortar fire laid down on us from the

Beuville and Benouville areas and then, in the Ranville area, a good deal of shelling from the direction of Houlgate. Most of it was aimed at the Orne bridges, which we had to negotiate. We had about 16 vehicles and I wanted to withdraw them from the bridgehead before daylight. The real attack was, in any case, timed for before dawn, so as far as deception was concerned the plan had already done its work.

'To draw fire was reassuring in itself, but a couple of days later David Strangeways visited the unit and said that he had seen a captured intelligence report from a formation which had been opposite the bridgehead area at the time. The intelligence appreciation confirmed that the Germans had thought that there was to be a genuine attack in that area.

'The news was a nice morale booster for the chaps, but you can never know whether there might have been other factors too in the German reaction which might have prompted the same response. You've got to be a bit hard-headed and not go overboard on these things.

'Later on, it was decided as part of the strategy of "banging at the hinge" as Monty called it [Caen was the hinge], that a full-scale attack [Operation Goodwood July 18] would be mounted in the area where we had simulated the build-up in Operation Hostage. On this second occasion the deception plan was to simulate movement into the Rauray area, west of the old Operation Epsom sector.

'This area, being near to the Caumont and Villers-Bocage region, was sensitive because the British had captured it once and then been driven back. It was thought that a diversion there would produce dividends. So this time we simulated tank sounds leading from Tilly sur Seulles and Audrieu on the road to Fontenay le Pesnel and beyond. It wasn't such a long run and it didn't attract the same enemy reaction as was given to Operation Hostage. Nevertheless a small air attack, dropping "ground effect" bombs on nearby artillery positions, did arrive. The gunners were firing to create "row" as part of the main scheme and I can't be sure if the air raid was in response to their efforts or ours.

'By that time the German forces in Normandy were greatly extended and feeling increasing American pressure from the St Lo area. No major reserves were available to them. They were also short of ammunition. So, even if they had fallen for the deception plan, they may not have been able to do much about it. In the circumstances even one small bombing raid was probably something worth attracting and indicative of the enemy concern about British intentions in that sector.'

Lieutenant-Colonel Curtis has had many years to reflect on the lessons he learned when in command of his Light Scout Car Companies in Normandy: 'The value of strategic deception can be enormous. It's going on all the time. It can be as valuable against the IRA as it was against the Wehrmacht. In wider military philosophical terms, intelligent use of deception is often what distinguishes a brilliant commander from a "good, plain cook". You find that Napoleon, Marlborough, all the famous commanders in history, have been skilful in how they deceived the enemy, both strategically and tactically. Deception needs to be controlled from the top and combined with well-trained troops to take full advantage of what it can offer.

'As far as tactical deception is concerned the important thing is not to devote too many resources to it. It can often be improvised like the false "going maps" or even the sort of simple deception in the trenches where you had a plaster soldier's head to attract the enemy sniper. He fired at the dummy and you located him and shot him. There are all sorts of things that can be done on the spur of the moment. In fact at Dunkirk we found a tractor and we managed to get it going, in the hopes that the Germans on the other side of the canal might think that we'd got a tank. I don't think it would have fooled them for a minute. But in any situation you need to be thinking of off-the-cuff deceptive ploys like that. They also help morale.

'The more formal kind of tactical deception, as developed in "R" Force, can be useful in a static or semi-static situation just as it was in the bridgehead. But once things become more fluid there is not time to produce elaborate deception ploys and once you have a great preponderance of your own forces ashore, then of course you can move real forces to confuse the enemy, not just notional ones.

'I think the Middle East "deceivers" were right that formal tactical deception was at its most effective in 1942–43 when we were stretched. I think it was useful in the first month of Normandy but after that it tended to diminish in significance. Nevertheless, some quite useful minor deception operations were carried out later in the campaign.[5]

'As far as sonic deception is concerned, anything that makes it difficult for the other guy, when he hears something or sees something going on, to be quite sure that he's getting a true impression must be valuable. It might only deceive him for a couple of hours but of course they may be the vital hours.

'Let's face it, he may *know* you've got loudspeakers making funny noises, but he's still got to determine whether you're using them that night or using real tanks. You might be doing a double bluff with two loudspeakers in front of a large force of very genuine tanks.'

Fred Willcox was another, humbler product of the training school at Laggan House in Scotland. He had been called up in the early part of the war, shortly after Dunkirk. He did his basic training with the Infantry in Dorchester, before being sent to Weymouth on the south coast of England. He learned to drive everything from heavy armoured cars to motorbikes: 'Every morning I used to do a Dawn Patrol around all the Coastguard stations. With the beach battalion we used to contact all the coastguards to make sure the Jerries hadn't landed during the night!'

After the invasion threat died down, Fred began one of those army odysseys that so many old soldiers seem to recall. His battalion became part of the Royal Artillery, he was then sent to Canterbury on a motor mechanics' course and eventually to Scotland. By this time his battalion had moved from Artillery to Ordnance and finished up as REME. If the deception-planners had been trying to confuse the enemy's operational intelligence then they had done well. They were not, of course. This was just the way the Services regularly operated. Fred and his REME unit finally came to rest at Laggan House in Ayrshire, where Fred found himself signing the Official Secrets Act in a Top Secret Unit.

In the Sonic Deception Unit at Laggan House, Fred's job was to service the jeeps that carried the full range of sonic deception that Lieutenant-Colonel Curtis has described. Willcox remembers that the jeeps towed small trailers containing generators for 35mm RCA film sound equipment. In the fields of Ayrshire the sonic deceivers set about recording the sounds of battle, shells being fired, bridges being built or destroyed, small-arms fire and so on. REME radio mechanics were trained to operate the film equipment and Royal Signals mechanics maintained it.

Once they had their tracks recorded they often had to edit, as Fred recalls: 'We all sat down to listen to what we'd recorded that morning – of course we always tested it before we used it . . . Right in the middle of the reel a factory hooter blew! So that gave the game away, straight away. So we used to cut it and join it up again, we used to have to do that a lot.'

Fred also worked with the Royal Engineers, who had their own rather more robust methods of sonic deception: 'The Royal Engineers used to make the firecrackers, like the rook scarers. They were like strings of sausages, laid out with tiny fuses between them. They'd go off at various intervals. They also used to set up Sten guns, old Sten guns with a few feet of time fuse. Next they'd light the fuses and a few seconds later, as soon as it was burned through, the Sten gun would start blasting away.'

While Fred Willcox was busy servicing the Light Scout Car Unit's vehicles, another sonic deceiver was learning how to operate the cumbersome recording replay equipment that the jeeps carried.

Colin Dennison was a soldier in 60 Special Squadron, Royal Engineers. The two troops in the squadron were labelled 'Visual' and 'Sonic'. 'Visual' unit specialised in Jasper Maskelyne's dummy tanks and other visual deceptions. But Colin Dennison joined the unit that concentrated on faking the sounds of battle. He has written in some detail about the equipment and the techniques of sonic deception, most recently in the magazine *Wheels and Tracks*.

Sonic troop was equipped with eight American armoured vehicles, known as White M3A1 Scout Cars. The most distinctive feature of these large jeeps was the loudspeaker assembly that relayed the sound from the RCA 35mm film equipment. Each of the two loudspeakers was a huge cube, roughly the size of a tea-chest. The operator would turn his swivel seat to the rear, while the driver was rolling the canopy clear of the 'cubes'. They used a small Onan petrol engine to work the hydraulic equipment which raised the cubes above the jeep. They fed the film sound tracks into the replay machine, threading them through the soundhead.

Colin Dennison describes the process in detail: 'It was possible to traverse the cubes by turning a crank at the operator's right hand. Between the driver and the operator was a compass, on which there was an indicator showing the alignment of the cubes. Owing to the magnetism of the armoured car, there were two iron balls to correct the deviation.

'There were three amplifiers, two of which would be in use and one spare, which would be instantly switched on in case of failure of one of the others. The decibels were indicated on a meter to show the amount of amplification. The maximum was 3.0Db, which was rarely used because of distortion. Zero Db was quite loud; so was minus one.'

In a later conversation Colin Dennison recalled more of the method of operation: 'We had a drill for turning the volume up and down. If we broke a film, we had to bring up the volume gradually when we restarted. That meant one minute to rethread and one more minute to bring up the volume again. If anybody forgot to turn down the volume when a film broke, the sound came on too suddenly and spoiled the effect.'

CHAPTER 7

THE SCRIPTWRITER'S TALE
John Dalgleish

John Dalgleish was one of hundreds who had to carry out David Strangeways' deceptions. His particular skill lay in writing the scripts for the mass of false radio traffic which had to accompany all the notional units and divisions that Strangeways and 'R' Force were creating.[1]

'I was on the staff of 5 Corps in North Africa and came back to England in early 1943 to go to the Staff College. After completing the course I was posted to 5 Wireless Group. This was a new unit formed to help with the deception plan for the invasion of Europe. A transmitter had been developed which, from one machine, would broadcast a whole wireless network, simulating conversations between a number of units. It was just people sitting round a table talking, but it sounded like a whole network of people taking part in exercises. We were told that, as the Germans had no air cover, they were unable to locate our troops by aerial reconnaissance, so they had to rely on information obtained by wireless interception. The unit consisted of a technical branch formed from the Royal Signals and a staff branch of three teams, each having a GSO2 and a GSO3. We had a lot of teething troubles on the technical side: there was only one man in the unit, a Captain Buchanan, who really understood how the machine worked, but we sorted out the technical problems in the end.

'Our next problem was to find out what the wireless traffic of an exercise actually sounded like when you were listening in from outside, so we were sent up to Yorkshire to sit in on a genuine exercise. I also went on a Combined Ops Course on the west coast of Scotland, to find out how we could simulate amphibious landing exercises. We'd listen to everybody taking part sending their orders, somebody else asking for clarification and we would make notes.

'After this introduction we were ready to start writing the scripts which would simulate a brigade or a battalion on exercises. We were given the area in which it was to be held and also the call signs of the various units. We would then make up an exercise, work out exactly what would take place and write a script to fit the action. For instance we'd write a script that would make it appear that these units were advancing. You'd advance up the road, you'd meet the enemy, attack them, call for reinforcements, that kind of thing.

'I found the difficulty when writing scripts was not to make it sound too slick. When you listened in on the exercises you missed lots of bits, and could tell that people were not hearing each other clearly. People were always saying "Say again" and so on. You write it and don't realise how often people in real life don't hear messages clearly the first time. You tried to imitate that effect and you hoped that when the Germans picked it up they'd only get bits of it just as we did. You hoped it wouldn't sound too "seamless".

'Having written the script we would find some troops actually stationed in the area to come and record it for us. One was told at the time this was terribly hush-hush and one mustn't say anything about it at all. But I always felt that if you'd got twelve chaps to read something out they'd think it was such a stupid thing to do – to be reading something for no reason – that they wouldn't really take it seriously. So, without telling them more than was necessary, I did say that it was meant to be taken for real, it wasn't just having a bit of fun. We were stationed in Kent at that time and our "actors" came from various units stationed around there.

'We produced a number of exercises in Kent to simulate the troops who were supposed to be preparing for an invasion across the Straits of Dover, the First US Army Group. On one occasion we took part in a combined operation for a practice landing at Studland Bay. We were in landing craft and had a lovely day out. I'll always remember it, it was such a beautiful sunny day. We'd recorded the exercise first, took the transmitter down there and put it on the landing craft and just broadcast it as we cruised in towards the beach. We thought it'd be nice to go and actually do the landing, even if it was all pre-recorded.'

All these preparations were an integral part of Fortitude South, persuading the Germans of the presence of the troops in East Anglia who were preparing for an assault on the Pas de Calais. Once the invasion had started, however, there was work to be done in the bridgehead and so six days after D-Day, John Dalgleish crossed the Channel.

'The unit landed in France on D+6, joined the bridgehead and camped in a very pleasant little field, through which a stream ran. There was a deep pool in which we could bathe. It was a quiet time for us, but we did carry out a few deception operations to help the American advance on the right of our front. This was the time when the staff side of 5 Wireless Group was run as a separate unit, working directly under David Strangeways, co-ordinating both the broadcasting by 5 Wireless Group and the dummy tanks and tank recordings of the Engineer Units of "R" Force. They were loudspeakers mounted on the back of tanks and they made a noise like tanks manoeuvring and getting into position.

'I recall sitting in Normandy, when the Americans were trying to advance on the right and we were trying to pretend we were breaking out on the left. We were stuck in a field with them, with one of the damaged gliders and a wireless. It was the day they had the thousand-bomber raid on Caen, June 23. I remember very early that morning sitting there, with our group involved in wireless and sonic deception. We were indicating that 8 Corps was crossing the Orne from west to east. It was a small part of the cover plan for Operation Epsom, the assault on Caen. The basic intention of the cover plan was to gain surprise for the attack by 8 Corps west of the River Orne and to try and persuade the enemy to bring more troops into his right flank east of the river. I can remember David Strangeways saying: "If they bomb that area tonight, then our deception plan is right." And we were standing there – in the deception area – and they dropped some bombs on us. So we thought we'd done some good. The bombers completely destroyed the town. It was dreadful. It was terrible getting through Caen afterwards, when the break-out came.'

5 Wireless Group also took part in Operation Hostage, which was the cover plan for Operation Goodwood, Montgomery's largest armoured attack, launched on July 18 to the east of Caen. The object of this cover plan was to persuade the Germans to move from east to west of the River Orne, in preparation for an attack by 8 Corps east of the river on the eighteenth. The responsibility of Dalgleish and his team was to simulate 8 Corps traffic in the wrong area. Dummy tanks and vehicles were also erected in the notional area, the noise of tanks moving in was simulated and special steps were taken by the 21 Army Camouflage Group to conceal the movement of the real 8 Corps. The operation was successful and elements of two Panzer divisions did

indeed move across the river from east to west. The day after the operation a map was captured, which showed 76 Division located in precisely the area in which 'R' Force had sought to place it.

'After Operations Epsom and Goodwood, there was little call on the services of 5 Wireless Group, in the mobile warfare which followed. "R" Force had turned much of its attention to intelligence-gathering in which I was not much involved. I had my own car, a driver and a tent, so I was completely self-contained. I spent some time carrying out some rather vague liaison duties with 1st Canadian Corps.

'There was one occasion when we were in the vanguard, approaching Rouen. We thought that the city might still be occupied by the Germans and a rather foolhardy Cavalry officer, Douggie Baker, who was attached to us, had gone forward to reconnoitre: we were sure he had been captured. Nevertheless, we set off in a little convoy. In the van went an armoured car followed by me in my Staff Car, with no protection at all, and then another armoured car from "R" Force Engineers. We went very slowly down the road into Rouen in the darkness, expecting to be fired on by Germans any minute, when suddenly a ghostly figure with a bandaged head loomed up. It was Douggie who had had an accident, but was able to report that the city was free of Germans. Rouen was already safely in our hands.

'When we arrived in Brussels we were established in the Chateau Lambert, a comfortable house a few miles outside Brussels. We were relaxing there when von Rundstedt made the Germans' last throw in what became known as "the Battle of the Bulge" on December 16. In the early stages there were no troops between the enemy advance and Brussels except a few American holding units. David Strangeways, however, had his Engineer units and he said, "Ah! We've got some troops here, we'll give them to you."

'I was sent rushing along the bank of the Meuse, wondering at each bridge whether we would find that the Germans had reached the river. I shouldn't have worried about the Germans, in the end I found myself captured by the Americans. I had called in at one of their units and an elderly "Blimpish" colonel promptly had me arrested as a German spy dressed up as an Englishman. There had been many rumours of Germans dressed in British and American uniforms. The old colonel kept asking me things: "You're a German, you're a spy!" And then he said, "What do you know about England?" I replied: "Well I was stationed in Salisbury for a long time." And he said: "What's wrong with Salisbury Cathedral? What's special about Salisbury Cathedral?" I didn't know. "It's the spire, it's slightly leaning." I said, "Well, I don't know that, but do you know the Haunch of Venison, where I had many good meals?" Finally I managed to convince a more intelligent brigadier, who asked me how many troops "R" Force had available and I replied that we had so many "bodies", an expression, he said, that no German would have used. "Bodies" was far too much like the vernacular.

'There was not much more for us to do before the final offensive across the Rhine took place and, on the defeat of Germany, we were disbanded.'

CHAPTER 8

THE TANK BUILDER'S TALE
Colonel Kenneth Robertson

Colonel Kenneth Robertson was involved in the first large-scale deception operation in the Middle East. It contributed to a victory at Sidi Barrani for General O'Connor under the command of General Wavell in Operation Compass, which began on December 9 1940. One of the simplest yet most effective of wartime deceptions was the dummy tank and Sidi Barrani is an early example of the successful use of this kind of deception.

Dummy tanks ranged from the elaborate fakes that, from a distance, were indistinguishable from the real thing to crude shapes that might convince enemy reconnaissance aircraft that there was, at least, a possibility of armoured reserve. At Sidi Barrani the disposition of forces was so overwhelmingly in favour of the enemy that there was no time to create any of the more sophisticated copies. Speed was of the essence. In the autumn of 1940, the Italian Marshal Graziani had successfully advanced into Egypt with almost 250,000 men under his command. He was supported in Eritrea by the Duke of Aosta, who could muster another 100,000. Facing the Italians was General Archibald Wavell, C-in-C Middle East, who at the time could field no more than 50,000. Wavell had been attacked and driven back to the town of Sidi Barrani. He knew that for the moment he was cornered and that his men were in no position to fight again until reinforcements arrived. Worse still, Graziani might now be able to drive through to the Nile. Wavell was a commander who firmly believed in the use of deception and had in his own words always believed in 'doing everything possible in war to mystify and mislead one's opponent'.[1] The odds stacked against him in North Africa made recourse to deception a natural step. The cover plans before the Battle of Sidi Barrani required that Graziani should perceive a threat to his flanks. To achieve this Wavell required the extensive use of a variety of concealment techniques, and wireless deception. He also started to co-operate with SIME in constructing a double-cross system, through which he could pass false information to the Italians.

Fortunately Wavell had on his staff the redoubtable Dudley Clarke and it was in the later stages of Operation Compass that on December 18, 'A' Force officially came into being. The Battle of Sidi Barrani had been a resounding success for the team of tactical deceivers under the command of Clarke. Faced with the problem of no reinforcements and inadequate armour, Dudley Clarke simply set out to create them.

Clarke turned to Major Jasper Maskelyne, a man who in Civvy Street had been one half of the conjuring act 'Maskelyne and Devant'. Employed as a deceiver and a builder of decoys, Maskelyne had gathered around him a group he called his 'Magic Circle'. They started to construct, at great speed, dummy Cruiser tanks and heavy field guns. In reality the guns were lengths of drainpipe filled with chemicals that produced loud flashes. Seymour Reit in his entertaining book *Masquerade* has recorded the Maskelyne 'gun flash recipe': '4 teaspoons of black powder, 6 dessert spoons of aluminium powder, 1 teaspoon of iron filings. The first provided the smoke, the second the flash, the third the red flame.'[2]

So, Marshal Graziani might yet be convinced that Wavell's heavy artillery was a real threat to his flanks. But what of his tanks? Maskelyne hired teams of native workers who drove their camels and horses relentlessly to and fro, trailing chains that whipped up the sand and suggested the incessant movement of large armoured columns. It seems that all this trickery at least gave Graziani pause for thought. He did not press home his advantage and, when the British counter-attacked with real tanks on December 9, it eventually led to an advance of 650 miles into Libya. Ten Italian divisions had been destroyed and 130,000 prisoners taken. That was the work of robust soldiery, not deception. But deception had played its part in allowing Wavell's troops to regroup. The fake reinforcements gave way to the real, their task accomplished.

Colonel Kenneth Robertson was involved in an exercise prior to the Battle of Sidi Barrani where a great many of these fake reinforcements, in this instance dummy tanks, had to be constructed very quickly. It was an exercise which never really stopped. Indeed it developed into the opening of the full-scale offensive against the Italians. At the beginning of Operation Compass Kenneth Robertson was a captain serving in 2nd Field Company, Royal Engineers. Here is the Colonel's tale, related with typical military precision:

'One afternoon at the beginning of December, when the pace of life was already speeding up, the Commander, Royal Engineers, hurriedly called his three company commanders together. His orders were to construct as many dummy tanks as possible by first light the following morning. The dummy tanks were then to be transported from where they had been garrisoned to Sidi Barrani where they were to be handed over to the commander of an armoured formation for him to deploy.

'The idea for these dummy tanks, I believe, came from General Wavell himself. As part of his plan he required a formation of dummy tanks to deceive Italian aerial reconnaissance, nothing more. The dummy tanks were to be deployed in the rear of our existing armoured formations to signify a formidable armoured reserve. Consequently only "low-fidelity" dummies were required. The design had to be very simple, constructed from materials either already in the Western Desert or immediately available in Egypt. There was no opportunity to obtain special items from elsewhere. Success depended on ingenuity and improvisation.

'The design for the dummy tank came down to us from headquarters in Cairo. Its hull was a timber framework covered in hessian canvas. The cross pieces between the two sides were removable so that the sides might be folded together for transport. Six hulls, folded in this way, could be loaded on to a 30cwt lorry. The turrets were constructed separately and also made from timber and hessian covers. They were designed to nest inside one another for transport. A gun was considered unnecessary. The completed framework was daubed with dye in the customary camouflage patterns. The appearance of a dummy tank from overhead was perhaps not so significant as the characteristic shadow it would cast in the bright sun on the open desert. They were very light but I never heard of any being blown away in the wind. Presumably they were lashed and picketed down if necessary.

'All the carpenters and joiners from the three field companies were concentrated into one working party responsible for the actual construction of the dummies. Other parties were formed in support and were used for the humping and collection of materials, and to fold the completed hulls and load them on to lorries.

'The first problem was to find somewhere large enough to be used as a workshop through the night. Finally, a large derelict hut was selected and the initial task was to put up some blackout for it. That done, illumination was provided by one of the lighting sets with which the Royal Engineers were equipped. All the lighting sets were already in use, which meant someone had to give up their set and make do with candles. While the hut was being prepared, tools and materials were also assembled.

'All through the night the hut reverberated to the sound of sawing and hammering. Individual components were mass-produced by small teams of carpenters. The pieces were then passed to other teams who put them together on two assembly lines, one for hulls, the other for turrets. Officers and NCOs were busily engaged in keeping the various jobs in phase with each other and transferring carpenters from one job to another as necessary. Work proceeded throughout the night and there was no slackening of effort. The cooks were as busy as anyone, maintaining a constant supply of tea and refreshments. By dawn, eighty dummy tanks had been constructed. A convoy of twenty vehicles conveyed them and their escort to Sidi Barrani.

'The ensuing battle around Sidi Barrani culminated in a resounding victory. Thousands of Italians were taken prisoner and the remainder put to headlong flight. Wavell pursued them for some three hundred miles, out of Egypt and across Cyrenaica as far as Benghazi. Regrettably, the effect the dummy tanks had on the battle is not known. The Italians were in such turmoil that they themselves did not seem to know what was real and what was not.

'The forward troops to whom the dummy tanks were originally consigned formed an attachment for some of them and carried them forward during the advance, more for fun than anything else. Some of the dummy tanks were reputedly seen in Libya, but I have no record of any having reached Benghazi. In the First World War, sappers like me had played a significant part in the development of the original tank. In the Second World War, they were relegated to producing only dummies.'

Kenneth Robertson's story bears out three of the principles which David Strangeways explained in his interview.[3] In the first instance the impetus to build the tanks came from a simple story based on a clear strategic objective. In this case the story might have been written:

'The enemy must believe that we have spare armour in the rear of our position.'

Second, David Strangeways found when he met the professional camouflage experts and decoy-builders that their designs were usually far too elaborate. To give an aerial reconnaissance pilot an impression it was not necessary for the 'machine' on the ground to have every rivet fixed in the correct space. Dummy tanks merely needed to cast a convincing shadow.

The third of David Strangeways' maxims, which Colonel Robertson's story reflects, is that there should always be a healthy chunk of truth included in the deception. As the Allies advanced they did indeed have a spearhead of heavy armour but when the enemy reconnaissance pilot overflew the battlefield, looking down on tank after tank, how was he supposed to spot when the real gave way to the fake?

As the war progressed, though, the construction of dummies did become more sophisticated – as we shall learn when we hear the tale of Mrs Hodgkin for whom dummy tank construction became a full-time cottage industry.[4]

CHAPTER 9

THE SAILOR'S TALE
Dr Peter Tooley

At the Teheran Conference attended by Roosevelt, Stalin and Churchill, between November 28 and December 1 1943, the decision was taken to invade northern France the following year. Once Normandy had been chosen as the landing ground rather than the Pas de Calais, a whole train of deception measures was set in hand. Bodyguard was the name given to the global deception plan. There were two main elements. Plan Zeppelin was the responsibility of Dudley Clarke and 'A' Force and their final mission was to pin down the large German forces in the Balkans, far from the beaches of Normandy. They succeeded. On June 6 1944, there were still some 24 divisions in Greece, Yugoslavia, the Dodecanese and Bulgaria. Fortitude North and Fortitude South were the threats to Scandinavia and the Pas de Calais respectively. The phantom army in Scotland whose menace had to be sold was the 4th Army, in south-east England it was FUSAG under the command of General Patton and the codename for all those cover and deception operations concerning FUSAG, the most significant part of Fortitude South, was Quicksilver. Bodyguard was a complex score playing from the deserts of Syria and Iraq to the estuaries of Suffolk in East Anglia and it was here, as a young naval officer in Combined Operations, that Peter Tooley found himself an important part of Quicksilver under the command of David Strangeways and 'R' Force, attempting to persuade Hitler and his generals that the *Schwerpunkt* was to fall on the Pas de Calais. When he took up his command he would not have been able to begin to guess how complex the deception plans for the invasion of Europe were.

Dummy tanks made a significant impact in several theatres of war from the campaign in North Africa to the reinvasion of northern

France. So too did dummy landing craft, and never more so than in the lead up to the Normandy landings. Not only did large numbers of real landing craft have to be secreted opposite the real invasion points, but the enemy also had to be deceived into thinking that an entire invasion fleet of landing craft was being assembled opposite the notional point of attack across the Pas de Calais. The architect Basil Spence[1] had already designed and built an entire fake dockside for Dover to reinforce the idea that the shortest crossing to Occupied Europe would be the one favoured by Montgomery and Eisenhower. During 1943 a small engineering firm in Watford started to turn out hundreds of fake LCTs (Landing Craft Tank). They were constructions of canvas and tubular steel, which floated above the water on empty oil drums. They were moored in creeks and inlets, only half disguised by camouflage netting, between Great Yarmouth and Dover. Most of them, though, were in the Suffolk river estuaries area, threatening the Pas de Calais. These were the vessels which, the enemy must believe, were going to carry General Patton's First US Army Group into the real invasion after the Normandy 'feint'.

The deception was fraught with difficulties but ultimately proved successful. Dr Peter Tooley was responsible for a small part of that success. He was involved in the building and deployment of an enormous fleet of dummy landing craft, the so-called 'bigbobs'. They were certainly big, but why 'bobs'?

'In this world of old school ties, most men knew that at Eton you were either a "wet-bob", someone who rowed for his house or his school, or a "dry-bob", someone who played other, land-based sports.

'At the meeting for "Roundup" in January 1943 it was decided that, although the invasion was postponed to the following year, they would mount deception exercises designed to mislead the German High Command. They decided to build a large number of dummy ships which were to be moored at strategic places around the coast.

'The London Controlling Section tried out several manufacturers for designs for these dummy craft, and settled on a firm called Cox's of Watford. Chris Toon, their senior design engineer and the managing director Howard Wilton submitted their plans to the LCS at Storey's Gate. They envisaged a 160ft long by 30ft wide model based on tubular steel, rather like the scaffolding used for building purposes today, with painted canvas stretched over the whole structure. It was to be a cantilever design floated on empty 60-gallon oil drums welded to the superstructure. Beneath the oil drums were little carriages with stub-axles and wheels so that the thing could be wheeled across land for short distances before it was floated. The prototypes were built at Cox's Watford factory inside a blister hangar nearly 220ft long and for security reasons, Chris Toon put it about the factory that he was constructing a mechanical elephant. He didn't say why. It seems a little far-fetched but people do seem to have kept quiet even if they were a little sceptical about the elephant.

'The initial flotation tests were carried out on Frensham Pond, near Farnham in Surrey. They only floated the central cantilever, so that there was no chance of anybody guessing what it was from its shape, which looked like a bridge section really. The trial was successful, so they were told to tool up for large-scale production.

'The prototype was photographed against the real landing craft anchored in the River Beaulieu in Hampshire. As was so often the case with dummies not only did it look good against the real thing, it looked *too* good!

'The problem was that the model looked too clean. It was something they hadn't considered. The real, sea-going version was often stained and weatherbeaten. Ships of the Royal Navy are never filthy! That problem was solved by splashing sump-oil around the superstructure and they even went so far as to paint rust streaks to the rivets. The whole thing was very convincing, with many pre-fabricated parts, a deck-house, funnel, guns, bollards, coils of rope, halliards, and masts. The bow-doors were also pre-fabricated to give the correct flare to the fo'c'sle. The whole thing was erected for the first time in a disused bus garage in Shepherds Bush. This was chosen because it didn't have any windows and was high enough to fit the model in without problems.

'The bigbobs were huge and the problem of keeping them a secret equally large. Obviously if the enemy or their agents caught a glimpse of one of these craft being constructed they would regard all sightings of landing craft thereafter as being inconclusive. So it was vital that the bigbobs could be constructed during the hours of darkness provided by the spring and early summer of 1944, in other words in less than six or seven hours. This would ensure that the various pre-fabricated sections could be transported to their sites along the south and south-east coast and assembled and deployed at night, so that the following morning German reconnaissance planes might locate and identify any apparent further build-up of invasion craft. Real LCT's were also moved continuously between the dummy anchorages to increase the sense of urgency to the build-up that the planners wanted to convey.

'The Cox's bigbob could in fact be erected in about four hours

110

by suitably trained men. If something went wrong and a bigbob was going to be left half constructed by daybreak it had to be dismantled and hidden away. Before morning a tractor with a harrow ran round the construction field scraping the grass up to disguise any sign of the construction activity.

'Originally, I was told that the operation was not sufficiently technical to warrant the use of Royal Engineers and so we had to make do with units of the Pioneer Corps. John English, the field training officer seconded from Cox's, described their work at the Virginia Water training site as "pretty disastrous at the beginning".

'He was there to help but the chaps just didn't know what they were doing. At one ticklish part, which was the erection of the funnel on the superstructure, a whistle was blown, everybody packed up work and the whole thing collapsed on top of John English. He climbed out of the wreckage not best pleased. However the training programme was completed and the first real launches were made in the River Beaulieu. Early in 1944 units earmarked for the final building operations were sent for training to Waldringfield, a small yachting centre on the River Deben in Suffolk and six coastal build and launch sites were selected between Yarmouth and Folkestone, where the dummies were to be concentrated. Eventually on May 20 the first completed bigbobs were deployed at Yarmouth. Not surprisingly for such Heath Robinson structures, which weighed about six tons and were designed to float on the water with very little draught, the bigbobs were very tricky to handle.

'I was stationed at Wolverstone on the River Orwell near Ipswich and I certainly had my share of problems. When these things were finished we used to run them down to the river on their wheeled undercarriages. The brilliance of Chris Toon's design was that the tubular steel struts were fixed to triangular plates with pins so that a certain amount of movement was possible. In other words they were articulated which was very useful when you had to push them down a slope into the water. But once in the water you needed four small craft at each corner to steer the beast. Two LCVPs, which were small assault boats, were tied either side of the bow with Royal Marine coxes to steer them. I climbed up on to the "Bridge" which was a piece of duck boarding tied precariously between 20 and 30 feet above the water. As the stern came into the water another two craft were tied on. So, in effect, I had four engines and by shouting directions I could just about manoeuvre the thing. We had no rudders, so if we wanted to turn to starboard then I had to get the starboard craft to put their engines astern and the port craft to go full ahead. They were very cumbersome and very, very difficult to handle, floating high out of the water and with all this canvas around them so that if there was any tide running or any significant wind it made my job even more difficult. In addition to what was already a pretty nerve-racking exercise, we had been told that under no circumstances were we to wreck one of these things. If I had run one of them on to a sandbank or worse still beached it, there would not have been enough time to prise it off before daylight. If the Germans then happened to come over and photograph the twisted wreckage of what was meant to be a fairly solid piece of hardware then we could have jeopardised a lot more than the well-being of a single bigbob.'

At the time Peter Tooley could not have had more than the tiniest suspicion of the full picture which his bigbobs were to play such an important part in. Nonetheless, they were clearly important. A lot of time and money had gone into them and having gone to all this trouble to disguise the construction and deployment of the bigbobs, Peter Tooley set about making them look even more like the real thing:

'During daylight we had the Royal Marines carry out animation exercises. We flew white ensigns at daybreak and struck them at sunset. Smoke devices in the funnels pushed out intermittent puffs of smoke. We hung up bits of washing, had men working on deck, sitting on the sides of them. We even used to run an oiling lighter, from craft to craft as if it was refuelling them. There were liberty boats as well as drifters, which took supplies from one boat to another. They would travel with their throttles wide open to give a good wash so that they could be seen more easily from the German reconnaissance aircraft, which appeared at regular intervals high over the Norwich coast.'

The German reconnaissance aircraft presented a difficulty. They were, of course, enemy planes and had to be fired at. Indeed, if the bigbobs had been undefended the Germans would soon have realised that they could not be a real invasion fleet. So the anti-aircraft gunners had to be seen to blast away, but they were told that they must make every effort to avoid hitting anything. After all this effort the pictures needed to find their way back to Germany. To those who did not understand that it was all a deception this failure to hit anything was a source of considerable amusement and for the Gunners themselves a source of embarrassment: 'The Gunners would go to the pubs in Ipswich at night and of course they were sworn to secrecy. The locals would say to them: "God! We could do better with catapults!" The poor chaps would have to grit their teeth and say nothing about it.

'Yet despite the ungainliness of these ugly ducklings I have since seen evidence from captured German intelligence reports that the bigbob deception was successful. At the time of the Allied landings in Normandy the Germans thought that there were 42 divisions and 500 major landing craft deployed in south-east England. In fact there were only 15 divisions held in reserve and no ships.'

Part Three

THE WORKERS

The elaborate schemes devised by the deception-planners had to be put into practice. The men and women whose tales follow in these pages, the plasterer, the electrician, the seamstress and so on, simply did as they were told, secure in the knowledge that they were making a real contribution to the war effort, the only way they knew how.

CHAPTER 10

THE PLASTERER'S TALE
Private Chuck Jones

'Where the bloody hell do you expect me to get a plaster technician at this time?' the brigadier bellowed angrily down the phone.

He felt a tap on his shoulder and an eager voice saying: 'I'm a plaster technician.' The voice belonged to Private Chuck Jones who had just been posted to Cairo and was not delighted by the prospect. The brigadier acted quickly. He organised for the invaluable plaster technician to be picked up within two hours. But there was a problem which Chuck Jones remembers vividly today, fifty years later: 'So this fellow turns up on a motorbike and says to me: "Are you a plasterer?" And I said: "Yes." I wasn't, I was a painter in the Royal Engineers, but the alternative was the paratroop regiment and they were only living nine hours at the time.'

Chuck Jones's reversal of the normal army maxim 'never volunteer for anything' was not only going to save him from the paratroop regiment, it was to present him in the next few years with a series of deception operations which ranged from the ingenious to the frankly ludicrous. He will describe the exploding camel dung later, but for the moment he had something of a problem with his plastering credentials. In the time-honoured manner he 'made his excuses and left'. He immediately claimed leave that was due to him and travelled to Alexandria, where he found a library and every book available on plastering. Chuck seems strangely unsurprised by the existence of one, never mind several, books on plastering in English in wartime Alexandria. He worked his way through the books and took careful notes. In civilian life he had been a painter working for Manders, a big firm in Wolverhampton, so he had seen plasterers at work. He returned after his leave with at least an inkling of what his

117

specialist trade was supposed to be. He was immediately sent on a three day refresher course. It was time to come clean.

'When I met the instructor I put my cards on the table and told him I knew nothing about plastering. I'd never done it in my life. So he says: "You expect me to make you a plasterer in three days?" And I said, "Yes." And that's how I became a plasterer.'

Why, in the war in Egypt were plaster technicians so much in demand? We come back to the figure on the motorbike who originally came to meet Chuck Jones. He was a Major Williams. In Italy his unit was known as MO4. In Cairo it went under the title ME60. Whatever it was called, it meant sabotage and deception. Major Williams had excellent credentials for the job. He had been trained as a soldier at Sandhurst and as an illusionist, a deceiver, at Warner Brothers in London where he had been an art director.

Major Williams had a job for Chuck Jones, his new plaster technician. He took him to a luxurious villa on the outskirts of Cairo and told Chuck to instruct a carpenter to make him a plasterer's bench. Once he had the bench and the tools, the job was to make 28 pounds of fake coal with explosives inside each piece. Chuck Jones was never entirely sure how the fake coal was moved around, but he did know that saboteurs mixed it in with real coal on the tenders of Axis trains. Once it was shovelled into the fire the plastic explosive would ensure that the boiler was ruptured and the train rendered useless. Listening to Chuck's description of how he made the coal, it is surprising that he and the rest of MO4 were not rendered useless themselves.

'How did I do it? First of all, I selected the best piece of coal so that it would look authentic and not be noticed if it was mixed in with real coal on a steam engine. Then I covered one half of the coal with clay about an inch thick. Then I covered the other half in clay and from these two halves I made a plaster mould. So these two plaster moulds are like two halves of a coconut. I made a device so that the two halves slotted together. So, now you've got what looks like a piece of coal made out of plaster. I'd left a little hole in the top and I melted plastic explosive and poured it into the fake coal.

'This Major Williams came in one day and I was melting this plastic explosive in a metal bowl on top of a primus stove. He nearly had a heart attack!'

Now that he was a successful deception technician, Chuck Jones began to refine his skills. He mixed in black colouring with his plaster and plastic explosive, put in a primer and detonator and sealed the top hole. When he painted it all matt black he said it looked 'ever so real'. He was worried that the fake coal would not be strong enough, so he mixed it up with real coal and shovelled it about for fourteen hours before the fakes disintegrated. By adding isinglass to his plaster he discovered he could make the product even more durable.

What happened to the exploding coal was, of course, on a 'need-to-know' basis. But Chuck Jones heard that in one month his fake coal disabled 12 trains in North Italy and Romania. It was a substantial, if bizarre contribution to the war effort.

Private Jones was a dangerous man to know. While in occupied Greece, Major Williams's unit identified a German petrol dump. It was an obvious target for one of Chuck Jones's 'specials'. And Major Williams had a contact, a Greek tradesman who worked inside the dump on the night shift. He was prepared to smuggle explosive into the petrol store but the Germans searched the men very carefully every day. They were, however, allowed to carry their own bag of tools into the site and Chuck Jones knew that the Greek regularly carried a hammer through the gates. He set about constructing a replica hammer which would have rather more impact than the real thing.

He made a plaster mould of the real hammer and then built a replica in papier-mâché: 'It was quite hard, but I also put a metal ferrule down the handle to make it even more rigid. This ferrule would take a detonator and an exploding time pencil and all around it, down the handle and the hollow head, I poured in plastic explosive. The papier-mâché hammer weighed about two pounds and I got in another one and a half pounds of plastic explosive. After I'd finished it I painted it myself, being a painter by trade. Then I tested it out on our carpenter to see if it would pass as the real thing. I slipped it into his bag of tools, and without noticing he picked it up and went to use it. Well, that was good enough for me.'

It is not recorded what would have happened if the carpenter hadn't been stopped from using the Jones hammer . . . But it *is* recorded that the Greek tradesman accepted the hammer, dirtied it up a bit and took it into the petrol dump one night. He set the time pencil, left the bomb in a critical spot, and the whole dump was destroyed in the explosion.

Major Williams's unit and Private Jones were becoming a very effective destructive force and so, in the nature of war, they also became a growth area. When they were still designated MO4 in Cairo there were just seven of them in the big villa. As the Italian campaign progressed they moved into a macaroni factory in Monopoli. This may sound more like a location from one of Spike Milligan's books about the war than a real-life history, but what Major Williams's unit actually did in Monopoli was even more strange.

Chuck Jones takes up the story in his customary detached manner: 'We made an exploding light bulb too. Major Williams said he'd got a window cleaner who had access to a German officers' mess. So I got a light bulb and took the metal base off it. I removed the filament inside the glass, then swilled the glass around in a very fine plaster solution. This made the glass opaque. Then I packed it with explosive and fitted in the detonator which we wired into the normal lighting circuit. Just for good measure I also put in some lead shot. But I was dubious about its effectiveness. So Major Williams tested it out on an empty room. He told me that when they examined the results, the lead shot was flattened out on all the walls and ceiling and floor. Nobody in that room could have lived. I know it was used but I couldn't tell you where.'

Perhaps it was just as well, in this world of ingenious deception devices, that people like Chuck Jones could so neatly distance themselves and their bombs from the reality of what the devices actually achieved.

One of Jones's other devices could achieve significant success on the enemy's railways. It was a set of fake railway fishplates, the joints that hold lengths of railway track together. Again, the newly accepted plaster technician's way of operating was simple. He would make a mould from a real fishplate and construct a papier-mâché fake. By the time his section was really succeeding he was being sent different models of fishplates from all over the world.

The papier-mâché was hollow and packed with explosive and a big magnet which would lock it on to the track.

'Of course, there'd be two fishplates either side of the track and there'd be wires painted black over the top of the rail connecting the fishplates and a battery and a detonator in one of the fishplates. This wire also made it look as if there was a real gap between the rails. So, when the train ran over the wires, it made an electrical connection, closed the circuit and the explosives would go up.'

Chuck Jones talked about his track-wrecking fishplates to an explosives expert from ICI. He suggested that the team should pack more explosives on either side of the rail 'for a bigger punch'. Chuck saw this device tested, with the added weight of plastic explosive, about three and a half pounds in all, and it wrecked eighty-five yards of track. Again he knows that the fake fishplates were used on tracks and *did* derail trains, but he was never offered any details, nor did he expect them.

His other deceptions were, perhaps, rather less lethal – a clothes line that concealed a wireless aerial and a jerry can that concealed the wireless itself. Both these devices were used by the Long Range Desert Group in Africa. But there can be little doubt that in the annals of war Chuck Jones's most bizarre contribution came with the simple but human observation he made in Africa: 'I realised that if anyone is driving for hours in the desert it gets so bloody monotonous, if he sees a pile of dung ahead, he'll drive through it – just for something different. So I came to the conclusion that if we made dummy dung and put in a tyrebuster, a small charge with a metal pin in, we could blow the whole bloody wheel off a German vehicle.'

As he warmed to his theme Private Jones the perfectionist was heard again: 'Of course, with donkey dung, you could only get a small charge in. With camel dung, which is a big cake, you could get a bigger charge in it. Blow up a jeep or something similar, no problem.'

From the moment when the Wolverhampton painter decided to volunteer as a plasterer nothing seemed to present him with much of a problem.

CHAPTER 11

THE ILLUSIONISTS' TALES
Stan Perkins, Fred Bateman and Geoff Selwood

The need for deception at home in Britain was at its most desperate in 1940, as the British tried to pick themselves off the floor after Dunkirk when they faced the real possibility of invasion. In the end, the bravery of 'the few' in the Battle of Britain was to save them and convince Hitler that Operation Sealion, his plan for invasion, should be postponed.

During those touch-and-go months another deceiver was to come into his own. He was Colonel Sir John Turner, the head of what was simply known as 'Colonel Turner's Department'. Even before Dunkirk, Colonel Turner had developed a simple system for decoy airfields. He would lay down two parallel rows of flares at a safe distance from the airfield that he wished to protect and making sure that they were at least partly visible as enemy aircraft approached the real and, of course, blacked-out airfield. Colonel Turner was able to show that the deception could work, because his fakes often attracted real bombs. One site at Watton, according to Seymour Reit in his book *Masquerade*,[1] was even bombed two nights in succession. With the Battle of Britain raging, it was obviously time for Turner's deceptions to move into a new phase. And so they did.

Colonel Turner was the inventor of 'Q' sites, much more elaborate decoy airfields which boasted electric lighting systems, taxi aprons, and fake beacons. He was soon installing these all over the country, on sites between 1800 to 3000 yards away from the real airfield. There is evidence of how successful these decoys could be at night – several RAF pilots 'cracked-up' trying to land on them until a suitable lighting code was devised to alert them to the decoy.[2]

The 'Q' sites *did* attract German bombs and Headquarters Coastal

122

Command suggested that the effect would be lost unless the Germans believed that they were inflicting dreadful damage on the ground. Coastal Command were concerned 'that the enemy should not be depressed by his lack of success'. In response, Colonel Turner came up with Starfish sites to create an illusion of success, as Leading Aircraftsman Stan Perkins tells us in detail below. These locations, which must have looked like junkyards by day, became pyrotechnic displays for the benefit of attacking Luftwaffe planes by night, convincing the enemy from time to time that he had scored successful 'hits'.

When the Luftwaffe began serious daytime bombing runs, the challenge for Colonel Turner's Department was obviously even greater. He turned to the British film studios for help. They created dummy Spitfires and Hurricanes, Blenheims, Whitleys and Wellingtons and they produced entire airfields built with canvas and fibre-board. These were codenamed 'K' sites and famous wartime airfields like Biggin Hill and Marham had their ghost 'K' site a few miles away.

As Seymour Reit reports, 'Q' sites could be run by just two men, but 'K' sites required a team of twenty men under a flight sergeant to make the airfield look convincing to enemy reconnaissance and enemy bombers. Striving so hard to create the illusion, the men sometimes forgot their true purpose, as RAF Flight Lieutenant Robin Brown recalled. He overheard this conversation in the middle of an air-raid:

Flight Sergeant: (agitated) 'Sir! We're being attacked!'

Pilot Officer: 'Splendid, Sergeant! Good show!'

Fl. Sgt: 'They're smashing the place to bits!'

P. O: 'Yes, excellent. Carry on!'

Fl. Sgt: 'But, sir, we need fighter cover! They're wrecking my best decoys!'[3]

According to the British Air Ministry there were 500 decoy targets throughout England during the critical months of the Battle of Britain. In terms of the success of the decoy airfields alone, the 'Q' and 'K' sites, Colonel Charles Hinckle of the United States Department of Defense reported that they 'attracted' over 440 enemy raids, compared to 430 on the genuine RAF airfields.[4]

The labours of Stan Perkins, Fred Bateman and Geoff Selwood, recorded below, would seem to have been much more than mere illusion. They diverted enemy firepower and saved lives.

Leading Aircraftsman Stan Perkins's war of deception began with a telegram to his station headquarters in Cleedon Hill, Hereford. He was to proceed to Cleadon Hill, County Durham, where he was to become a 'Starfish Electrician'. It had all the makings of a classic

Services blunder – as the cynics had it, it was bound to be a 'SNAFU', 'situation normal, all f***** up'. Clearly some bungling bureaucrat had confused the two almost identical place names and, in addition, had misread the normal description of Staff Electrician, Stan's real metier, for the rather more exotic 'Starfish Electrician', a job Stan could not even begin to understand.

The grimly familiar wartime train took him north and then RAF transport dumped him at No. 15 Balloon Centre, Longbenton, County Durham. While Signals checked on the provenance of the telegram, Stan was attached to the electrical section of the Balloon Centre. The centre provided some of the vehicles and the barrage balloons which were flown above the major industrial installations of the north-east, notably of course the dockyards of the Tyne and Wear. The barrage balloons were known as Dumbos and they flew from long, stranded steel cables. Stan recalls that one old Geordie woman who lived nearby said to the men at the centre: 'That must be a very stiff wire to push that balloon right up there.'

Stan was soon on the move again, picked up by a taciturn sergeant and taken to Whitburn, County Durham. It was not until they were within sight of Cleadon Hill that the sergeant broke his silence, pointing to the top of the hill and asking Stan what he made of it. 'It was all mysterious and I couldn't make head nor tail of it. The hill looked as if rubbish had been scattered all over it in large clumps. The wagon came to a halt by a concrete pill box and Nissen hut. Inside the pill box I was introduced to a corporal and some airmen. Finally it was explained to me that I was now an electrician on a Starfish, a decoy site for enemy aircraft.

'During the day it really did look as if the fields were cluttered up with useless, scattered junk and Heath Robinson gadgetry. But at night time, because of the clever electric lighting, the shadows thrown by all this junk would create shapes that would look like dockyards to marauding enemy aircraft. Throw other switches and the site would look like a railway marshalling yard. We also had twelve rocket projectors on the site, known as Zed guns. They were actually harmless-looking assemblies of scrap iron, pointing heavenwards.'

In reality, this small site at Cleadon Hill in Durham was three decoy areas in one: a dockyard, a marshalling yard and an anti-aircraft emplacement. This latter was designed to simulate the large Zed gun site which covered Sunderland and Newcastle. If any of these ploys could entice the German bombers to waste their payload, they had made their own important contribution to the war effort.

There were of course real dangers in all these illusions: 'From time to time some bombs would hit the edge of our site, but we were safely tucked up, three quarters of a mile away in the concrete pill box, which housed all the switchgear.

'But one night, during a snowstorm, the site was struck by lightning which lit one of the dummy fires, designed to let the enemy know that his bombs were "doing some good". So we had to turn out in the dead of night, scramble up the hill and frantically shovel snow on to the fire in the hope of quelling it, but the fire had really got going and we had to give up. Luckily for us the weather wasn't suitable for enemy aircraft and lightning didn't strike the same place twice!'

The daily routine on the site consisted of typical Service chores. The dummy fires were separated by shallow fire breaks which had to be weeded constantly to make them effective during the blaze at night. Each site would contain literally hundreds of lamps, some on the ground, others mounted on poles and some with enamelled shades and various fittings to cast the correct kind of light and shadow. All of these had to be kept clean and bright. Stan Perkins always chose a day when the typical North Sea fret was drifting in over Cleadon Hill. The decoy site had no running water but, with the grass soaking wet, he could keep his cleaning cloth damp.

The pill box was Stan's own little command post. Inside, a map of the site allocated numbers to all the installations. Push-button selector switches were wired to a GPO selector unit and miles of twin rubber cable snaked away to the various gadgets that needed electrical power. It was, of course, essential to know that the individual circuits were always working. They could be tested before each night's activity with a galvanometer on a very low voltage. Even the electrically operated incendiaries which set off the fake fires could be tested without actually setting them off.

The entire Starfish idea was an intriguing mixture of slapdash scenery and witty improvisation. Stan's dockyard scene represented the hulls of two ships which were presumed to be under repair or even construction. Lights were placed on short poles with baffle boards behind them, so when the light was switched on it was thrown outwards and the shadow inwards, producing a shape like a hull. They placed two huge box-like shapes in the middle to represent the ships' holds. Around these specific effects they placed general dockyard lighting and even dummy rivet fires made from old enamelled washing-up bowls. Two lamps were put inside and red glass covered the top. All the lighting could be brightened or dimmed depending on the weather conditions. Large canvas flats, grey and sloping, represented the dock sides. But there was still the problem of simulating water on top of Cleadon Hill . . . Stan's men had the answer: 'Dotted about on the ground were boxes containing lamps. They were covered by loosely woven bamboo mats. To an observer flying overhead it looked as if lights were twinkling on water that was being ruffled by the wind. I would have liked the opportunity to have flown over the site during darkness to see the effect and how real it appeared.'

Had Stan been able to fulfil his wish he would also have seen the effect of his railway marshalling yard decoy. Here, apart from the general lighting they also created the effect of 'steam engine box glows', the red light which streams out of the boiler when the footplateman throws more coal on the fire. Elsewhere, safely outside towns, he might have seen decoy 'tram flashes', attempts to simulate the flash from the overhead wires as the tram's contact arm pulley ran over the gaps. An even more confusing effect was created by the 'Greyhound' which attempted to reproduce the sight of planes taking off at night. It was, again, crude and simple, consisting of nothing more than a large frame in the shape of a letter 'T' which carried navigation lights. It was suspended from an overhead cable and propelled by a small rocket which was shrouded to make it invisible from above. As soon as the 'plane' was deemed to have taken off the navigation lights were doused and the frame hauled back to the beginning of its run. This little illusion played endlessly in fields and wasteland a few miles away from important targets.

For a full decoy site like Stan's at Cleadon Hill to be effective it had to have some firepower to convince the enemy that he was attacking a real target, one worth defending. Stan Perkins remembers his Zed guns in remarkable detail: 'The main parts were first the nose cone with adjustable height settings. This then had to be screwed on to the explosive part and this in turn on to the long three-inch-diameter pipe containing the rocket propellant. Four fins had to be fitted at the base. The fins formed part of the electrical circuit for firing the rocket and they were wired in parallel, so that it didn't matter which way the rocket was loaded on to its firing rails. This was important since we were almost always reloading in the dark.

'The gun was no more than two support rails on which we laid the rocket, pulling it back on to its electrical contacts. The most important thing to do before reloading was to switch off the electricity supply.'

That was by no means the only danger that Stan and his mates found themselves facing. If they were successful in their deception they lured fully laden German bombers to their site. They fired their rockets, then they must reload in the dark, blundering around with their heavy rockets and remembering to interrupt the electrical circuit before they armed the Zed gun. 'I trembled at the thought of banging the nose cone on something solid in the middle of the night and being blown to Kingdom Come.

'The nose cones were pre-set for exploding at the correct height. Inside they had four venturi holes. When the oncoming rush of air entered it pressed on a flange against a strong spring. As the rocket gained height and accelerated the flange was pressed further down, releasing the firing mechanism, with a bit of luck at the correct height for the incoming aircraft. The twelve Zed guns we had were set on three different fixed compass headings in groups of four. The instructions for firing them came to us direct over a special phone from the G.O.R., the Army Gunnery Operations Room.'

The term 'Heath Robinson', fashionable to this wartime generation, occurs regularly in Stan Perkins's account of his deception activities. It is the term he uses to describe the constructions they built to produce fire and smoke to convince the German bombers that they were indeed not only over a real target but scoring 'hits'. They built two huge, square metal tanks on top of scaffolds fifteen feet high. One contained water, the other oil. Beneath these tanks they fitted ordinary domestic lavatory cisterns, one fed with the water, one with the oil. Stan still recalls how this Do-It-Yourself system worked: 'The outlet pipes from the base of the cisterns forked into one long pipe sloping down to a long iron trough about ten feet long. The trough was supported on massive cast-iron fire bars. Beneath the trough, kindle was packed in abundance, cotton waste, wood, coal and so on. It might be three feet high. Electrically operated incendiaries tied to wax wicks were wired up to the circuits. The cistern chains had heavy weights on them. These were raised and incendiaries were attached to the string. Let's assume that an enemy plane is dropping bombs indiscriminately, close to an important target. The orders go like this: "Draw off the enemy! Number Four Fire selected!" Incendiaries ignite wax wicks, which in turn fire up the kindle. Just a minute or two pass, the flames are licking up under the trough. On this occasion oil has been selected so the oil incendiary is fired, this burns the string, the weight falls and pulls the chain, flushing the oil out of the tank. The oil pours down into the hot trough, sending up plenty of flames and smoke. After a while we select water and this flushes down, creating steam

127

and more smoke. As far as Jerry is concerned he's scored a good hit.'

Stan worked happily enough with his lavatory cisterns and decoy lamps for much of the war. But after D-Day a new posting came through. It was to prove an even more interesting assignment yet his initial reaction was to panic. What could he do with his large collection of handmade model aeroplanes? He packed them with great care and dispatched them to his wife Alice at home. During the long shifts at the Starfish site in Cleadon, Stan had carefully constructed scale models of a Wellington, Lancaster, Sunderland Flying Boat, Mosquito, Lysander, Spitfire, Hurri-bomber, Thunderbolt and Typhoon among many others. To his everlasting delight they arrived undamaged, even in the midst of wartime Britain.

His skill and dedication as a model-maker was, in fact, the reason for his new posting, as he was about to discover: 'Transport turned up and I was taken to RAF Shepperton which turned out to be Sound City Film Studios. What was all this about? Was I getting a film part? Had they heard that I'd done film projection? No. The studios had been commandeered by the RAF for special projects.'

Stan had been drafted to Colonel Turner's Department where all camouflage and experimental work was concentrated. This was where the full-size dummy aircraft and tanks were created which would either fold up or deflate into small, easily portable packages. These packages could then be transported all over the south of England and assembled to simulate the armies that the Allies still pretended were to be the main attack force across the Pas de Calais and elsewhere. In Colonel Turner's Department Stan learned to paint aircraft so that they blended into the buildings. Only in the early morning or late afternoon sunshine would the long shadows reveal the deception. He learned to use cowdung as the basis of camouflage paint, because 'it stuck very well and dried with a matt finish'. He learned too that not everyone on the site was completely aware of the principles of camouflage when, after a heavy snowfall one night, a particularly dim corporal ordered a group of airmen to sweep the snow off the roof since it was covering up the camouflage paint.

Stan had arrived too late to contribute much to Colonel Turner's Department. His memories now are of success for the Allies in Europe, the bombing of Japan, and the wrapping up of the huge industrial war-machine that had finally defeated Hitler. Satisfactorily, for Stan's story, it ends with a great conflagration.

He and his group were detailed to destroy 100-yard lengths of fast-burning fuses. One at a time, the fuse rolls were to be pegged out on the ground. Electrically operated incendiaries were to be fitted and the whole thing detonated at a safe distance of 100 yards. But this was not good enough for a man whose entire war had been firework flashes and bangs: 'This one-at-a-time procedure browned us off, what with all the walking up and down a hundred yards at a time. So we noticed this small bomb crater on a hillock and we filled it with kindling and got a good little fire going inside it. When it had really heated up we tossed a complete roll of fast-burning fuse into the blaze. Within seconds it caught fire, screaming and leaping into the air like a giant pyrotechnic octopus, all the loosened ends trailing from it. It sounded like a monster Chinese cracker. This was much quicker and great fun. Soon we got more daring and were throwing in two and three at a time. It was Merry Hell.'

'Merry Hell' was a fitting epitaph for Stan's decoy war.

Stan Perkins gives the most comprehensive account of work on the various decoy sites, but two other veterans also remember important details of their wartime deceptions.

Fred Bateman was an apprentice electrician before the war with Frank Burton Electrical Contractors in Birmingham. When war broke out they were taken on as subcontractors by a Birmingham building company, Bryant & Sons, who, Fred recalls, worked for Colonel Turner's Department at the Air Ministry. 'Funny that, *Colonel* Turner's Department, because Colonel isn't an RAF rank. Bryant's had the job of building these decoy sites and we did all the electrical work. Our side of the business all moved up to Bristow's Timber Yard at King's Lynn Docks and there we were soon involved in making the so-called "Starfish" sites.

'They had all different kinds of fires and we installed the electrics so that they could be detonated remotely from a safe distance. Sometimes we worked with fire baskets, which were large wire netting cages filled with shavings and other combustible material. Then there were other decoy fires which used huge 1000-gallon oil and water tanks and steel troughs with coal fires set with detonators.'

Fred remembers how they rigged up the oil and water tanks so that, after a suitable delay, they would pour on to the coal fires and create the effect of blast furnaces being operated. 'We knew they were secret. We never talked about our work when we were away from it. But there's a funny thing. When we went out to start work on a decoy site – and they were all controlled by the RAF – we'd go to the village and ask, innocent-like, if there were any RAF chaps about. Sometimes the locals would tell us that the RAF were working at the secret decoy site. Some secret!'

Another type of decoy Fred worked on was the false airstrip. These were the 'Q' sites that Sir John Turner had been so successful in creating. Fred recalls a straight line of lights about a mile in length including lights to indicate a plane's angle of glide. 'These were so real at night that our own pilots tried to land there on returning from a bombing raid, especially if they had been damaged and were unable to return to their own airfields. Eventually we had to devise a special red bar with about ten or twelve lights on it. This looked realistic enough to the enemy but it also helped our own pilots to distinguish the decoy airstrips from the real ones. This was more interesting work because there were more lights to put up and they had to be in a straight line across the country. If there was a tree in the way, we chopped it down.'

Fred also worked on a decoy factory at Leamington Hastings near Rugby. It was built of tubular scaffolding with hessian and canvas sides. The windows were painted on: 'There were fake chimneys too and a couple of chaps used to burn rubbish so that smoke would be seen pouring from the chimneys. Around the factory they placed scrap cars, some without wheels but they were propped up to look as if they had been parked there by the factory workers. We also had a few dummy aircraft so it looked as if it was a factory making aircraft. It could, for instance, easily have been mistaken for the Armstrong Whitworth works at nearby Coventry. We put the lights inside this factory in such a way that it looked like stray light was leaking from a skylight that had accidentally been left open in the blackout.'

Fred was just a young man and he worked 'all hours, from dawn till dusk in all kinds of weather'. He calculates that he must have worked on thirty or forty sites during the war. 'We all mucked in together. Even though I was an electrician I did everything. I dug the holes, mixed the concrete and laid it. I even erected the girder work. I remember one job we had at Felixstowe. We were making a decoy site for the docks and the marshalling yards. We had to fix the poles that held the lights right out in the mudflats and I remember we rowed out and we had to sink three 20-foot scaffolding poles before we reached the bottom, the mud was so deep. But we never minded the work, just so long as we could fool Jerry.'

Geoff Selwood was an electrician who joined the Territorial Army before the war and reached the rank of sergeant. When war broke out he joined the Regular Army as a master sergeant. Eighteen months later the cry went up for a soldier with experience of electrical work and Geoff soon found himself 'volunteered'. He takes up the tale of how he spent a large part of 1940 and 1941: 'A young man came up to Chilwell where I was posted. He told me to pack some stuff for a day or two. He wouldn't tell me where we were going. Apparently it was deadly secret – even the young man himself had nothing but a map reference. In the end it turned out to be Strines Moor just the other side of Sheffield. They were building an elaborate dummy lighting scheme to imitate the prominent points of Sheffield itself. In particular, they were trying to simulate the effect of the Brightside furnaces. They wanted to copy all the marshalling yards too, and what they'd done was to borrow three KVA diesel sets from the new radar people and they'd borrowed three people to operate them. They'd spread the whole lot out over something like one and a half acres.'

One site was at a place called Strines End and another at Grindleford. Geoff and his crew erected long wooden poles on the site, held in place by guy ropes. In between the poles they ran cables which carried the current to hooded lamps on the top of the poles. The lamps were laid out to correspond to the main points of Sheffield, including its furnaces and marshalling yards. Geoff was impressed: 'If anybody flying above at night saw this layout, and they were working to a map with a pattern of the city on it, they'd be damn sure it was Sheffield. And it *was* Sheffield, in a sense, moved so many miles north. For the furnaces we had some big floodlights and a very ancient water dimmer to dim them and big orange glasses in front of them. The idea was that if an air-raid was coming, they would have the lights up at full brightness and then, as the planes approached, they would dim them at the last moment as if the furnaces were rapidly being closed down. But they'd leave the pretend marshalling yards' lights on, to help Jerry out a bit!'

Geoff was working with 'a small army of ex-Dunkirk lads' who had also been 'volunteered' to lay the miles of cables. But for some reason the local deceivers decided not to proceed with the Sheffield site, a decision they were soon bitterly to regret: 'After a while it all folded up and they decided to dismantle it. I was left in charge with about a dozen men to carry on further experimental work in Warwickshire in a little village called Radway just underneath Edge Hill where the Civil War started. I did hear that just after we'd ripped everything down above Sheffield, they had their first blitz. The lads we'd left behind were hopping mad because they couldn't get any lights on or anything. You've got to remember that at that time Jerry

131

would bomb any lights he saw. That's how they bombed – viciously, no quarter given.'

Geoff's deception war was not over. He was moved to a big mansion that the government had requisitioned at Compton Verney in Warwickshire. He carried on further experiments in decoy and deception with what he describes as 'a lot of boffins'. One of the most important aspects of deception they worked on concerned water. Water is notoriously difficult to disguise. To make matters worse almost all cities have important rivers or waterways connected with them or running right through the middle of them. When bombing by moonlight any distinctive stretch of water was as good as a signpost to the city. The Germans in Hamburg became so concerned about the distinctive shape of their inland lake, the Binnen Alster, that they covered the entire area, 225,000 square yards of water, with wooden sheeting mounted on hundreds of wooden poles. It took them from January until April 1941 and when they had finished the construction they painted the lake's new roof with roadways, cars and houses. Even though the British knew about the deception the RAF had still lost a vitally important landmark and found Hamburg a more difficult target as a result. At Compton Verney Geoff and his 'boffins' came up with a less expensive technique for disguising waterways: 'Somebody had the idea of spreading coal dust on top of the water. It was a beautiful idea. You mixed it with a bit of old sump-oil to get it to lie on the water. In calm weather it completely stopped the reflection. The trouble was that when the wind blew, the coal dust and oil skin would roll up just like a roller blind. My lads used to come back looking like the Black and White Minstrels when they had been playing with that particular trick.

'We tried this coal-dust experiment on the two small lakes that belonged to Compton Verney. We had a connection with the RAF at Wellesbourne just outside Warwick, they used to take us up in their planes to give us an idea of what the experiments looked like from the air. And, I have to say, they looked terrific.'

Geoff Selwood's men teamed up with an RAF officer called Peter Sugg. According to Geoff they made this man an officer just to bring under their control because he was so inventive about decoys and deception. Again, they had to maintain strict secrecy: 'We all acted like civilians. There were about twelve of us and they built us Nissen huts in the fields as our billet. We became a unit with this Peter Sugg as our officer. We must have formed the smallest unit in the British Army. They called us the ADEE – the Air Defence Experimental Establishment. We got a War Office number and we could indent for any damn thing we wanted on that number. We also had a squad of Scots Pioneers who did the donkey work for us.

'We tried various experiments there. I remember we got a load of scrap cordite and we blew that up in a barrel. The idea was to simulate bomb blasts to confuse the Jerry bomb-aimers. I was flying that night as an observer in a plane from Wellesbourne. Well, we landed in real trouble with that one. One of the nearby RAF stations thought one of their planes had crashed. And we'd forgotten to notify them.

'On another occasion we got the sappers to dig a huge circle about fifty feet in diameter. We "puddled" it with clay to make it watertight. Then we flooded it with diesel and floated a couple of hundred gallons of petrol on the top. When we flashed the whole lot off it made the kind of dramatic fire that no enemy pilot could possibly have missed.'

Like the other electricians, Geoff remembers the simple method they used to simulate planes on their dummy airstrips. He also describes how they gradually refined the method during their experiments: 'We built what we called a Running Rabbit. This was just a long curve of two wires with a light and when it was working it looked as if it was a plane turning off a runway into its dispersal area.

'Peter Sugg got hold of a load of balloon cables. He also procured a whole lot of steel towers about nine feet high. We fixed the balloon cables to these towers and incorporated the Running Rabbit at the end of this device. We designed a little trolley which ran on the rails on top of the towers. There was a little rocket engine for propulsion and a lighting rig on the trolley. So what happened, we powered this trolley along the rails with the rocket, then we would switch the lights on and the Running Rabbit would take over. The whole effect was just like a plane coming in to land very fast. It would slow down and then the Running Rabbit took over and for all the world it looked as if a plane had landed and then turned off the runway to the dispersal area.'

Peter Sugg's team also made a Bailey Bridge out of nothing more than electrical conduit tubing and canvas webbing held together by wires. They fitted painted canvas on the top and sides so that it looked real from both angles.

'It was dead simple and convincing. We threw two wires across a river and fixed them tight. Then we just hauled this Bailey Bridge across because it folded up flat, just like a concertina, and more or less erected itself as we pulled from across the river. The "roadway" was just a piece of hessian. There's no doubt it was convincing because we actually had to stop a group of soldiers who were just about to start driving over it. The truth is it wouldn't take the weight of a child let alone an army truck.'

Geoff Selwood never told a soul what he was doing during the war. He did not even tell his wife and that, he admits, 'still doesn't go down well with her'. The days of decoys and deception were soon over though. His unit packed up just after D-Day. Geoff was to end the war as he had begun – as a warrant officer at Chilwell, where the man with no orders other than a map reference had picked him up in 1940. 'The fact was that after D-Day they didn't have much use for us!'

CHAPTER 12

THE RAILWAYMAN'S TALE
Jim Rowe

This is the tale of one man's experience of the Operation Fortitude deception. He was just one of thousands who saw, heard and perceived events they could not fully understand. They did as they were told to help fulfil an official plan they could not even begin to guess at.

Operation Fortitude was described officially, in words attributed to SHAEF's General Harold R. Bull, as a plan to: 'cause the Wehrmacht to make faulty dispositions by military threats against Norway . . . deceive the enemy as to the correct target date and target area of Operation Neptune . . . induce the enemy to make faulty tactical dispositions during and after Neptune, by threats against the Pas de Calais.'

It was this last function that Railwayman Rowe was to assist in his own bemused way. Just as a real build-up of men and materiel for the Normandy beaches was being disguised, so the notional concentration of stores, armaments and men was being constructed opposite the Pas de Calais. Obviously, as a part of that concentration, General Patton and his First US Army Group would need significant tank reinforcements . . .

Jim Rowe is a railwayman through and through. He's a professional, not a professional soldier but a man who helped the railways to help win the war. His story is a minor classic of how the ordinary man could help the war effort by his own professionalism and his ability to follow orders and, just as importantly, to keep his mouth shut. In an age that increasingly expects to be told everything through the media and television in particular, Jim's story is a reminder of the 'need-to-know' principle during the Second World War.

Jim Rowe became a railwayman in 1937, starting as a cleaner and rapidly graduating to the footplate as a fireman, stoking the steam trains. Originally he worked on the Waterloo/Portsmouth line, but when that was electrified in 1938, Jim moved on to Reading, where he was to spend an eventful war. He was called up in 1941. Reading became a major railway junction since it was the ideal distribution point for ammunition, troops, tanks and guns without touching the dangers of London in the Blitz. The number of locomotives at Reading soon rose from 20 to 40. A new junction was built to increase the ability to move large freight trains in and out of the station. It was a big enterprise which involved filling in an 80-foot-deep chasm and building retaining walls, which was completed by a team of stonemasons from Gloucester. It was, says Jim, 'an achievement at the time. Reading became a major junction for the Midlands and the North. The munitions and all the stuff that was being made for the war effort which was required in the South had to come through Reading to avoid London.'

Jim did not immediately realise that even a railwayman like himself could be drafted into the ranks of the deceivers, without even knowing it. It happened late in the war, as the prospect of D-Day approached. Jim's routine, with his engine driver, was to inspect the train and the freight that they were supposed to 'work' before they joined the train.

'This day it was tanks and there were 36 of them and we knew that it couldn't be our train, not all of them, because it was just a load that you couldn't possibly have taken with one engine. 12 to 15 was the top whack, that's as many as you could take with one engine. And it wasn't just pulling them, it was being able to stop them! The gradient going down into Guildford, for instance, was such that they'd have pushed you down into Shelford or such like! The trouble was they were "loose-coupled" and you didn't have a continuous brake throughout the train. All you had for brakes was the engine and a bit of help from the guard in the caboose at the back.

'Well, there was a big row with the guard we were taking the train over from. He says it's 36, equal to 60. What he means is that there are 36 vehicles but they are equal to 60 normal wagons. We'd worked our trains before and we knew that this couldn't be our train – I mean even half of them, even 18, would have been a few too many. If you had more than 12, generally you were double-headed, so you had two engines.

'Anyway, the guard has his "tally", which told him that there were 36 vehicles and the load was equal to 60. And it was just ridiculous. Twelve tanks was equal to 60. And here we are with 36

– it's just not on. And it's a hell of a slog pulling away from Reading. There was an argument and my mate, the driver, says: "If we find we have any trouble with them, we won't be going down into Guildford with them." If that train was pushing us so hard that we weren't able to stop, there was no way that we were going down that gradient into Guildford.

'Well, after a load of protesting, we set off from Reading. We put on an extra big fire and my mate was all ready to give the engine a hammering. We really were, both of us, prepared to have a go with them, but knowing really that this load must overcome us, they must be too heavy for us.

'Believe it or not, within a mile there we were whistling along like a passenger train almost. We just stood and looked at each other and scratched our heads and said: "Don't know what's happening." We kept looking back to see what *was* happening, were they still coming? And they were just sailing along behind us. And these are Churchill tanks. Then, next thing we're going down into Guildford. We had good command over them. That was when I got down off the engine. I had quite a big key in my pocket, it was a carriage door key. So I went back to the first bogie and climbed up on the wagon and started tapping. There were no metallic sounds at all, just the dull sound of wood all the time. I checked the second one and the third one – all the same.

'When I got back to my mate I said: "Here, Bill, these tanks are made of wood." Well, Bill looks horrified, don't he, he says to me: "Jim, don't tell me we're fighting this bloody war with wooden tanks!" '

As far as Jim's part of the war effort was concerned, the secret was out. From now on he was able to spot the trains with their decoy loads. But it never occurred to him or his mates to discuss this new phenomenon. Imbued with the wartime injunction that 'Careless Talk Costs Lives', they simply went ahead with their tasks, either transporting twelve real tanks on a journey to the real invasion army on the south coast or shuttling many more dummies to the deception sites around Dover and Folkestone. Jim never seems to have discussed the implications of what they were doing, and yet he must have known that the real tanks, Bren guns, Bren gun carriers and petrol tanks were heading for the coast opposite Normandy and the fake cargoes, made of wood and rubber, were on their way to join the dummy build-up opposite Calais. Yet he says, 'At that time, we weren't sure what they were for, we weren't sure that they were decoys.'

In the end, it was better not to speculate, not to know. Because he knew his railways, he knew that the decoys he was ferrying to Ashford would end up around Dover and Folkestone, but he would never have said so at the time. He knew that these trains of fake tanks were being berthed in sidings all along the coast in the area opposite Pas de Calais. He even knew that some were having sidings especially built for them.

'There could have been no doubt when the German reconnaissance planes came over, they *were* tanks – there wasn't no argument about it. They were wonderful fakes, right down to the guns on them and the dark green camouflage. Excellent workmanship to have produced them like that. Practically the whole coast of Kent, wherever there was room, these trains were berthed.'

Jim also knew that the real cargoes were bound for the New Forest, Hampshire and Dorset, where they were camouflaged. 'But we didn't talk about it too much, not then.'

Jim never felt that ferrying trainloads of dummy munitions around was somehow less than a real job. He had implicit faith in his masters: 'We had a lot of clever people in this country at that time, the boffins, working out all these schemes. They knew what they were up to and you just did as you were told. As a footplateman in those days that was your train and that was what you had to do with it.'

CHAPTER 13

THE SAPPER'S TALE
Private Ron Turner

Jim Rowe and his railwayman mate wondered how on earth the British were fighting the war with wooden tanks. It fell to others to fight it with rubber tanks and rubber guns. It may all have seemed innocent fun for a time until, that is, you found yourself, with Monty's blessing, actually sent into battle, into the greatest invasion in history, with such weapons. That's what happened to Sapper Ron Turner:

He enlisted in January 1942 at the age of just 17. He was desperate to get into the war. His first posting was to Maldon in Essex. Shortly after his company's arrival, a large consignment of materiel arrived for unwrapping and deployment. Here at last, Ron had the chance to contribute to the nation's fighting prowess. An officer barked at him to bring over a tank, another told his mate to grab an anti-aircraft gun. Neither of them could imagine what was going on. They had never been near anything like a tank or a big gun – they did not know what to do. They need not have worried. After they had unwrapped the hessian, everything they found was made of rubber. In among the rubber tanks and guns they even found cardboard soldiers. There were strings of lights to represent flare paths for aircraft, in fact every conceivable piece of practical deception that the experts could come up with.

Soon, the training started. The company was based in a mansion in Maldon, surrounded by a low hawthorn hedge. Ron remembers how ridiculous they all felt: 'It was laughable! The farmworkers would cycle past the hedge on the edge of the country park, and they'd fall off their bicycles, 'cos there'd be four men carrying a tank. Of course, we were the talk of the village. They thought we

139

were all loopy! We kept them blown up all the time and, dafter than that, we parked them on the football ground in full view. Well, my army training told me that they should all have been concealed. But of course, even then we still had German reconnaissance planes flying over, so we realised that must have been the aim to make them think that there were thousands of tanks at Maldon. In fact there were two companies of us there.

'About three months before D-Day, one of our companies disappeared. It was all top secret. We knew nothing about where they were going. They just took off about 5 a.m. They took all the lorries and some of these tanks. I found out, ages later, that they'd gone off to Dover and Folkestone. They were putting these tanks up all around the Kentish fields. Not only that, there were thousands of dummy units there. A unit ought to have been about four or five hundred men, but when you went into a pub there on the South coast there'd just be two blokes wearing the flashes of the Grenadier Guards and pretending to be a whole division. You just wondered what was going on and, quite honestly, whoever organised it must have had marvellous brains.'

As far as the dummy tanks and guns were concerned, Ron thought that, if anything, they were actually too good: 'They looked *too* real. Because a normal tank, you don't see any shine or glint on it, but these had a sort of shine painted on, like glitter. The turret or the gun would glisten like silver – I don't know how they did it, Dunlops made them as far as I know. The only thing that gave them away to the locals is that two or three men could pick them up and carry them away. Of course we had a real tank as well, so that we could make real tracks. But we had to keep blowing the dummies up and moving them around. It got really boring in the end.'

Ron's description of his war sounds rather more like the preparations for a particularly elaborate children's party: 'We had to blow up the tanks, we had to blow up these anti-aircraft guns, we had to lay out the Bailey Bridges, put the cardboard men up. And of course they took us up in planes to see the effect from the air. Three times I went up from Colchester or Chelmsford airport.'

After six weeks at Maldon the purpose of all this effort became clear in a particularly dramatic fashion. 'We suddenly had a lot of spit-and-polish forced upon us by our major. We were told to paint the black coal white, the brown grass green. Just to make the barracks look spick and span – load of nonsense if you ask me!

'Then Montgomery came in a jeep, surrounded by military police.

' "Gather round, lads!" he said, and then he told us what our job was going to be. "I've just come back from the Middle East, and you've been chosen to be part of 21 Army Group and you're going to crack Hitler's Fortress Europe. You're going to be the first in and you're always going to be in the forefront of the battle. The equipment you've had issued to you is what we developed in the Eighth Army in Africa – the purpose is to deceive the Germans into thinking there is a mass of military armour out there when there isn't. And that's what you lads have got to do in France." '

Ron remembers that Montgomery told them, a month before D-Day, that they were going to France, although of course he was not specific about where in France. Ron assumed that, since the route to Calais was the shortest distance, that would be the most sensible crossing point. The rumour was that the invasion would be launched in late May 1944, but at that time Ron and his sappers moved to Worplesdon in Surrey. REME units arrived and waterproofed all their vehicles.

By this stage, Ron was beginning to have his doubts about fighting Jerry with rubber tanks and cardboard men: 'I knew it was deception, but I didn't really know the purpose – to me it was stupid. I thought, hang on, the Germans are not *that* daft. They're sure to see through this and they've got spies and so on. Even the local farmworkers used to laugh their heads off at us. We used to go in the pubs at night, we were the talk of the town. I mean you felt silly. I thought the war was a very serious business, Hitler had said total war and I thought we were wasting our time, in a way.'

Despite these occasional misgivings, Ron and his mates were soon on their way to the final camp before the invasion and their own strange part in it.

There are many points of detail which old soldiers naturally forget or mistake, but not one of them apparently has forgotten the stomach-churning detail of the last few hours before D-Day itself: 'When we moved into Southampton we were sort of prisoners of the Yanks. They guarded us in our tents with fixed bayonets. We had to sleep with all our uniform on, our boots and everything. We were told that at any hour of the day or night we might hear the ship called out over the tannoy system. We had a white label, like a luggage label, tied round our necks – mine read SHIP LST 46. So I thought, "This is the real business." Then they gave us a field letter to write home to our parents, wives or sweethearts, saying we were going on an exercise, not to write back but we'd send an address care of an army post office when we arrived. That's all we were allowed to say, because everything was censored.

'We were in this camp on Southampton Common, there were more than half a million men in that particular area, and every night we used to go into the Americans' PX, the equivalent of the NAAFI. We used to drink lots of beer. Anyway, on this third night I had a feeling that it was going to come off that night. I said to my mates, six of us in the tent, I said: "Tonight's the night!" They said, "Don't be silly! We won't go tonight, the wind's getting up, it's stormy."

'I couldn't sleep. It was 2 a.m. All my mates were snoring their blinking heads off. Suddenly, there it was on the tannoy: "Ship LST 46." I scrambled up, woke all my mates and we tumbled out into the pitch black. I said to my mate, don't worry, Southampton Docks are only two miles away. We'll get a lift – our trucks with all the dummy equipment will take us, I told him. But they'd gone, they'd been loaded on to the boat at seven or eight o'clock that evening. So we marched from the common to the docks, about two and a half hours. It was right in the middle of the night, yet all through the streets there were Red Cross workers, WVS, NAAFI girls, all throwing packets of sweets, packets of Mars. Some would shout "You smoke, Tommy?" "Yes," you'd shout back. Twenty cigarettes would come skimming through the air.

'We got to Southampton Docks, boarded this American landing craft. All down below, where it stank of diesel, I felt a bit sick, even though I was born in a seaside town and the lads called me the Admiral of the Fleet. We moved out at 10 a.m. If you could have seen this sight. I've never seen anything like it. You couldn't see any water. You could've walked to the Isle of Wight across the boats. It seemed like a million landing craft, battleships, you name it. I was amazed.'

But the D-Day storm was brewing in the Channel and Ron's landing craft got no further than the Isle of Wight. The greatest military invasion in history stood still for 24 hours. Ron sat in his landing craft, consuming a meal that someone had contrived to rustle up.

Then, on the morning of the following day it really *was* time to go. The ungainly landing craft seemed to crawl and crab its way to France. Most of the men were, says Ron, 'sick as dogs'. Then his major told them they were approaching the beaches, they were to wear steel helmets and carry their gas masks, because the Germans were already bombing the beaches. 'I said, "I don't care what happens, I'd sooner be bombed. I just want to get off this boat. I'm as sick as a skunk." The Major said, "You're Churchill, the Admiral of the Fleet, you should be a good sailor!" Everybody had a bit of a giggle at that.'

But there were few giggles to come. And from the moment they landed they had plenty of other things to think about beside all the deception they had been trained for. More immediately useful than all the dummy equipment – and far more comforting – were their personal rifles and a real tank that someone had thoughtfully provided. Their primary task, once ashore, was to clear mines and, where necessary, build bridges. Ron's unit was attached to the 3rd Canadians and they made for Ouistreham, which was situated between the Americans at Omaha Beach and the other beaches, Gold and Juno. They were in one of the most dangerous areas of the whole invasion. The Canadians took terrible punishment, while the Americans attempting to storm the cliffs at Omaha were mercilessly cut down by German fire.

Ron is still vividly aware of the sacrifices of those few hours when more than a hundred men from British Ninth Para knocked out the Merville battery which could have thrown the Canadians and the sappers back into the sea. At the end of that Commando action, just twelve of the Paratroopers were still alive.

Ron's sappers landed at 7.30 a.m. on June 6 1944. Their first task had nothing to do with deception whatsoever. It had everything to do with survival. Near the beach were large cornfields. At varying distances offshore were ships full of vital supplies and materiel. There were two essential considerations: obviously these supplies must be landed as fast as possible and stored on areas adjacent to the beachhead, areas like the cornfields. But also the ships themselves must be released to return to Britain to pick up yet more supplies. Before the supplies could be landed the cornfields had to be cleared of landmines. It fell to Ron's sappers to find and eliminate them. 'We had to get our Polish mine detectors out and sweep the whole damned area. It took us a week to do all those fields around there.'

It was not until 10 days after D-Day that Ron and his sappers finally turned their minds and their energies to deception. When they did the results appear to have been not only demonstrably effective but quite spectacular into the bargain. They reached a village called Courcelles where the Allies wanted to impress the Germans with their strength of armour. Ron's unit was split up. Another section went out into the fields and erected some of the dummy tanks. It took about 20 minutes of heavy effort with a hand pump to blow up a rubber tank.

'When I took my turn with the decoys, I finished my duty about nine o'clock. That same night the Germans sent about six planes over. Of course, we all had fires lit – that was our job, to attract enemy planes. Well, that night we were successful. They bombed us and killed about 18 of our chaps.

'We had about three or four hundred tanks out there, Shermans and Churchills, all in glorious rubber. Well, they set every tank on fire. They couldn't tell that the tanks weren't real because they couldn't get low enough to see what was going on. It wouldn't have been safe. When the tanks got hit they just shrivelled up and burned. They didn't half stink.'

Rubber tanks may have been ridiculous, they may have been anti-social as they burned like old tyres, but they had the great advantage of being very cheap and therefore easily replaceable. Within an hour of the Germans destroying a field full of tanks, another three or four hundred tanks were apparently filling the gap. In reality, they had all just 'come off the back of a lorry'.

The tanks were more easily replaced than the dead men. Ron now found himself working endless shifts to fill in for his dead comrades. The bombing ceased but the dummy tanks still succeeded in diverting the enemy's attention: 'What they did, they mortared us every day. They obviously got a fix on us and trained their 8mm guns on us. I'm sure they thought that we were real armour, because it was so natural. You had this tank making tracks all day long. You had the Signals giving out all this false radio information. The Royal Signals had this white jeep – they kept pumping out all this information about troops – that's what a tank set-up would have been called. We were just companies.'

By this stage, Ron and his mates knew that they were successfully fooling the enemy. The Military Police played their part in this charade as well, painting roadsigns which read '200 Armoured Squadron, The Royal Tank Regiment'. 'All that sort of rubbish', as Ron called it, contributed to the illusion that the Allies had even more strength than the remarkable success of the invasion had in reality provided. Ron's deception unit was issued with black berets and the correct shoulder flashes for the Tank Regiment. 'You didn't know what you were going to be wearing the next day! You were RTC, the Royal Tank Company. I don't know who organised it, but it was marvellous.'

The remainder of Ron's war seems to have been a mixture of the marvellous, the tragi-comic and the plain dreadful. The Army equipped him and his mates with a phrase-book which, he says, contained such memorable and helpful sentences as: 'How old is the mother of your aunt?', just the thing a young Tommy needed to know in France in 1944. Nevertheless, Ron constructed a knowledge of the language from this source and, it seems, a string of pretty French girls. Apart from his increasing familiarity with the local maidens, he also struck up more than a passing acquaintance with the vin du pays, Calvados, the Normandy apple brandy. This was to be his downfall, literally.

Ron was injured soon after he reached Brussels with the bulk of the Allied forward forces. He broke his leg. Was this further evidence of the evil of the Boche? No, it was a tribute to a combination of German beer and Normandy Calvados. He was so busy worrying about whether the equally drunken driver of his army truck could get them all home, that he fell off the back of the lorry and broke his leg. It was effectively the end of his war. He returned to Britain and to the sad part of his tale. He had chased the French girls, he had over-indulged in the heady air of liberation, but he had also been one of the first sappers into Belsen, and had bulldozed the corpses into their mass graves. He had seen his comrades killed in the bocage of Normandy. In short he had become in his own phrase 'bomb-happy'. He spent many months recuperating in hospital. Gradually, he says, he 'got a bit happier'. Today he seems happy enough, even if he cannot really understand why the central most exciting, illuminating and intriguing incident in his entire life involved the deaths of millions of men and women. Monty told his company that their deception operations probably saved thousands of lives and shortened the war by as much as a year. It's a pretty good epitaph.

So is Bill's own coinage: 'They used to call us Fred Karno's army.'

CHAPTER 14

THE SEAMSTRESS'S TALE
Mrs Margaret Hodgkin

As the war progressed the business of manufacturing decoys gradually became more professional. As the effect of dummy tanks and vehicles seemed to be more and more successful in fooling the enemy the demand for such decoys naturally increased, culminating in the enormous demand leading up to D-Day.

Of course, somebody had to make the rubber tanks, rubber trucks and guns. Mary Hodgkin was one of the thousands who did and, like Ron Turner, her war of deception also damaged her health.

The construction of dummy vehicles was Margaret Hodgkin's entire work for five years, and in the end, despite the ostensibly pointless nature of the task, she was invalided out of the job.

At the age of 19 she volunteered for work in a factory making barrage balloons in Cardington, Bedfordshire.

'My sister and I and another girlfriend, we all decided we'd go to Cardington. We weren't in the forces but we were under Air Force supervision. We had to get passes to go in and out. We were the civilian people working at the Air Force base.

'We were making and repairing barrage balloons. I was in the "Fin and Rudder" Section. You had to blow up each part and go inside and make any repairs that were necessary. Sometimes we had to blow the entire balloon up in the big hangar at Cardington, go right inside and tape all the seams. All the seams, of course, had to be sealed to make sure that none of the gas or air escaped.'

It was hard work. They worked on the floor, kneeling on rubber cushions. Most of their job was sticking the rubber and canvas together with a strong pink latex solution, rather like rubber welding.

The technology required to make an effective barrage balloon was exactly what was required for decoys and dummies as well, as Margaret Hodgkin soon discovered: 'The forelady came round one day with a chargehand and selected a number of us. We all had to march out into the main hangar in front of the officers' quarters. One of them came out and told us that we were going to be doing highly secretive work and we mustn't tell anybody about it. He didn't really tell us what we were going to be doing. It wasn't till we actually got the work that we realised we were making these imitation vehicles.'

Margaret now graduated from the floor to a long bench, where she sat with forty other girls, manufacturing rubber parts to make up into jeeps. She moved from 'Fins and Rudders' to 'Wheels and Engines'. 'They were all done in parts, like tubes, so that if one part of the engine or wheel deflated that part could be patched and blown up again. The wheels were done with thick rings or tubes and the engines with tubes going across and going down. When all the parts were done they were taken down into the bottom room and covered all over with balloon fabric, a sort of rubber fabric that is linen covered on both sides.'

To begin with, while the work may have been more secret, it was hardly more exciting than making barrage balloons. The same repetitive chores went on hour after hour. They worked from half past seven in the morning to half past seven at night. And sometimes long into the night. But that could not diminish the thrill when, eventually, the factory girls were taken 'down below' to the assembly room to see what their bits and pieces actually added up to: 'They were marvellous! When you looked at them you'd have thought they were the actual vehicles and that you could get in and ride them. They were marvellous imitations.'

Cardington turned out jeeps and lorries in their hundreds. They were carefully painted with spray guns. The painters, who were all volunteers, could only work for about half an hour at a time because of the smell and toxicity of the paint. 'All the little Bulldogs and all the flashes were put on the finished vehicles and the windscreens were also made of balloon fabric but covered with a paint that made them look just like glass.'

The wonder at this neat deception is still in her voice today as Margaret remembers being shown line upon line of rubber jeeps and lorries. When they had begun they really were not sure what they were doing. Now it seemed to all of them a major part of the war effort. Margaret admits that, like many of her friends among the factory girls, she became a workaholic. She worked long hours in the Cardington hangar, the very place where the Airship R101 had been built. The work was predominantly gluing up the seams on the rubber balloon fabric. The combination of hard work and the 'dope' effect of the strong rubber solution eventually harmed her health. She had to be invalided out of the job.

'We all used to get droopy at the end of the day. It's a wonder we're not all glue sniffers!'

During this time, her husband was fighting in Italy and later in Germany. On several occasions he saw concentrations of dummy vehicles and guns, usually half hidden under trees. He recalls that you had to be closer than fifty yards to them before you could begin to suspect that they might not be real. Of course, he and his mates knew that there just were not enough vehicles available, so that such high concentrations must be fake.

The Germans, on the other hand, only able to watch from reconnaissance aircraft high overhead, must have found it almost impossible to distinguish fact from rubber fiction. Margaret's husband has no doubt about the effect of all this effort at deception: 'I don't think the war would have finished so quickly if it hadn't been for us bamboozling the Germans about how many vehicles, tanks and guns we had.'

CHAPTER 15

THE GUNNER'S TALE
Gunner Sergeant Shawler

Margaret Hodgkin was decidedly in the nuts and bolts category in the deception war, yet the products she made contributed to both the tactical and the strategic successes of the war. Sergeant Shawler saw those successes on the ground, with equipment manufactured by both his own men and the Margaret Hodgkins of this wartime world.

After the shock of Dunkirk, the British were badly in need of a military victory. They had to wait two years for El Alamein in North Africa. It rapidly became clear that El Alamein was a great triumph of arms. But it has taken decades for it to become apparent that it was also a considerable success for deception, particularly since it was at the expense of one of Hitler's best and most cunning commanders, Erwin Rommel, who was away on leave when the attack came.

Monty had decided that his real attack would be made along the northern sector of the El Alamein line. He wanted to avoid the dangers of the Qattara Depression to the south. Lieutenant Colonel Geoffrey Barkas was asked therefore by Montgomery's Chief of Staff, Freddie de Guingand to fake a build-up in the area of the Qattara Depression and, an even more difficult task, to disguise the real build-up in the north.

Brigadier Dudley Clarke[1] co-ordinated the results of Barkas' camouflage work. He was required to conceal 80 battalions of infantry, thousands of vehicles and over 6000 tons of stores. De Guingand told Clarke bluntly: 'You can't do it, of course, but you've bloody well got to!'

What Dudley Clarke, Geoffrey Barkas and the other camouflagers 'could not do', they had one month to accomplish before Operation

Lightfoot, the El Alamein offensive on October 23. They called their task 'Plan Bertram'.

In slit trenches near their proposed front they hid 2000 tons of tank fuel, carefully checking the shadows to make sure that the cans would not give themselves away to the enemy. The other, massive stacks of stores that the 8th Army had to conceal were built up into structures that looked like 10-ton trucks. Four hundred 25-pounder guns were dovetailed together in pairs and covered by truck canopies.

Dudley Clarke and his team produced canopies that, from the air, looked like 10-ton lorries – they called them sunshields. These they deployed along the genuine attack point in the north. The real armour was still in the rear, some 60 miles behind. During the build-up to the battle, they gradually moved up and secreted themselves underneath the lorry 'sunshields'. At the same time, the tanks that had moved up to the real *Schwerpunkt* were replaced each night by dummy replicas. The tanks which moved to the front dragged chains after them to obliterate their tracks.

As a result the enemy planes found it almost impossible to tell the difference between fake lorries at the real point of attack and fake tanks at the notional point of attack. In any case they kept changing.

Gunner Sergeant Shawler was a very small cog in this elaborate machine. But he, in his own way, fooled the Germans as well. He embarked for the Middle East with his battery in the summer of 1942. He was in the 59th Anti-Tank Regiment, which was due to join the 73rd Anti-Tank Regiment, who had been in service there for a long time.

During the spring of that year the British had been driven back to El Alamein, where they defended what was a very short line. Rommel tried to attack the line, but was driven off. To begin with Gunner Shawler's battery had to manhandle their guns into position. But later in the year and before the decisive battle of El Alamein, they acquired self-propelled anti-tank guns. These were not quite as grand as they might sound, since they consisted of guns mounted on armoured lorries. Indeed, even the armour was not as impressive as it might sound, since it was merely bits of armour plating attached to the cab. On the flat deck at the back they 'just stuck the gun on in the middle'.

All this may have been a trifle 'Heath Robinson' in design but there *were* 16 of them and so far Rommel did not know that the anti-tank provision of the British 8th Army had been reinforced with self-propelled guns. It was, of course, important that he should stay

(Above) General the Hon. Sir Harold Alexander, C-in-C Middle East *(left)*, with Lieutenant General Montgomery, Commander Eighth Army.

(Below) Alexander before Operation Diadem, Italy 1944.

(*Above*) Churchill's support for the London Controlling Section was vital to the success of deception operations in the Second World War.

(*Opposite above*) General Sir Archibald Wavell, a firm believer in the value of deception, conferring with British staff officers in India in December 1942.

(*Opposite below*) Monty talks to troops, post D Day.

(*Above*) Colonel David Strangeways worked closely with Dudley Clarke in the Middle East and commanded 'R' Force, Monty's tactical deception unit attached to 21 Army Group.

in ignorance of the new British mobility. So Shawler and his men conjured up some tubular metal frames and stretched hessian over them, painted in desert camouflage. From the air, the self-propelled guns looked like any other large lorry. These were a version of the 'sunshields' that were used to disguise tanks.

The German pilots used Storch planes for their North African reconnaissance and they would make sorties three or four times a day. Shawler's ploy was to allow them to approach closer than would normally have been sensible. But once they had had the chance to see the 'lorries', he and his men would open up on them with Bren guns. The situation was rather like 'Heads you win, Tails I lose'. The Storchs would fly very slowly in order to get their photographs, so there was always a slight chance of actually being able to bring one down. But, equally, it did not matter if they all returned to base since they would be revealing false information about the transport convoy. Similarly, if the Bren gun attacks seemed furious enough it would reassure reconnaissance aircraft that they had really seen something that the British were desperate to disguise. For many weeks, the self-propelled guns remained a camouflaged secret, their shells unfired.

There are only two dates in his war service that Gunner Sergeant Shawler remembers clearly: October 23 when the Battle of El Alamein began and November 4, when it ended. The order to end the self-propelled gun deception came, he believes, on the night before the battle of El Alamein commenced. The guns were duly uncovered. But it is wrong to say that the deception ended there. In many ways, the cleverest part of it was just beginning.

The gunners removed the large tubular frames covered in camouflaged hessian and left them in exactly the same place as the self-propelled guns had been when spotted by the enemy reconnaissance aircraft. Only the most vigilant of German pilots would have noticed that the 'trucks' down below looked slightly different in outline. By the time some expert photographic interpreter back at base spotted that the lorry shapes no longer had any cabs on the front, his information was redundant. The battle of El Alamein was under way and it was now perfectly evident to the Germans that the British were using self-propelled anti-tank guns.

Gunner Sergeant Shawler remembers that when the British opened a gap in the German lines, he and his men broke through along with the British tanks (real ones this time) and followed them into the widening breach. In fact they followed the battle through all the way to Tripoli the following January.

One tiny postscript to Sergeant Shawler's story testifies to the Germans' ability to intercept, if not understand, British wireless traffic. One of the contemporary field regiments called their guns 'Priests', while Shawler's outfit called theirs 'Deacons'. Apparently the Germans had been heard to ask why the British had so many Reverend Gentlemen among the ranks.

CHAPTER 16

THE DRIVER'S TALE
Percy Nunn

Percy Nunn, an Army Driver, moved up to the Highlands from Central Scotland in spring 1942 to train as part of a Mountain Division, the only one in the British Army. His unit was posted to the Grampian and Cairngorm area and it was soon quite apparent that they were going to train for an invasion of Norway. At the time this possibility seemed very reasonable. Although they were never exactly told, they regarded it as the worst kept secret anybody could imagine.

'The training was absolutely 100 per cent and very tough. We were issued with mountain clothing, windproofs, heavy pullovers, string vests, white oiled socks, soft leather mountain boots, rucksacks, sleeping bags and two-man tents. That meant two lots of kit, the normal army kit and the mountain gear. The mountain kit was never used to parade around in – it was only used in exercises. We did various exercises, some lasted a few days, some a few weeks. I remember one of them was called "Operation Snowshoe" and there were two other very big ones, "Goliath 1" and "Goliath 2", where a lot of troops were used over a wide area in northern Scotland. Together they lasted about two weeks and we were simulating operations in mountainous country. We were in the RAST, supplies and transport. That meant we had to practise supplying a division up one very narrow road or track. Everything had to be exactly timed and very well disciplined, because you couldn't get past a vehicle that had broken down for maybe several hours.

'The accent was very much on fitness, so we did mountain marches in full mountain gear. We spent some nights out on the hillside in our two man tents. The trick was to get two of you in the tent with the

153

primus stove going and it got very warm, whatever it was like outside.

'Physical fitness was at a premium, particularly when General Ritchie came back from the Middle East and took charge of the division. We reckoned we were on to something big when a big name like him arrived to take over. He was determined that everyone should be fit, so he had each unit doing commando exercises, swinging on ropes, scrambling through ditches and crawling under tarpaulins.

We had Norwegian officers who had rallied to the colours in this country, attached to the division, one for every unit. There were some who had escaped from Norway, so there was really a small Norwegian Army in Britain. And of course, their arrival in Scotland was even more significant than everything that had gone before. We actually started to have lessons in Norwegian, which I've now, needless to say, practically forgotten. It seemed to be a cross between German and Flemish. I certainly got the impression that that part of the training was there to create a mood, rather than in the serious belief that we'd all suddenly become fluent in Norwegian. But we never believed that all the training we were doing was a ploy. In fact I'm still not convinced that it was entirely a ploy. It was used very skilfully. Anyway, we had a few lessons in Norwegian, "I see a man in the street" in Norwegian, you know, all the sort of stuff that you'd never want.

'It was said at the time that 52nd Division must have been the darlings of the Imperial General Staff, because we could get stuff that nobody else could. We were the first to get vehicles called "Weasels", these marvellous small tracked vehicles for travelling over soft ground. They were developed in America and a small detachment of our people actually went over to America to watch the trials. They were reckoned to be the vehicles for travelling over soft snow and we were issued with scores of them.

'At that time we also had two companies of the Royal Indian Army serving up there. The officers were British but the men were Indian of course. It was very strange to see these dark men in the unlikely setting of the north of Scotland. There was also a Mountain Artillery Regiment which had these small guns you could take to pieces and transport over mountainous terrain.

'As a potential invasion force for Norway I tell you we looked the part. Throughout most of 1943 we took part in innumerable small exercises, trying to keep our interest up. I think by the end of 1943, probably some of the more adventurous among us were beginning to say, "Hang on a minute, all this training, when are we actually going to do something?" Eventually, we were told in a roundabout kind of way, "Look you're here, the Germans *know* you're here, they are very interested in what you're doing. Just by training here you're keeping thousands of German troops tied up in Norway." I think they reckon that there were 150,000 German troops in Norway just held there to counter the threat of an Allied invasion.

'I suppose some of the more adventurous spirits were getting a bit restless, thinking "Come on, let's go and do something," because there was all this glorious news coming in from the Middle East and the successes in North Africa. Then another rumour began to circulate that Monty had asked for us to go out and fight in Italy. We thought this was quite feasible if we were going to a mountainous part of Italy. We realised that if Monty had asked for us he had obviously been refused and this made us think that we really were in reserve for Scandinavia.

'Then in December 1943 we were told that we were moving south to the Dundee area to mobilise. The major exercises ceased and we just did small exercises to keep us on our toes. Then we were issued with shoulder flashes which said "Mountain". They were quite obvious. We all sewed those on and that was added to our divisional sign, so that we were a pukka Mountain Division. In Dundee, down in the harbour area, you couldn't miss a considerable display of snow-clearing equipment, giant snow-ploughs, and bulldozers. It looked like business.

'I remember – this must have been in the spring of 1943 – one evening I saw a German fighter plane come in very low from the sea, probably from Norway. It flew up the Tay and about 10 minutes later it came back again very low, obviously on a photographic reconnaissance mission. I'm sure the anti-aircraft pooped off at him a bit. And, of course, all our transport was lined up very noticeably down by the Tay. He must have got some good photographs.[1]

'In June 1944 we went down to the west coast of Scotland for amphibious training. We waterproofed all the vehicles, so that they could be driven through several feet of water and we practised driving on sand, of all things. This was just about the time of D-Day. Where are we going to land, we thought? We were absolutely mystified about what was going to happen. There was no point in asking any questions – I don't suppose our officers even knew the truth.

'Then, suddenly, the whole thing was dropped. We had all our transport taken away from us. We came down to the Midlands, to Shropshire, and we collected 450 jeeps and trailers. We were going to be reorganised as an air-portable Division. That's when, if it was a sham, it was all dropped. They were doing quite well in France by that time.'

Percy Nunn is still reluctant, all these years later, to admit that all his hard training – so hard that men even died during exercises on a few occasions – was all deception. And, who knows, if D-Day had not succeeded, a new front in the North might have been necessary in the course of time. But further problems lay ahead for the new Air-Portable Division.

Their training now consisted of loading jeeps and trailers into Dakota aircraft, preparatory to an air assault on some as yet unspecified coast. They went on to load supplies on to Dakotas, lash them down and then fly them to check whether they were correctly stowed. So convinced were they that they were about to be parachuted into the battle zone that they asked their officers whether they would be allowed to wear the famous red beret of the paratroopers. The answer was a firm no.

In fact, as Percy later learned, they were being held in reserve for the Battle of Arnhem. They would have been flown in by Dakota as reinforcements if the Allies had captured the airfields and prevailed at Arnhem. 'It would have been a very hairy experience, I think. Myself and another six drivers were attached to the Glasgow Highlanders, we were going over with them. By this stage we were up in Lincolnshire and waiting for the word to go. And the Battle of Arnhem started and we were: "Stand-To, Stand Down, Stand-To, Stand Down". We had twenty four hour ration packs and lifebelts. We had no idea where we were going. But because of the situation at Arnhem they cancelled it about nine hours before we were due to take off. Of course, they had to evacuate Arnhem and we never went. There again, we were left in limbo.'

The combination of training for mountain warfare, amphibious landings and desert driving on sand, all of which proved to be useless and impractical, might have driven a less sane man to distraction. However years of army experience allowed Percy to treat it all philosophically: 'By 1944, I'd completed going on for five years in the Army and I'd got quite used to the rough rule that if you were told something was going to happen, it was a fair indication that it wouldn't happen. You got very hardened and blasé – you just thought, "Oh well! there's another cock-up for you!" We didn't know that we were leaking information that was absolutely correct, but was designed to deceive.'

The Air-Portable Division was the next plan to be scrapped.

156

Eventually, Percy did reach the enemy coast, four months after D-Day. He almost sounds regretful when he recalls how quiet the beaches of Arromanches were so long after D-Day. He finally got ashore in a Canadian three-ton truck after a voyage across in a tank landing craft: 'We had to drive all the way to Belgium to catch up with everybody.'

It was only much later when Percy Nunn began to read about the activities and dispatches of the German double agent Garbo, that he realised how effective 52nd Division had been in convincing the Germans that an invasion of Norway was a possibility.

CHAPTER 17

THE MERCHANT SEAMAN'S TALE
Wilfrid Chambers

Wilfrid Chambers was an engineering officer on merchant ships throughout the Second World War. The deceptions he was involved in were neither grand nor strategic, but they give a very real flavour of wartime Britain. This story underlines Britain's desperate lack of resources in the early part of the war and the pervasive fear of the 'Fifth Column'. Men like Wilfrid Chambers were not to know that the German agents in Britain had been rounded up *to a man*. After Dunkirk, people who had lived with the threat of invasion were, quite understandably, capable of seeing a German round every corner. And Wilfrid was a fervent believer that 'Careless Talk Costs Lives'.

Wilfrid Chambers says the best cartoon he saw was in the *New York Times* at the height of the American war effort. The American manufacturing machine was in top gear, turning out materiel at an unprecedented rate for the continuing and decisive fight against Hitler. The cartoon showed a dowager lady on the launching ramp of a shipyard, accompanied by one of the great shipbuilders of the time. She has a bottle of champagne in her hand ready for the launch but she's complaining: 'There's no ship there!' The shipbuilder replies confidently: 'Start swinging, Lady!'

It still amuses Wilfrid today although, as he struggled to survive as a Merchant Seaman on convoys, there must have been precious little to laugh about. Although the story was American it might equally well have applied to his own native area, the North East. He is rueful today when he considers the much-discussed north-south divide in Britain. In the 1940s, the shipbuilding power of the north was one of the nation's greatest assets. The shipyards of his native Sunderland were 'working flat out and turning ships out very quickly, but the Germans were sinking them quickly too'.

Ron joined the SS *Empire Eve* as Fourth Engineer Officer in June 1941. She was a rather special and deliberately deceptive vessel, known as a CAM. Only three were ever built and Ron believes that the initials stood for 'Catapult Aircraft Merchantman', but, typically, no-one ever confirmed this during wartime.

There were two deceptions involved in the SS *Empire Eve*, one quite beguiling in its naivety and the other potentially important. But before they can be described, the Geneva Convention rules about merchantmen need to be rehearsed. Broadly speaking, the SS *Empire Eve* belonged to a class of merchantmen known as Defensively Equipped Merchant Ships, DEMS. The rules stated that the ship was 'defensively armed' if all guns were mounted aft of the bridge. This resulted in many neat designs, where guns that could traverse through 180 degrees were mounted just a few inches aft of the bridge. But that was not the first deception practised on the SS *Empire Eve*. It was not that Wilfrid's ship had an illegal gun or a gun that might contravene the Geneva Convention – he himself is scathing about the Germans' willingness to observe such niceties. No, Wilfrid's ship had no gun at all, merely a pretence at one, made out of a length of tubular steel, two oil drums and a tarpaulin draped across it. Why did they go to all this trouble? It was because of the prevalent fear at the time throughout Britain of what they called in those days 'Fifth Columnists'. Hear Wilfrid on the subject: 'Fifth Column were the kind of people who might have looked favourably on the Germans – maybe they saw the chance of a little bit of power for themselves if Hitler succeeded. They worked as tip-off merchants, supplying information. Wherever you went, even into a toilet, there was that thought "Careless Talk Costs Lives" echoing in your head, "The Walls Have Ears", that kind of thing. Because the bloke standing here, the woman walking along beside you, anyone could be picking up titbits. People in public houses could get a little bit loose-tongued. So if anybody saw the ships being fitted out and it wasn't hard, for instance, to see into George Clarke's yard in Sunderland where I served my time, they would see this "gun" sticking over the stern. It was all just a bluff so that information might filter back to the Germans that the merchantmen were armed.'

It was hardly a sophisticated affair with oil drums purporting to represent the breech of the gun and, as Wilfrid says, 'It wasn't a lot of good if you got attacked by a U-Boat. I suppose we treated it as more of a joke than anything else.'

The second weapon carried by the Catapult Aircraft Merchant-men was more sophisticated, and more deadly both for the enemy and occasionally for the Allies themselves. The CAM ships would steam to each side of the convoy. They carried Hurricane aircraft on their bows which could be catapulted into action. If the convoy came under attack from enemy aircraft they would launch their Hurricanes in counter-attack. But the SS *Empire Eve* was hardly the *Ark Royal*:

'When an aircraft was fired off it was only on a trolley that went the length of the fo'c'sle, then it was in the air. The trolley pushed it to 60 miles per hour. In the experimental stages two pilots suffered broken backs. You see, they went from rest to 60 miles an hour in about 2.5 seconds. The reaction on the seat was too much. They didn't have the design quite right at that time.'

At least the Hurricanes did represent some form of surprise to those attacking the convoys. But they hardly constituted Defensive Armament in the sense that the Geneva Convention had outlined. So their presence had to be disguised when the ship put into port: 'When we went to the States, first we went down to Halifax, Nova Scotia, and took the aircraft off along with the crew who were in fighting personnel uniform. Our merchant uniform didn't matter, but RAF uniform was belligerent. So we went up to the States in mufti, loaded the ship and returned to Halifax to pick the plane up and off we went.

'We were supposed to be a Defensively Equipped Merchant Ship, but the Hurricane was forrard of the Bridge and she had eight cannon. So really we could have been sunk at any time without any complaint. Mind you, the Germans were sinking without warning anyhow. While we were in the States we fitted Oerlikon guns either side of the ship. We were careful to fit them exactly two feet aft of the centre line. It seemed a bit daft, because we still had the Hurricane. So really they could have sunk us and had no regrets.'

Wilfrid Chambers and his mates became used to deception in various forms. Even when loading ships back in his home port of Sunderland he would spot 'the deliberate mistake'.

'We went down one day to Corporation Quay in Sunderland and the crates were all stacked up there. Every one of them was stencilled about four inches high; Calcutta, Bombay, Karachi and I think Columbo. Well, we're busy loading the ships, obviously off to the Far East, when down comes this squad of laggers. All the winches on the deck were steam, in those days, and they put three or four inches of lagging on all these pipes and four inches of insulation on the deck housing, the accommodation. And we had this cargo marked for the Far East! It was so obviously a flipping red herring. If we'd had any of our Fifth Column "friends" creeping about, God knows what they'd have thought!'

Part Four

THE TALENTED AMATEURS

The talented amateur has a particular place in the British tradition, and not least in the organisation of the British war effort. Like so many British wartime deceivers, Douglas Fairbanks came from a privileged background; though Lady Jane Bethell was of course very young during the war she sat at the very centre of wartime planning. It is a characteristic of the talented amateur that he or she will grasp the opportunities that present themselves in extraordinary times and offer a unique contribution to their jobs and responsibilities. That can certainly be said of the actor and the secretary whose tales we now hear.

CHAPTER 18

THE ACTOR'S TALE
Douglas Fairbanks Junior

Douglas Fairbanks Junior was already a famous Hollywood star when America entered the war. It was somehow most appropriate that a man who had lived his life in the Hollywood Dream Factory should become part of the machinery of Allied Deception. After all, film technicians from Shepperton and Elstree Studios helped the British. The famous actor helped too. Before the Americans entered the war after the Japanese had bombed Pearl Harbor on December 7 1941, Fairbanks had worked tirelessly to persuade a reluctant American public that the fight in Europe was their fight too. Once America had joined the hostilities he joined up and spent the early part of the war as a Junior Grade Lieutenant on convoy duties. Later he was to become what he calls a 'two-striper', a full Lieutenant, escorting convoys to Malta and Murmansk. He sailed in destroyers, cruisers and finally in aircraft carriers. By the end of the war the list of the places in which he had fought sounds like a catalogue of the war itself.

'I was in the North Atlantic, Murmansk, Russia, North Cape and the Arctic Circle, across the Channel in France and then the Mediterranean, North Africa, Sicily, Greece, Salerno, Anzio, Naples, Corsica, back to France, you name it.

'My entree into deception came about as a result of my long standing family friendship with Lord Louis Mountbatten. He wanted some American representatives on his staff. There were already one or two, but he asked for more and he asked specifically for me as an old family friend. He knew I'd been at sea several times and thought that it might be interesting to get me involved in the dirty tricks department, in deception and tactical diversions. The relationship with Mountbatten went back as far as my childhood, because he and Lady Mountbatten spent their honeymoon with my father at his house in California. He was Godfather to one of my children, she was Godmother to another one. The families have always been close.

'I suppose it's like anywhere else. You go for the people you know and trust. If I'm making a film and I know somebody who's very talented in building ships down in Florida, I would still have to convert him from making ships, however good he was at that, into making movies. But at least I would already know that we spoke the same language. When I was in London, Mountbatten's influence and indeed my many connections meant that I had no problem being taken seriously but out in the field it was a little different. In fact it was a freakish, difficult position for me because being a name that was familiar to a lot of people, they would suspect that I was just there for show. Well, that was a good thing for them to think, that I was a decoration, a "do-nothing". But they were sometimes rather astonished to discover that I would go on actual operations. Mind you they didn't know that the operation was part of a deception plan. There was a sort of bewilderment on the part of others, "What the hell was I doing there?" In a way that reaction was useful because they'd never suspect that I was in something as subtle or as top secret as this. I know that on this score Mountbatten was worried at first that I'd be a compromise to security because I'd be recognised. That was the case at first but eventually it worked the other way around.

'In terms of sheer rank I was often out of my depth. I had such a humble rank and yet I was moving in high circles. The Army was able to make spot promotions so that people could fit into their jobs. So people in the Army were promoted to Lieutenant, Captain up to Colonel and Brigadier. The Navy just wouldn't play that game. I just stayed at my humble rank until promotion was due and then, little by little I moved up.

'I came to London to work on the planning side of deception and then travelled to Inverary in Scotland where they were working on the tactical side, mostly for the Army. When I was up in Scotland I was asked to consider how the army work on tactical deception could be adapted to naval warfare. I had been briefed to make a particular study of sonic deception at sea and was also intrigued by the use of false radio broadcasts to confuse the enemy wireless interceptors. I came across people like Disney Barlow when I made my way across to Laggan House in Ayrshire, where there were all sorts of experiments going on in sonic deception. Montgomery at

El Alamein had some success with that at sea when he simulated an amphibious landing, which threw the German Commander, General Stumme, into a bit of a panic. But it was in Scotland, which was a lot colder, that I first learned all about it; how they made the recordings and how they experimented behind trees to see what the reaction was. Then we had to adapt that to amphibious warfare and put these devices on small boats. The amphibious side of tactical deception moved to a base in Southampton, where we built up a group of Special Operations people who were involved in raiding, dirty tricks, deception, diversion, a little of everything that was off-beat. I was a sort of liaison with the British for Special Operations. We had some small adventures across the Channel and finally we had the North African invasion in November 1942 and established bases out there. On my trips out to the Middle East I met Dudley Clarke on a number of occasions. He was taciturn, pleasant, very retiring, physically small, a deception in himself because he didn't look very important. He looked to be an amiable little fellow, a classic professional soldier, not very impressive to meet until you started talking to him, then he became very impressive indeed. In fact it was Dudley Clarke who was sent out to Washington on a mission to brief the American Chiefs of Staff on what he had been doing out in the Middle East, in September 1942. Out in Cairo, I also knew Noel Wild, who was a very smart Hussar, Clarke's right hand man. I seem to remember that Clarke and Wild had their headquarters in what had been a brothel before the war. At one time or another I came across David Strangeways, David Hunt, and the conjuror Jasper Maskelyne, they were all involved, in one way or another, with Dudley Clarke, who really gave a lead to the whole thing.

'I was still doing a liaison job and in the early summer of 1943, after Rommel had been chased out of North Africa, the Americans established small sonic and tactical deception units at their bases in Algiers and Tunis. By this time I had gone back to the States for a while and was helping to train those units at a base in Virginia, before they were posted. Recruiting for the units was interesting. We went to the universities and asked for volunteers with backgrounds in electronics. They were not told what they were volunteering for except that it could be dangerous. There was no shortage of young men wanting to come along and see for themselves what it was all about. Once they had undergone their basic training, we had them shipped out to the Mediterranean and equipped with pre-recorded sonic deception devices.

'How did it work? Well, we would pre-record sounds of landing-craft, voices talking in the middle of the night, signals back and forth. At night, one or two boats would sound like twelve or fifteen. Of course, sound travels further over water than anywhere else. Or we might arrange for a single plane to fly overhead, giving out signals as though there were a whole flock of planes.

'And then we went into the visual end of it, in fact every kind of diversion on the tactical side. But that had to mix with the strategic, like the famous story of the "man who never was". Well, it all had to fit into a pattern. Except for the High Command on the American side, I was one of the few Americans who knew what was going on on the British side. First of all I liaised with the British and then tried to make our own people adapt to the deception plans.

'At the outset, the American High Command hated the entire idea of deception. The Chief of Naval Operations, Admiral Ernest King, thought it was "just boy scout stuff". His attitude was that if you were going to fight a war then just get ahead and fight it, don't do that kind of thing. They thought that War should be fought as War. Trojan Horse stuff was not for them. As far as they were concerned we were just a bunch of small boys wasting our time with tricks, instead of getting on with the business of fighting. Headquarters in Washington took a long time to be convinced of the value of deception but my Commander, Admiral Hewitt, Eisenhower and indeed Roosevelt himself simply saw the results the British were achieving and they were in close, friendly relations with the British, so there was some fairly high powered support, which won the day in the end.' Douglas Fairbanks Jnr was unusual in that despite being a member of the planning staff he was allowed to be both a planner and an operations man. Normally the information the planner carried in his head was considered too valuable to risk if he were taken prisoner.

'As I was the only one who had had experience with the British on these commando raids and on deception and diversionary operations, I would help to write the diversionary plan but there was no-one available to carry it out. They would assign a senior officer to do the job, but often he couldn't understand the kind of thing we were up to, so I had to change hats and go with them to advise the senior officer, which was very unconventional.'

But Douglas Fairbanks Jnr has no doubts about the theory and the practice of deception. This is how he summed it up:

'I suppose at first, in the very simplest way, the purpose is to confuse the enemy as to your target. For example, when we landed at Sicily in 1943 one of the earliest things we did was to make them think we were landing in Sardinia. Once it became obvious that we were going to land in Sicily then we planted the idea that it could be there, or there or there. Finally, we persuaded them we were going to land *there*, but actually we landed *here*. That was the trick. The second thing was to give an impression of much greater strength than we actually possessed, with dummy parachutists, an illusion of many more ships than we actually had and so on.

'At the beginning of 1944 I was appointed as representative on the Joint Security Council (JCS) which was the American organisation under the Joint Chiefs of Staff responsible for co-ordinating deception operations. It was the American equivalent of the LCS. In the run up to D-Day we co-ordinated with things happening in the Mediterranean on the strategic side, air traffic, radio traffic, movement of ships, false information and so forth. We also did some tactical deception with dummy craft and "beach-jumper" units. Beach-jumper was a codename for the American Tactical Diversionary Groups. They were small boat operations. It was the BJs who created the effects out of small boats of sounds of battles and bright lights, a sort of "son et lumière".

'There were two operations, Taxable and Glimmer, which although I was not involved personally, were for me a culmination of a lot of the amphibious deception, that I had been involved in throughout the war. The plan was to persuade the Germans early on D-Day itself that there were two very substantial convoys heading right for the French Coast. They were meant to draw attention away from the real landing zones. Taxable made its way towards the bit of coast between Cap d'Antifer and Fecamp and Glimmer steamed towards Boulogne. They used all sorts of things that had been developed during the war: something we called Chaff but the British called Window, thousands of little pieces of metal dropped out of the air which showed up on the German radar screens as a blizzard. There were balloons called Filberts, which had their own radar reflectors, and something called Moonshine, which just bounced the enemy's radar right back at him and magnified it too. Once the two fake fleets had almost reached the French coast, the next stage was sonic deception, and that involved loud speakers sending out all the noises of a huge invasion fleet. By the time the Germans came out to see what was going on the whole party had disappeared. I think that the Germans had really been led to believe that this was it, the big one, and in the early stages it did help to take some pressure off the Normandy beaches. I think anyone would have been fooled, because the deceptions were expertly worked out in detail. Sometimes the

Germans might have suspected that one of these operations was not all it was got up to be, but they didn't dare take a chance. What made all this so impressive was the amount of resources that the Allies were prepared to throw at their deception plans. It's not enough if the enemy is disabused of what he thinks you're going to do. You must make him think positively that you are definitely going to do something else and that takes planning and manpower. Not only does he think I'm not going to hit with my right hand, but I make him think that I'm going to hit with my left hand. In actual fact, I'm going to kick him!'

CHAPTER 19

THE SECRETARY'S TALE
Lady Jane Bethell

It was said of Dudley Clarke that he was worth an Army Corps on his own and during the early years of the war, 'A' Force Headquarters in Cairo was undoubtedly the hub of deception activity. In the end, London naturally became the place from which deception on a global scale was controlled and it was to this end that the LCS had been established in 1941. Once Colonel John Bevan had taken charge of the small deception headquarters under the pavements of Whitehall, the LCS gradually began to increase in confidence and stature.[1]

Ronald Lewin has summed up the function of the LCS with characteristic elegance.

The principles on which the LCS operated were as old as war itself. What Bevan and his unit brought to them was sophistication and finesse. But all the main elements in their technique can be observed for example, in this account of an episode during the American Civil War, when at the time of the battle of Gaine's Mill in 1862 Robert E. Lee needed to keep the bulk of the Union Army under McClellan out of the fight. General John B. Magruder did the trick.

Magruder all day long played the part of a general who was just about to launch a shattering offensive. His skirmish and patrol parties were constantly active, his batteries were forever emitting sudden bursts of fire, he kept bodies of men in movement on open ground in the rear where the Yankees could see them, and with drums and bugles and human voices he caused noises to be made in the woods like the noise of vast assembling armies – and all of it worked. It worked, partly because Magruder was very good at

171

that sort of thing, and partly because the Federal command was fatally infected by the belief that Lee had overwhelming force at his command. This was the grand illusion that brought other delusions after it.

To distract Hitler and his High Command from the real intentions of the Allies by fatally infecting them with grand delusions, and by convincingly creating a threat where none in fact existed, was precisely the task of the London Controlling section.[2]

Early in 1944, Lady Jane Pleydell-Bouverie joined the LCS, as personal assistant to Colonel Bevan, at a time when he and his colleagues were fully engaged in the planning for the grandest delusion of them all, Plan Bodyguard. Lady Jane is the youngest member of a famous picture of the LCS, taken around a big table in their underground bunker in 1944. She is also now the only surviving member of that group.

Lady Jane Pleydell-Bouverie grew up in the country, as the eldest of six children. After leaving Godolphin School for girls in Hammersmith, she went to secretarial college and then, in February 1942, at the age of eighteen, she joined the ATS.

'We had six weeks of initial training, in very bad weather at Aldermaston, which was enough to break anybody in. After that I was given a clerical job at Southern Command for nine months. This was followed by an Officer Cadet Training Unit (OCTU) course in Edinburgh and a stint as a platoon officer with cooks and orderlies in London. I was living at Eaton Place at the time and it was early in 1944 that I got the interview for the job at Storey's Gate, the headquarters of the London Controlling Section. One was just told that one was being interviewed for a "Staff" appointment, which sounded frightfully grand, but one knew perfectly well that it meant a little bit more money too.

'The competition was fairly hot – though I don't know exactly who else they saw because I never saw them. You didn't wait in a queue. I was interviewed by Colonel Bevan and I think Colonel Wingate was there. They were both informal and friendly. I don't think they were terribly interested in what small skills I had. I was a shorthand typist which was, I suppose, necessary although, in the event, I don't remember ever using my shorthand. Filing was what was really needed. Anyway, I seem to have been suitably qualified because I was offered a job and I joined them in February 1944.

'On my first day Mr Rance showed me round the entire labyrinth of underground offices. He was the old caretaker, and it was quite a tradition that if you were new he took you in hand and gave you a

172

conducted tour. When you arrived at Storey's Gate you went down the stairs and into the dungeon, down the passage with a dreadfully old-fashioned air conditioning system all in great big tubes. The impressive thing was that one knew that upstairs there was General Ismay and loads more important people. Of course Churchill himself was not very far away. Mr Rance's tour included a moment of great pride and reverence when you were shown the bedroom that Churchill used when he had to spend the night down there. We were also shown the map room which was all quite historic during the height of the Blitz. The nature of the place where I had come to work, the Cabinet War Rooms built underneath Whitehall, meant that it was difficult to remember what time of day it was. There were permanent electric lights and rather noisy air conditioning. Some of the rooms were quite large, with very high ceilings, but Colonel Bevan had a small office and his door came out into a room in which other members of the LCS worked. Further down the passage there was a big room where we had the morning meetings and this too was used as office space by some of the team. There was one other room for the Civil Servants, the Chief Clerk and two girl clerks, and one or two junior people just passing through. So basically there were four offices, the one with the clerks in, the big one which had three people and the meeting room, then the smaller one, and the last one in the passage where Johnny Bevan worked. That was where all the files for the most secret things were stored – the ones that didn't go to the Civil Servants and lower grades to be handled.

'The thing that really shook me was that, on the very first day, I was told the date and the place of the invasion. Since practically everybody in the country at that time spent a great deal of their conversation speculating as to what was going to happen, once you knew, you became a kind of social pariah. You could no longer take part in those sort of conversations. I had, of course, signed the "Black Book" and, in those days, one was certainly led to believe that you would never be allowed to say anything of the secret work you were doing for the rest of your life. I don't even know whether there was a 30-year rule at that time, one just didn't mention that sort of thing. You were bound to secrecy for life.

'Perhaps that is the reason why one tends not to have very clear recollections because once you had put it behind you you tended to make no effort to recollect anything just because it was safer not to. On the whole, the less you knew the better. I don't think that anybody was told anything that they didn't need to know to do their job. Maybe certain people knew certain secret things but

173

they didn't know the whole story. It just demonstrates how frightfully 'safe' we were. You didn't discuss anything, even with your nearest and dearest. I had to be terribly careful what I said to my friends, we all did. I just said that I worked in the Cabinet Offices, which covered a multitude of ideas. It could have been any sort of job in the whole building really. The designation "LCS" was chosen as a specifically non-committal title. It didn't really give any guide or clue to what we did at all. Even if people knew that it stood for the London Controlling Section, nobody knew what exactly we were controlling. In the end it was nothing more than a notice on a door. There must have been quite a lot of people in the building who had no idea at all what we did.

'When I started I worked alongside Margaret Donaldson, who was the only woman officer there. There were two Civil Service clerks, but they never handled top grade secret material, that was handled entirely by Margaret and myself, and eventually by me alone. When Margaret left I assumed responsibility for all the top secret files, so I had the opportunity, over the time I was there, to study the previous plans. I was able to look at deception plans like Mincemeat for "The Man Who Never Was" and Operation Copperhead, when just before D-Day an actor impersonated Montgomery. Most of the plans that had been done as part of cover operations for North Africa and the invasion of Italy were there.

'I would think that in our office we knew more of the whole story than probably anywhere else. The job of the LCS was the overall plan, and the strategy. That's where it was determined what the deception planners wanted the enemy to believe we were going to do or not do. It wasn't really up to the LCS as to how it should be implemented. The implementation was farmed out to all the other agencies, the double agents, the diplomats, the tactical people, the ones who arranged all these bogus armies with wireless communications. LCS did not much mind how they did it as long as they gave the right impression.

'One was aware that Winston Churchill took a very personal and a very close interest in the whole concept of deception. It seemed that if he hadn't been who he was and where he was, he would very much have enjoyed getting really mixed up in it because most of the plans went to him personally and came back with notations in his own handwriting. I saw comments and suggestions which demonstrated that he read the deception proposals very carefully from cover to cover. I think he fully appreciated their importance. He often sent for the Colonel personally.

'Colonel Bevan was also in touch with the operational commanders at the highest levels. He would be in no doubt as to what the real plan was, and once he was sure of that, he and the rest of the team would fabricate a suitable cover plan, with sufficient truth in it to be plausible. This was the great thing, every plan had to be plausible. If it wasn't you couldn't expect the enemy or anyone else to swallow it. In some cases, to be absolutely fair, they didn't *appear* too plausible but it was amazing what the Germans swallowed.

'Of considerable importance was the feedback that we received from Ultra. Colonel Bevan took the Enigma decrypts very seriously and by no means everybody in the LCS was admitted to the Ultra secret. We had the messages between the different German Headquarters, the different Generals and even Hitler himself. We were given all the extracts that were pertinent to our plans and security was very tight. Funnily enough, Colonel Harold Peteval, who worked in the same office as me and his wife who worked on Ultra at Bletchley had been married for two years before they realised that there was any connection between their work.'

For Lady Jane one of the strongest memories is of files, many of them Top Secret: 'My real job was personal assistant to Colonel Johnny Bevan. So I did whatever he wanted, which entailed filing everything or, if he shouted for something and he wanted to refer backwards which, of course, he frequently did, I had to be able to find the right file. I inherited the filing system in an enormous cabinet, which went right back to the beginning of deception operations. I expect it's all there still somewhere. I don't remember it being very scientific. The different cover plans provided the names for the files because members would often need to refer back to previous plans, since it was vital never to cross your tracks. If the LCS were busy giving one false impression then they had to be careful not to give a diametrically opposite one in a later plan, hence the frequent need to refer back to see what had been said and what had been the reactions. These, as far as we had been able to ascertain them, were also in the files. Very important information came from diplomatic sources for example. The enemy's ambassador in Portugal would be heard to say something or other and every nuance would be carefully logged. Information filtered back from many countries, but predominantly from Europe. We didn't have the reactions from the Far East. There *were* plans for the Far East but we didn't actually handle them in detail, all that was handled in Delhi.[3]

'I also had responsibility for typing anything very secret for the Colonel. Everything that was too secret to be handled by the civil servants would be my responsibility for either Bevan or Wingate or Peteval who were, so to speak, the Colonel's right hand men. They were the most senior.'

Lady Jane Bethell still has a clear memory of how the planning meetings ranged over the various options before the LCS.

'First of all it would be made clear, probably by Colonel Bevan that the operation was so-and-so and we wanted to mislead the enemy. How shall we do it? Any ideas? That meant, literally, *any* ideas? People tended to have their specialist things – secret channels for instance. Or somebody would look at it from the Royal Air Force or Royal Navy point of view. The vital question was always: "has anyone got any good ideas for making the Germans think that this is going to happen as opposed to that?" Plans used to be drafted at great length and eventually through a process of refinement they would agree on a final plan, which could be put to the Chiefs of Staff.

'Compared to most other army establishments the working atmosphere was very relaxed. You have to bear in mind that nobody was "regular service" at all, they were all war time volunteers. Their careers varied from stockbrokers to manufacturers of soap to a small part character actor. We didn't really have a barrack room life because none of us lived in service establishments. We all lived at home or in flats or clubs. There was none of that discipline that one associated with the Services. There was simply a personal discipline that grew from the job. You did what you were told regardless of the hours or the effort. Things like leave were all arranged on a very friendly basis when it suited you, or, if you wanted leave for something special, you asked for it and it was probably granted unless it was wildly inconvenient for somebody. Mind you, there wasn't exactly a lot of leave going.

'It worked well because they each had a very clear idea of how the others' minds worked. More than that, they could approach each other by ringing at home in the evening or talking to them over lunch or dinner at White's or Brook's or at one of the favoured restaurants like the Hungaria or Rules. Very often a great deal more can be achieved that way than on a totally formal basis and I think that what they called the "Old Boy Network" was influential, was important and was effective. Lots of people would like to decry it but I think that they would be wrong. It was based on the Public Schools and the Universities. Everybody either knew somebody or they knew their friends or somebody quite close to them. In a biggish office you would be able to find somebody who could approach almost anybody on a personal basis. You simply get more done that way.

'Johnny Bevan was very "laid back", that would be the current phrase. He was very kind, very quiet with a nice, gentle sense of humour. He hardly ever raised his voice and didn't really give the impression of being very clever or very influential, but I think he was both. He was a great friend of "Pug" Ismay, Churchill's Chief of Staff and of Menzies Head of MI6 of course. The truth was that almost everybody that he dealt with on the top level were personal friends. I think that that applied to quite a lot of the top echelons of the Services in the War.

'Ronald Wingate, his second in command, was a most amusing man. I saw him several times after the war because he lived at Wilton which is near my home. He was very lovable, very volatile, terribly keen on making his pennies on the Stock Exchange. When he got sent away the thing that really worried him was that he couldn't ring his stockbroker up every day. He pretended that he was older than he was and he had a smart wife who wore very dashing hats. He was the oldest person there, a cousin of Orde Wingate, and his father had been very distinguished in the Sudan, so he came from a line of very distinguished public servants. He was a very clever man and a great personal friend of the Colonel's, with a lovely sort of twinkle, always pulling people's legs.

'Dennis Wheatley was very flamboyant. How would you describe him? He had a very red nose and looked like the bon viveur that he was. He loved his success. He was a great admirer of Churchill. He even built walls like Churchill. Dennis provided the Dancing Faun, the elegant Graeco-Roman statuette that sat in the middle of the LCS board-room table, in the middle of our deliberations. I can't remember what its history was. And I think the carpet, a very smart Persian carpet was his too, it certainly was not Government property. I don't know whose the table was because that wasn't very much like Government property either, so I suppose that that might have been his as well. He liked the luxuries of life. The Civil Service girls, the clerks, did their typing in the outside office. They were normally responsible for typing up Dennis Wheatley's brainchilds. I did this once but only once. His grammar was non-existent, full of split infinitives and dreadful spelling. My spelling is not very good either and with seven copies, all done on carbons with no Tippex, it was truly unbelievable. I was well and truly stuck. Hours of rubbing out and overtyping.

'Major Harold Peteval was, if anything, slightly out of keeping with the rest in that he took life quite seriously, but was extremely hard working and I suppose, in some ways, less imaginative than somebody like Dennis. Perhaps he had the role of shooting down the more far-fetched ideas. I am not quite sure how he came to join the office. But he was a good friend. I didn't much care for his pipe, but because I smoked myself in those days I had to put up with it.

'Alec Finter was charming, but rather sad in a way. I suspect that his previous life hadn't been very successful. He was a small part character actor, and I imagine that is a hard life. He was a bachelor, friendly and nice. Derrick Morley was very much on the social plane, a personal friend of the Colonel with a very beautiful wife but she lived in Ireland. We used to meet occasionally across the dim lights of night clubs and occasionally we sat slightly bleary eyed in the office. He was totally un-military. It would have been impossible to have made him march. I think that he might have had arms and legs that didn't go in the right rhythm, but, of course, he was very clever and, like everybody else, he got stuck into the job. James Arbuthnott was very urbane, very charming and Neil Gordon Clark was never anything but charming to me. I think that you wouldn't have looked twice at half of them if you met them in society in ordinary clothes. They were just ordinary people. Nobody wanted to do anything else. It was exciting. You felt that it was very important, which indeed it was, and you felt, even then, that we were quite lucky to have that sort of a job. Other people used to come to the office, when they were in London.

'Peter Fleming of "D" Force in the Far East was a real character. He used to visit us every time he was in town, a very flamboyant, very attractive, very smart Guardsman. He had a good figure – altogether a glamorous man who used to blow in or blow out when he was in England, which wasn't often. He was also a personal friend of Johnny Bevan's. Of course we maintained a correspondence with Peter Fleming and his team but they were so far away that basically they formulated their own plans and deceptions.

'I remember Dudley Clarke very clearly. At the end of the war he came back and started to write the history of what we'd done, but he didn't get very far. Eventually the plan to write a history of deception was abandoned. But whose decision it was to abandon it at that stage I don't actually know. Maybe there wasn't too much enthusiasm because obviously they knew that they were just writing something that was going to be locked away.[4]

'Everyone was a bit war-weary and tired by that stage. I think that a lot will have been lost because it was not all recorded straight away with the people who actually took part. Despite my responsibility for filing I don't think that what you file gives you a complete picture. It can't do. A lot of that sort of thing is between people, it wasn't ever written down. And the way people's minds worked dictated the sort of impression you wanted to create in the mind of the enemy. You knew what you wanted him to think. Of course there were a great many wild and scatty ideas, which tended to be tenfold greater than the final plan, but a good final plan could not emerge unless every possibility had been explored. The essence of the whole office and the people employed there was the fact that they had good brains and fertile imaginations. They dreamt up all sorts of ideas which were never put into operation or even recorded. You arrived at your final plan by a good deal of roundabout thinking, a mass of possibilities and a roundup of everyone's bright ideas. There was a lot of paper torn up, and a good many of those ideas were never put to the test.

'As we moved towards D-Day we worked longer and longer hours. People smoked rather more cigarettes than they did before and it was pretty tense. One scanned the papers and listened to the wireless to see what reactions your deception efforts had created. Then we looked at them again, for any mention of people who'd got drunk and said things they shouldn't, people who knew more than the average, though to be honest the enemy didn't seem to pay much attention to the press. We compiled a scrap-book, mostly about people who'd gone too far, a lot of them drunken sailors. How they came to know so much I don't know. Some of the comments were just inspired guesses, of course, but if they ever got to the enemy there was a chance he'd think the drunks knew something worth knowing. But as I said, I don't think he took much notice.

'On D-Day itself we knew that the invasion had had to be delayed. That was an awful day because it was postponed for twenty-four hours and I remember those long hours in the office. It meant that we had one more day to sweat it out. Then it was the morning of D-Day. It was when I was still living in Eaton Place and my bedroom was what in the old days would have been a servant's bedroom, right at the very top looking over the rooftops. With my specialist knowledge I knew that the Paras and the Gliders would be towed out at the crack of dawn or before. I spent most of the night hanging out of the window and listening to the drone of the aircraft going over, which was probably so great that almost anyone would have realised that there was something a bit different afoot. It was much bigger activity than an ordinary bomber raid would generate. They came from all over the whole country.'

Exciting it undoubtedly was, but waiting for news of success or failure was nerve-wracking. It involved sitting hunched up over the message traffic: 'Of course we were waiting for every possible reaction from the decodes for the next day or two. We were also watching for any reports of troop movements, because it was in the first few days that it was so important that the plans should work and that vital German divisions should remain in the Pas de Calais instead of coming streaking down to the beachhead. Thank God they did! We were hanging on every possible bit of information about enemy troop movements to see how successful or otherwise we had been. It was quite difficult to judge the level of success, but as the days passed by we began to realise that the deception operation had gone very well indeed. It really had worked, so everyone heaved a great sigh of relief. It didn't stop there, of course, because the deception operations carried on in the beachhead, though the whole business moved from the strategic to the tactical.

'The basic FUSAG deception was maintained for some weeks because we were still giving the impression that we were going to land in the Pas de Calais as well as in Normandy. We were still trying to convince the enemy that the other notional army was just waiting and that the main attack was still to come. It was quite amazing how effective it was. Goodness knows what would have happened if it hadn't been, or if we hadn't had deception at all. I really think that the course of the war might have been quite, quite different, not just in Bodyguard and Overlord, but in earlier operations as well. Invasion landings were always traumatic and in many cases there were a lot of casualties and a lot of opposition. But it might have been much, much worse, with much stiffer opposition and many more casualties. You even had to consider the worst possible thing, that we might have been pushed back into the sea.'

Lady Jane Bethell recently had the chance to revisit the Cabinet War Rooms, which are now, of course, open to the public. It was a nostalgic experience for her:

'I noticed odd little things that brought so much of the war back to me. For instance I saw that the ash tray had a little sign on it saying "ash tray". It made me remember that Colonel Harold Peteval was an inveterate pipe smoker. He used to have two pipes because when one got too hot he had to put it down and light up with the other one. So presumably they were balanced in these amazing tin ash trays. And all around there were endless bottles of Stevens inks and these marvellous old-fashioned telephones. One had really forgotten what they looked like.'

Part Five

THE ACTION MEN

While the brains laboured in Storey's Gate; while Lady Jane Bethell picked through her files to confirm or deny details of past deceptions; while the tales of deception were being constructed, another breed of men was putting elaborate deceptions to work. And often they were risking their lives in the process.

The SAS men and the other special operations soldiers were often in danger and they describe such occasions below. But the double agents, were also forever frightened of being discovered by the German masters they affected to be feeding with information. It remains an extraordinary fact about the Second World War that *all* the German agents in Britain were rounded up early in the war and many turned against their German controllers.

The two double agents 'Mutt' and 'Jeff', whose account follows, were in real life John Moe and Tor Glad. Today they live in Oslo and look back with mild astonishment at the world they inhabited in the early 1940s.

(Above) Colonel David Hunt, a university don who became involved in intelligence and deception work.

(Above) Dr Peter Tooley, the young naval officer who supervised the launching of the Big Bobs during the build-up to D Day.

(Above) Terence O'Brien, the Australian pilot who flew on many deception missions for Colonel Peter Fleming in the Far East.

(Above) General Sir Charles Richardson, the mastermind behind the deception operations prior to the Battle of El Alamein.

CHAPTER 20

THE AGENTS' TALE
John Moe and Tor Glad

John Moe is the son of a Norwegian father and a British mother. Tor Glad is wholly Norwegian. Both today enjoy presenting themselves as 'innocents abroad'. And that is exactly what they tried to do when they finally reached England on April 7 1941. They had been sent as paid agents of the German Abwehr, destined to sell the secrets of the British to their German masters. In fact they had been trying to subvert the Nazi cause by every means they could find. We shall return to April 7 1941, again, as both of them do constantly. But from the beginning of the war in Norway they had been involved in trying to undermine the Germans.

Tor Glad was a trainee NCO with a Sapper regiment at Akershus. When the Germans invaded he helped to blow up four railway bridges to halt their advance: 'I don't know what we thought we were doing. The bloody German tanks just drove around the ruins.'

John Moe remembers the ultimatum from the Germans to the people of Oslo: 'Surrender or be bombed!' They surrendered.

Tor Glad had spent time in Germany and spoke the language fluently. He describes himself before the war as 'German-friendly'. 'But when those bastards raided us all that changed.' With his fluent German, he was soon approached to work for the German authorities. He accepted 'in order to stop a real Nazi getting the work.' He was soon working for the German Censorship Department in Oslo and passing lists of suspected Norwegians to John Moe, who in turn was warning the suspects that they were likely to be under surveillance or even to be arrested by the Gestapo. Tor Glad vouched for John Moe as an ardent Nazi and managed to get him into the Censorship Office as a colleague, despite the fact that the Germans were naturally suspicious of his English mother and English background. But John Moe had already taken the trouble to join the Norwegian National Socialist Labour Party which he knew the Germans regarded as a replica of their own Nazi party. He had obtained two membership cards for himself and Tor and had them back-dated so that both men would appear as keen and long-standing supporters of Hitler's ideas.

Eventually Tor Glad was asked to work as a back-up man for a radio operator who was to be dropped by parachute into England. But in the event the radio man decided to back out. When Tor told John Moe about this John immediately suggested that Tor try to convince the Abwehr that he would make a splendid substitute. 'We seem to have reacted like eager boy scouts.' John Moe recalls their youthful enthusiasm: 'We were already planning a deception operation. We now had a radio and a chance to feed false information to the enemy. We were like little boys with a Meccano set. At that time I didn't even know what MI5 or MI6 were all about. My idea was just to get over there to England and report to the nearest police station.'

Again, Tor had to intercede on John's behalf, trying to get him on the same mission. He reminded his German masters that John spoke perfect English, complete in those days with a Lancashire accent. (Later on in his career in England Oxbridge men eradicated his Northern accent and replaced it with a studied English upper-class one.) 'Herr Moe is a convinced Nazi,' he told the Germans. 'It's essential that he comes with me to England.' It worked, and to Herr Moe he said, 'Now we'll take the Nazi bastards if we can!' In a scene straight from Le Carré they were eventually both summoned to a hospital where the local head of the Secret Service was propped up in bed recovering from his latest bout of alcoholism: 'He took out two pistols from under the bedclothes, handed them solemnly to us and declaimed: 'You are now members of the Abwehr.'

Today, the two double agents remain amazed at how easily the Germans were fooled by them. 'We had learned to see through the Germans. We knew which ones were real Nazis. Believe it or not you could tell just by the way they said "Heil Hitler!" '

They were given very brief training in Morse transmission and radio techniques. To Tor Glad's amusement they were also given instructions on how to fuse and plant incendiary bombs, and how to manufacture explosives from ordinary substances like sugar and sulphur. As a trained Sapper he soon discovered that he knew more about it than his instructor.

'We were given money as well as the pistols. We had a hundred pounds in English money and a hundred American dollars. We had false ration coupons and clothes brushes with ignition caps, fuses and detonators concealed inside them. We showed them to MI5 later and they were fascinated.'

But before they could begin to play their double-cross game they had to reach British shores and contact the secret services there. They were flown by German seaplane to the waters off the Moray Firth, transferred to a boat and landed at Crawley Bay in what was then Banffshire in the north of Scotland on April 7 1941: 'We rowed ashore and we were supposed to cut a hole in the dinghy, fill it with stones and sink it, but we didn't bother, we just pulled it ashore.' The two Abwehr agents were also supposed to have buried their radio and the ski-suits they'd travelled across in, but since they intended to give themselves up as soon as they landed, they deemed these precautions unnecessary. 'We decided to knock on the door of one of the houses. An old man opened the door and saw me holding a pistol in my hand. He obviously thought we were something nasty, in blue ski-suits and peaked caps. I told him that we had just come ashore and asked him to direct us to the nearest police station or military camp. He indicated a narrow path going up the hill behind his house and said we would find the coastal road at the top.

So John and Tor climbed the hill and when they reached the road they set off on their bikes to find the nearest police station or military camp. They remember with amusement that a truck full of Women's Land Army girls passed by and waved gaily at them, quite unaware that they were newly-arrived German spies. Finally they found the policemen they had been so diligently seeking: 'There was an Inspector and Police Constable,' Tor Glad remembers, 'their car drew up and the Inspector demanded: "Where have you come from?" "Norway," I said. "Here's my pistol." "Have you got any loose cartridges?" "Yes, here's a whole box of them." '

Then John Moe arrived on the scene: 'I come up and I make my "Statement of the Year". It was to be thrown back at me in my meetings with MI5 later on. I said: "We were landed as German agents." '

John Moe meant to say 'as if we were German agents', but he used 'as' in the Norwegian way and so his first words made it seem that he and Tor really were spies. 'It was a bloody silly thing to say. I got that back at many meetings later. But they knew what I meant in the end.'

They were taken to Banff under police escort and the splendidly named Major Peter Perfect was flown up that evening to interrogate the captured 'spies'. Fortunately Major Perfect's judgement seems to have been the match of his name, for he quickly decided that this unlikely pair were genuine in their wish to act as double agents for Britain.

But not everyone was so enlightened. By this time the small Highland community of Banff was becoming highly excited. Here in their midst were two dastardly German spies, spies who had already admitted their crimes, as far as the local folk were concerned. 'There again we'd made fools of ourselves,' says John Moe. 'ARP wardens had come in to look at the "spies", the butcher had come in, the local publican had come to see us. We were standing there in the police station against a mantelpiece. They said to us: "Where do you come from?"

' "From Norway."

' "What are you doing?" And we told them what we were doing, we said we had a transmitter with us and we were going to be very clever and fool the Germans.'

They were not believed – and by this stage the crowd were ready to lynch them. Peter Perfect told them: 'Gentlemen, there has been quite an uproar outside. We can't put you up at the local hotel because it is also a pub and if people see you there will be trouble.'

The Police Inspector explained to Major Perfect that the worthies of Banff had all paid a visit to the new arrivals and heard their story. He ordered the Inspector to round them up. The following day they were all investigated by Special Branch and ordered to sign the Official Secrets Act and say nothing of their knowledge of Moe and Glad.

It was suggested to John Moe that perhaps he and Tor Glad had acted a little naively in telling the Banff butcher, baker and candlestick-maker the truth about their mission: 'Not a little! *Bloody* naively! My God! Oh yes, we told anybody who came in exactly what we intended to do. Anyway, Peter Perfect asked us very politely if we would mind being accommodated at the local prison. We were dog-tired, we didn't mind where we slept. So we were taken to the local prison, given a cup of tea and left in open cells for the night. We slept very well that night and we were wakened in the morning by the jailer's wife with another cup of tea and some biscuits, and she said "There'll be breakfast in half an hour." We went down the stairs following the smell of freshly fried bacon and eggs, toast and marmalade. The tea was marvellous.'

The jailer and his wife had a young daughter whose eyes, one might imagine, were as big as saucers as she surveyed these alien beings at her breakfast table as she prepared to go to school. John Moe was wearing a Norwegian flag badge in his lapel and he told the little girl about his country and gave her the badge as a memento. 'At this point her father brought down a jug from the dresser. I assumed it was milk but in fact it was whisky from the distillery where he was working in his spare time. So we had two quite big noggins in our tea, and when we went out to the car to be driven to Aberdeen, we were quite soused!'

From Aberdeen they were taken on the night train to London. 'We were so elated at having landed in Britain and, in our minds, having fooled the Germans. It was euphoria!'

It still does not seem to have occurred to the two adventurers that their lives might have been on the line. When they reached King's Cross they were presented with the first of a series of tests: 'We were dumped on the platform with our rucksacks and our bikes and left alone. The people who'd been looking after us disappeared. "We're going to get a taxi," they said. They were obviously watching to see if we'd make a break for it. Well, we sat down and we watched a lot of free taxis go by and then one of the policemen came back and said "I managed to get one." '

They were taken to New Scotland Yard, by now attired in their brand new Burberry raincoats 'like English actors in the latest Cops and Robbers drama'. Still convinced of their new status as superspies, they marched into the Police Station and up to the Desk Sergeant well ahead of their 'captors': 'We were pushy. I said to the Desk Sergeant: "We have come from Aberdeen." "Yes, Sir," the Desk Sergeant says to me: "Are these the prisoners?" And he pointed at my plainclothes police escort. It was wonderfully funny at the time.'

They were soon on the move again, this time to what turned out to be the Internment Centre at Ham in Southern England. A second, even less sophisticated test of their allegiance awaited them: 'This Corporal met us and you could see his contempt – you could see him thinking "Bloody Nazis, I'll hit them below the belt!" So he produced these drawings of Hitler and Mussolini. The one of Hitler showed him with a prick in the shape of a swastika. The Mussolini drawing showed him holding up his Roman Emblem of Office, which was also like a gigantic prick sticking up. He showed us these and gave us a hard look.

'Well, we burst out laughing. "Good Lord," I said, "look at that, Tor. Have you got any more?" The Corporal's jaw just dropped. "Do you think it's funny?" Anyway, he shut up then.'

John Moe and Tor Glad were split up and taken for medical check-ups to a doctor and a dentist. The dentist's job, among other things, was to check them for cyanide tablets concealed in their teeth. John Moe had just had a series of new fillings done before he left Norway and this made the dentist doubly suspicious. But nothing was found.

'And then the great moment when I was let into the big room at Ham Internment Centre. Up at the end on a dais were nine gentlemen, with Colonel Stephens in the middle. I saw our radio set on the mantelpiece and, with crazy confidence, I marched straight up to it and said, "Would you like me to set the radio up now and show you how it works? Maybe we should contact the Germans straight away?" I was full of go, there was no doubt in my mind what we were going to do.'

He was firmly told to be quiet and to speak when he was spoken to. The questioning began. They asked John Moe about his family. His grandfather had been a Colonel in the Ninth Manchester Infantry Regiment of the British Army. His name was Colonel Doctor Herbert Wade. There ensued another moment of farce:

' "Ah, he was in the Medical Corps," said his Interrogator.

' "No," I said, "he was in the Infantry."

' "No," he said, "The Medical Corps, he was a doctor."

' "No, his father was a chemist in Oldham and my great-grand-father's best customers were doctors, so when he had a son he christened him 'Doctor'."

'Well, I could see the reaction on the faces of the interrogators as they tried not to burst out laughing. Imagine a German spy trying to spin a yarn like that.'

At first, the panel did not believe him, but the Army List was fetched and the point proved. That seems to have been the turning point for John Moe at least:

'And then, the great moment in my life. The Chief Interrogator looked down at the subaltern at the end and he said:

' "Would you get Mr Moe a chair, please?" Terrific, just a little thing like that.'

From then on, John Moe was destined to be used as a trusted double agent, transmitting information and misinformation home to the Abwehr. At the time, he had no idea how close he had come to death, but in 1945 he met a Captain who had been one of his interrogators at Ham, who asked him, 'Do you know, John, when you were on your way to the Internment Centre in that Army truck, we were planning to have an early lunch? We were all assuming that you would either be sent to the Tower or that you would be shot or hanged.'

John went on to work effectively for the Allies as one of their many double agents ostensibly in partnership with Tor Glad. But the MI5 and MI6 people were not prepared to take the same risks with Tor that they took with the half-English John Moe and, as a result, Tor spent much of the war interned at Ramsay in the Isle of Man, and on Dartmoor.

'Everything went wrong,' Tor Glad says today. 'I must admit that it was partly my own fault, because I behaved like a bloody idiot! I was too impatient to get into action. And I never could stand discipline. It was a scandal though, not only the way MI5 treated me, but also how they treated all the others I was meeting who had also passed through interrogation at Ham. We called ourselves the "Bad Conscience of MI5".' It seems a shame that Tor was not able to put his courage to work. Fifty years on there is no doubting his sincerity.

The British were still deeply apprehensive of a German invasion at the time and they were suspicious of many Scandinavians in Britain. So Tor spent much of his war 'twiddling my thumbs and fretting my life away'. One of the Secret Services' people looking after Moe and Glad had to learn Tor's radio 'signature' so that he could transmit in the same mode, convincing the Germans that both were still successfully operating behind enemy lines.

What Tor could not achieve his partner certainly made up for. After the British had decided to trust John, his first task was to contact his German Controller. His code was SOW. He claims he always thought of PIG when he transmitted to the Germans! Somewhere in the text he had to include the word 'Henry'. If that word was left out of the body of the text it would reveal that he had been captured.

The Germans were no doubt delighted to hear from their 'agent'. But a problem arose. Since he was operating his radio set under control he was transmitting in ideal conditions. The Germans radioed back that they were receiving him strength four or even five – almost perfect. 'What sort of antennae do you have?' they wanted to know. A rapid cover story was required. They told their controller that they had been lucky enough to find an attic room in a wooden building on high ground. They expected their transmissions therefore to be particularly high quality. Better still, the old lady they had rented the room from was deaf. It sounded a bit like the perfect second-hand car – one owner, vicar's wife – but their controllers seemed satisfied. It was time for John Moe to go to work at the same time as his colleague

Tor was notionally in an observation ship in northern waters.

John Moe played all the games that he felt he could get away with. Every now and then he would deliberately break his transmission as if he was suddenly fearful of discovery. This ploy had two beneficial effects for the double agent. It made his controllers aware of the dangers he was running and the fact that he was operating for them in the tough reality of enemy territory. Second it sometimes gave the agent more time to answer difficult questions, time to refer to his British controllers and construct the most effective response in terms of misinforming the enemy.

'We would pretend that there was someone knocking on the door and we would break off. We would already have received all of their message. But they had only received part of ours, so they could not decode it. We had one, two, three days or as long as we wanted to read their message, see what question they asked us and decide how best to respond.

'I was then ostensibly a Sergeant in the Intelligence Corps. They swallowed this on the basis that as my English was so good, I would be valuable within the British Intelligence Establishment. We had established Tor as the man on the North Sea observation boats, in order to explain his long absence from the centre of operations.'

John Moe did a lot of his work in Scotland, observing for the Germans and misinforming them skilfully about the supposed build-up of forces confronting Scandinavia. Although he could not be allowed to know it at the time, he was taking part in the deception plan for Operation Torch, the invasion of North Africa. If the enemy could be persuaded to 'take his eye off the ball' by focussing on the north of Scotland and Scandinavia, then an invasion in Africa would clearly have more chance of success: 'I was up in Scotland, I was in Inverness and Inverary and I saw all these white-painted skis and rucksacks. I saw Austrian military ski-specialists training Allied troops in winter warfare. I saw ships being loaded with white anoraks. My stories included titbits of information I had picked up in pubs. I *did* realise that the reason for all my invention was that we wanted the Germans to believe that we planned to invade Norway or at least somewhere in Scandinavia.'

The German controllers were also, of course, extremely interested in what was going on in the South of England. They wanted Moe to find out the truth about a fuel pipeline being laid on the South Coast. He sent back a stream of false messages suggesting that pipes were being ferried to the Coast by the lorry-load. Among the messages were some true stories of glimpses he had had of real lorries carrying pipes and other cargoes. The Germans, he believes, were concerned that the fuel line was designed to pump inflammable material onto invasion beaches and ignite it in the face of an enemy trying to land. Whether this was ever more than a fanciful German notion is not clear. But, in the best traditions of good deception practice, John Moe was able to take a fear the enemy already harboured and make it far worse by a mixture of verifiable truth, judicious exaggeration and total fabrication.

John Moe had every reason to believe that the Germans regarded him as a highly effective agent. With the help of his British controllers he developed a dramatic and elaborate method of keeping them convinced: 'In the autumn of 1941 I began to carry out acts of sabotage in London. I caused an explosion at a sugar store in Wealdstone. Of course, I didn't do it at all. The explosion happened sure enough but it was done by Special Branch, who helpfully left a Norwegian compass among the ruins.

'Through the Ministry of Information we informed the *Daily Mirror*, the *Telegraph*, the *Express*, the *Observer*, in fact all the papers that went to Lisbon and to Stockholm, that this act of sabotage had taken place.'

Before that, of course, he had told their German masters that he had the sugar dump in his sights. He had identified the target and reported that he had a chance of 'throwing in a bomb'. Then, a few days later, after Special Branch had carried out the attack John Moe would physically go out and buy the relevant newspapers and report what they said to his German controllers. 'It was all a trick, all a deception. And the Germans came back with a message, "Congratulations on your sabotage, you naughty boy, you. Well done!" '

When involved in complex acts of deception it is difficult to pick one's way through a maze of actual and fictitious events. In the case of double agents the problem is, quite literally, doubled. If you cling to the idea that in John Moe's stories of sabotage the explosions on the sites were real and that everything else was propaganda, it may help to keep the thread clear.

Plan Bunbury was another of the pieces of sabotage that John Moe was supposed to have carried out. He was travelling by bus in the countryside near Bury St Edmunds in East Anglia when he saw an electricity station which was no longer in use. He noticed that it had thick pipes running down the side. His sabotage training told him that the best way to rupture the pipes would be with magnetic mines. He told his German controllers about the target, which for Moe's double agent purposes had now of course become 'an important working electricity station' and asked for a supply of magnetic mines.

The Germans duly delivered a bagful to him at a pre-arranged dropping zone. It must have been a fairly relaxing life for him in many ways as he did not even need to turn up to collect his own deliveries: MI5 did that for him. The following morning he went to see the local Chief Constable who joked: 'Here's your bag of tricks and they've enclosed five hundred pounds. Shall we split them fifty-fifty?'

In reality, the money the Germans sent went straight to help the British fight the war. John Moe was given one pound a day in expenses.

Christopher Harmer, one of Moe's MI5 Case Officers, asked him if he had ever tried to blow up an electricity station before. Did he have any relevant experience? He admitted that he had little idea of where to place his newly acquired magnetic mines. He suggested that to make the whole event seem even more important he should send a message to the Germans, outlining what the works looked like and asking for advice on where to place his bombs. Harmer, who always preferred operational ideas to come from the 'agent' himself, thought this was a brilliant suggestion. 'The answer came back from the Germans, "Place them in a cluster around the biggest pipe, so that you blow up as much as possible and the greatest volume of water or coolant will escape. You may succeed in damaging the generators." '

While John Moe's involvement in the actual attack was to be purely notional, he really *did* take part in the initial reconnaissance of the electricity station: 'During my observation of this area, I was lying in a ditch overnight, seeing how often the patrols were going by and so on, I saw American jeeps full of GIs, girls and cans of beer. They would flash by, shouting and braying at all hours of the night. So we reported to the USAAF Chief what we had seen. He said that yes, he knew it was difficult for his men "sitting on their arses waiting for the invasion". We also told him that a special operation was going to take place in his area. He promised to alert his security officers but nothing more. You wanted to keep these things as close as possible.'

In due course, the electricity station was blown up by the bizarre combination of British Special Branch expertise and freely provided German magnetic bombs and the story of this dastardly sabotage duly appeared in the British press, courtesy of the Ministry of Information. The German reaction is not on record, but the USAAF Chief's response came in the form of a thank-you letter: 'Thank you very much. Our guard shifts have been doubled. There are no girls in the jeeps and the men don't drink any more! We appreciate your effort, my security outfit is now top-notch.'

One of the classic deception ploys is the leakage of apparently vital operational intelligence that can only really be interpreted by the enemy *after* the event has safely taken place. This serves two excellent purposes: it raises the credibility of the double agent in the eyes of his German controllers and it is most unlikely to jeopardise the operation it purports to reveal. The Red Triangle is a fine example of this genre.

'This was an idea that Christopher Harmer came up with. The story I was to put out was: "As a security officer in a camp in Scotland, you have come across a folder with a Red Triangle on it, or a red pyramid. It's a war plan of something or other."

'Well, the Germans came back and said, "Try to find out more. Very important! Sehr wichtig!" But I told them I couldn't find out any more.

'Then one morning I read in the newspaper about a commando raid on Spitzbergen. Now, on the west coast of Spitzbergen at the bottom of a fjord there was a village called Pyramid. I had used the word triangle but it could equally have been a pyramid. So I went back to the Germans and pointed this out. I said I warned you about an operation, I gave you the clue and you still didn't manage to find it. I think there was quite a ruckus in the Abwehr back in Berlin when they realised they'd missed out. So that enhanced our value immensely. We'd forewarned them about a raid on Spitzbergen. They forgot it was only a brief message and was open to misunderstanding. As far as they were concerned they *had* been informed by their two star agents in England about an imminent raid. Our controlling officer in Berlin was so proud of us that he had our pictures hanging on his office walls. Ha!'

Doubt can be cast on the efficacy of secret agents at the best of times. It is probably only sensible to look at their work in the light of the sudden, single important message you may need to pass. The most startling example of this was the message that the celebrated double agent, Garbo, was able to pass to the Germans confirming that the main invasion thrust would definitely be made into the Pas de Calais. This at a stage when, for the first time, Hitler was beginning to doubt his long-held belief that the Allies would indeed invade through Calais. Garbo had been an important agent, but never more so than then.

Moe and Glad were certainly worth cultivating in the hope that one day just one vital piece of misinformation or advice from them would alter the course of the War. Tor Glad, despite his own miserable incarceration in England during most of the war, is still proud today that he was able to convince the Abwehr that John Moe was a reliable Nazi. Both are sure that they managed to confuse Hitler over the pipe lines on the South Coast, just when his invasion plans were being finalised. There can be little doubt that they also played a part in the D-Day deception albeit, as John Moe says, 'indirectly and by implication'.

Despite their occasional, farcical naivety which they so readily admit today, their brave spirits can in no way be doubted.

CHAPTER 21

THE BOMBER'S TALE
Ronald Chamberlain

Planting false ideas in the enemy's mind can be a dangerous business. The planes that dropped subversive leaflets or dummy paratroopers flew through the same flak as the planes carrying bombs. Ronald Chamberlain never wanted to bomb anything. He wanted to be a professional tennis player. But the years from 1939 to 1945 were denied to him. Instead he learned a different set of skills, skills he did not seek and did not want. For six years he played no tennis at all.

It is idle to speculate what his nickname might have been if he had been able to become a winner at Wimbledon in the early 1940s. Since the war chose a different career path for him, Ronald Chamberlain's nickname is a matter of record. The Canadians with whom he flew called him PB or 'Pickle Barrel', because they firmly believed that Ronald could drop a stick of bombs into a pickle barrel from 18,000 feet. A reputation, which according to him today was 'Absolute nonsense!'

'I worked as a navigator, a bomb-aimer and, from time to time as a P2, the second pilot. Most of the missions we flew were real enough but some were also clearly something to do with deception. There was so much deliberate uncertainty surrounding these jaunts that, even today, it's hard to pinpoint exactly what they were intended to do. One mission I do however remember particularly clearly. It was a Sunday and it is clear to me now that it must have been organised after we had run into the horrible impasse of Arnhem on the day before, the Saturday.' In early September 1944, the Allies were confident that the road to Berlin was now going to be a short one, and Eisenhower was saying that the German armies were as good as defeated. It was a confidence that was to have disastrous consequences. The ill fated Operation Market Garden was the Allies' attempt to outflank the German defences along the Rhine by a massive turning movement through Holland into the north German plain. The bridge at Arnhem was to be the key. The first gliders in the war's biggest airborne operation took off on the morning of September 17. 2023 troop-carriers and glider towing tugs made their way slowly towards the drop zones protected by 1500 fighters.[1] The British 1st Airborne Division, which included a brigade of Polish parachutists, were met by resistance, whose ferocity none of the senior Commanders, including Montgomery and Eisenhower, had expected. The Germans were organised by Field Marshal Model, who was only by chance in the Arnhem area. The resulting losses on the Allied side were very heavy.

'When my orders came through there was nothing special about them and I certainly did not know how serious things had become at Arnhem. At the time my unit was based at Witchford near Ely in Cambridgeshire and we were ordered to load our bomb bays with small bomb containers. Nobody told us what these clusters actually were but we were told that, if we were shot down over enemy territory then we had to destroy them. Nobody told us how we were supposed to achieve this destruction. The assumption must have been that we would leave everything in the plane and fire a Very pistol into the craft to destroy it, along with the bomb containers. Fortunately, it never came to that.

'On this particular mission the strangest instruction we received was related to "Window", the anti-radar device[2] that bombers regularly dropped to confuse the enemy radar about the size of the assault and its whereabouts.

'We were dropping Window at an enormous rate. We always dropped plenty, but on this occasion the plane was practically overflowing with Window. There were more than a hundred aircraft in the sortie, each containing about eight crewmembers. The other strange factor was that the "aiming point" seemed to be in the middle of nowhere. Only much later did I discover that it had been around fifty miles from Arnhem.'

His plane reached the target and 'Pickle Barrel' took his usual careful aim. 'We went through the usual flak, had a couple of fighter scares, and then did our bombing run. Normally we'd have been carrying incendiaries. But these bomb containers seemed to be carrying something else. As they went down they looked as if they were bursting into parachutes, and we assumed that maybe they were something for the Resistance. Then when they hit the ground they all went off like firecrackers, not like incendiaries but like Roman candles or something. We never learned what it was all about but we guessed that it must have been something to do with a dummy attack by paratroopers, maybe with fake battle sounds, to take some of the pressure off Arnhem.'

Ronald's subsequent brush with deception was rather more cruel: 'Airfields were so vast that anyone could get in, however hard you tried to make them safe. There was an incident in which I was involved when we did a "daylight" on the Ruhr. There didn't seem to be much flak, then, all of a sudden, three of our aeroplanes went up, just like that. You see, everybody had heard this story that there was such a thing as "invisible flak", the Americans had started the rumour. So we were all more scared than usual. We had to go back to the same place the next day, and the same thing happened. Again, there seemed to be very little flak, apart from what we usually got. It really unsettled us. There was no explanation then. It wasn't until after the war that I ran into the man who had been our intelligence officer at the time and I asked him about the mysterious explosions.

'He said to me: "You know what it was?" I said, "No." "Well," he said, "you were being infiltrated. They were getting onto the airfield and wrapping gun cotton around the bomb releases. As soon as certain of your Wing released their bombs, up they went." Saboteurs were infiltrating the airfields after the operational planes were fully "bombed up", closed down and ready to fly and transforming them into "flying coffins".'

CHAPTER 22

THE SAS SOLDIER'S TALE
Colonel David Sutherland

It was Winston Churchill who, within days of accepting the Prem-
iership in May 1940, foresaw the need for Special Forces. He wanted
what he called 'troops of the hunter class' to make 'butcher and bolt'
raids against the Germans. The Special Operations Executive, whose
mission was 'to set Europe Ablaze', the Commandos, and the Special
Air Service could all slip in and out of enemy lines, work with local
resistance movements, carry out acts of sabotage and, as their work
developed during the war, they could also be put to use by the
deception-planners. Used carefully – Colonel Bevan at the LCS was
always wary of SOE – the kind of pressure that these small units
could bring to bear on the enemy at well chosen moments became
a valuable operational tool.

Colonel David Sutherland's military training was a classic one:
the Cadet Corps at Eton followed by the Royal Military Academy,
where he was still an Officer Cadet at the outbreak of war.

In January 1940 he was commissioned into the Infantry and
went to France to join a Scottish Battalion. At the age of 19 he
found himself commanding 'Lucky Thirteen' platoon of the Sixth
Battalion of the Black Watch. He describes it today as 'rather a
nasty time, attacking, holding the line and finally withdrawing in
much discomfort and confusion to the broad, open beaches near
Dunkirk.'

He returned to England, 'being bombed rather badly on the way
back' and soon learned of Winston Churchill's plans to regain the
offensive initiative after Dunkirk by creating 'special forces to harass
the enemy'.

The scramble back from France took place in June 1940. By

August he had managed to join one of the first Commando units then being formed. His special training in infiltration and survival took place in the North of Scotland, near Mallaig at Lochailort where the Commandos had taken over a shooting lodge. Here, in the grounds of the lodge watched over by its Victorian Gothic turrets he was taught groundwork, sniping and how to operate behind enemy lines, which meant killing others silently and staying alive yourself. By now he was a second lieutenant commanding a small Commando sub-unit of about 20 men.

During his training Sutherland found himself in the company of Randolph Churchill, Winston's son, the novelist Evelyn Waugh and the man who was to become the leader of the SAS, David Stirling. He met others who made an equally lasting impression on him.

'There were these incredible knife people. Messrs Fairbairn and Sykes, who had both been policemen in Shanghai. They taught me how to disarm a man coming at me with a knife. They showed me how to stick a knife into somebody else's ribs you didn't like. In particular they demonstrated the silent approach to dealing with enemy sentries.

'The course in deception at Lochailort was organised by the Chief Instructor. He had his so-called stalkers who taught the commandos how to use a spy-glass, a telescope. He also taught them how to approach a target unseen. Once that target had been stalked the final lesson was how to eliminate it, again with the minimum of noise.

'It was a fully integrated course in "knock-out". Certainly, there were assassins there, these Shanghai policemen. There was also a man called Grant Taylor who was a particularly good shot, he taught us to handle all manner of small arms and to shoot really well with a revolver.'

During this comprehensive course on subversion and deceptive operations, Sutherland's team were also trained in all manner of small boat activity and the problems of getting in and out of enemy territory.

In 1941 he joined the Small Boat Section (SBS), which at that time was called the Folbot Troop, after the German for collapsable canoe, *Faltboot*. At this stage they were simply two-man teams operating in collapsable canoes from submarines. The section was founded by Roger Courtney, who had paddled down the Nile in a folbot, before the war. Sutherland describes him as a 'kind of White Hunter, definitely one of Churchill's "troops of the hunter class".' Courtney saw the German folbot's potential as a canoe for reconnaissance and the infiltration of small raiding parties behind enemy lines and enemy positions near the coast. The canoes were carried by submarines, from which Sutherland and his team would surface, pull the canoe out on to the forecastle of the boat and assemble it. Then they would set off, usually in groups of two canoes.

During this uncompromising training there was also room for learning about deception from some more entertaining sources.

'I used to go and watch Maskelyne and Devant at a theatre in Upper Regent Street. They were one of London's best known pre war variety acts. Maskelyne was everybody's picture of a traditional magician. For his 1930s act he dressed in white tie and tails and of course a top hat, out of which he used to produce rabbits and Heaven knows what. I couldn't believe my eyes when Jasper Maskelyne turned up at Lochailort.' The employment of Jasper Maskelyne is a good example of how imaginative the British Establishment could be when it came to combing the country for people whose talents could be used to help to defeat Hitler. Sutherland's surprise on seeing Maskelyne in the midst of all his hard physical training was natural, but then so is the choice of a magician to work in a world of illusion.

'I think he produced a number of cunning devices which he was to improve upon throughout the war. The most useful of these was the compass made from a tunic button. I came across that in Scotland. Later, when I met him again in the Middle East he produced these special escape maps printed on silk. The two things that any escaper wanted were a map and a compass. Maskelyne had thought of a particularly good compass. It was an ordinary metal button cut in two and magnetised. Inside there was a pin and by balancing it correctly you could always find North. Since everybody in those days had brass buttons it was a jolly useful wheeze. Everyone had at least one of these. I can remember having one sewn on the inside of my battledress trousers. The other ruse he came up with was the secret maps, which were pure silk with the relevant fighting area printed on them. They were beautifully printed, but more importantly, they lasted one or two dunkings in water. I had one of Jasper Maskelyne's special silk maps made for the campaign in Rhodes. I've still got it today and, it certainly did survive quite a lot of hardship. I also remember coming across explosive coal[1] out in the Middle East, which I think was another of his ideas. He was a past master in leaving around things that were not in fact what they appeared to be.

'I remember too that he had these marvellous long fingers, and beautiful hands. It was the first thing one noticed about him. He also had a very soothing, persuasive voice and was a cheery man, always telling jokes and always interested in how gadgets, like his silk maps, performed in the field. When I met him later in the war, I suggested that he should use luminous dots for the significant bits of the maps, since more often than not they were used by commandos in the dark. Maskelyne took a great deal of interest in the idea. He was a hands-on guy.' It was after he had arrived in the Middle East that Sutherland was involved in his first piece of tactical deception, essentially a camouflage operation, codenamed plan 'Alouite'.

'In 1942 before Alamein, Rommel was knocking at the gates of Alexandria. Everyone was very anxious about what might happen. GHQ in Cairo was concerned about what kind of resistance might be required if the Germans broke through into Egypt and beyond. Well, somebody thought up this idea of establishing arms, ammunition and explosives dumps in the Syrian hills, north-east of Tripoli, near the Turkish frontier. The codename "Alouite" referred to the tribe who lived in the hills.

'The arms dumps were hidden in caves, which in turn were disguised by camouflage made from painted papier mâché. I helped to prepare some of them and to log their positions on the operational maps. The idea was that we would be operating from Cyprus and that we would move in small bands to the Syrian coast and use these dumps of arms and ammunition with the local resistance to try to harass the enemy. In the event, Monty turned the tide and the Alouite plan was never used.

'After David Stirling's capture in March 1943 everything changed. 1 SAS went to Sicily. 2 SAS, commanded by David Stirling's brother operated in North Africa, and the small boat unit that I was with became the SBS. By this stage I was using the skills and experience I had gained from small boats operations. We were vaguely aware that we were engaged in the deception business, but working at that level of operations it is hard to say at what level or to what extent we managed to mislead the enemy.' This kind of tactical deception, using special forces to put pressure on the enemy, might well mean that there was a dual purpose to a raid or a mission, which those carrying it out could only guess at.

'The only major deception that I participated in was in the Aegean in the spring before D Day. It was quite obvious to everyone that a landing on the Continent was imminent, but nobody except the senior Allied Planners knew the location and the date. At that stage I was under orders from GHQ, Middle East. We were operating from the SBS raiding base situated north of Haifa and we received a GHQ directive to inflict maximum damage to the enemy positions in the Aegean during the spring of 1944.'

The background to the GHQ directive was Plan Zeppelin, part of Plan Bodyguard. The intention was to suggest that the invasion of north-west Europe would not take place until late summer and that consequently the Allies' main effort would be made in the Balkans. Dudley Clarke and 'A' Force were to represent threats to Crete and the Peloponnese and to Istria and the Dalmation Coast. In May Zeppelin was supplemented by Operation Turpitude, which suggested an assault on Rhodes followed by an assault on Salonika and a push up the Struma to link up with the Russians.[2] By this stage of the war Dudley Clarke and his team had become extremely deft manipulators of the truth. Propaganda leaflet raids, wireless traffic, visual deception, and the use of Special Forces were all used alongside the other techniques built up during four years of war in the Middle East and the Mediterranean. The go ahead for Zeppelin had been given on February 10 1944.

'We were trying to pin down German garrisons, attacking all sorts of things, machine gun positions and so on. We were capturing enemy shipping, in particular a lot of caiques, local fishing craft, small coastal vessels. We went for a number of radio stations which were, of course, vital for enemy communications. I was, at that time, responsible for all SBS operations that took place in the Southern Aegean. We were operating from a bay on the Island of Kos in Turkish Territorial waters, where we had a large base ship and carried out numerous raids. We'd go out at night in smaller craft, ten ton caiques with diesel engines which we had specially designed for the job. There were quite a few of them, with their ordinary engines removed and tank engines put in in their place. Very seaworthy they were too, and reliable. They didn't go very fast, but they could be quickly camouflaged and they did the job. And when I say camouflaged I mean totally camouflaged; when the mast was down and the boat was alongside some rocks, with a carefully cleverly draped camouflage net pulled across it, it was impossible to spot a caique even from 15, 20 yards.

'We operated on all the islands in the Southern Aegean, north of Crete. By this time we had gathered tremendous experience in operational planning. We prided ourselves on being able to use surprise and to get in undetected. We also had excellent air cover throughout the area and had pretty good maps.

'On some occasions, once we were ashore we would deliberately leave clothing, equipment, rations and stores behind for the enemy to uncover. The inference that we would soon return to the spot was inescapable. On a tactical level, deception became the norm during these missions. The SBS would regularly start fires as diversions, or fake a small arms battle away from our real target area. This kind of exercise was of value in misleading the enemy in action, but they were only small tactical successes, military deception of the most basic kind.

'One particular operation took place on a small island with a volcanic crater. As usual, the SBS lay up during the day and then at night we went ashore to reconnoitre the island. A plan was constructed for the following night which was designed to write off the German garrison, together with the radio station. It was a significant target and the attack was successful.

'That was probably the most significant operation we carried out at that time, April 1944. We were, of course, conducting other operations throughout the Aegean in March, April and May of 1944. SBS were also operating with Greek commandos, and they were doing exactly the same in the North of the Aegean. We now know that the Germans were sufficiently worried about all this activity to send four thousand men to the islands. And those men were stuck there until the end of the War.

'There's no doubt about it, our activities in the Aegean just before D-Day were of enormous importance in getting the enemy to reinforce the wrong theatre of war. Though of course it's only with the benefit of hindsight that it is possible to see just how many of our operations were a part of those broad strategic deceptions.'

CHAPTER 23

THE BRIGADIER'S TALE
Brigadier Michael Calvert

Brigadier Michael Calvert is in very much the same mould as David Sutherland. He too grew up in a group which included David Stirling, Lloyd Owen of the Special Boat Squadron, the Long Range Desert Group and many others who would become involved in special operations behind enemy lines.

After a Royal Engineer's commission and a degree from St John's College, Cambridge, Michael Calvert was reduced to the ranks. But it was his own choice. He volunteered to join a ski battalion that was just being formed. Discovering that all the officers' positions were already filled, he agreed to join the battalion as an ordinary Guardsman. Their training took place on the steep slopes of Mont Blanc, where they perfected their skiing with the help of the French Chasseur Alpin. Since the Ski Battalion's most likely destination was Finland, where the soldiers would spend their time on the flat, pulling sledges, Michael Calvert admits that the Mont Blanc training may have had more to do with excitement than practicality. To him the Ski Battalion became almost like a second period of Higher Education:

'It became like a university in the Renaissance, that was my impression. We were all determined not to fight another 1914–18 War, where your skill appeared to have no bearing on whether you were killed or not. We felt that in the next war we should go for the enemy's guts, his communications, his headquarters and we should start revolutions behind his lines. We were all first and foremost soldiers, who wanted to be where the action was but we also began to see that deception should play a part in this war. If you've got brute strength, whether muscular or financial, you tend to use it. But if you're weak, you have to use your brains and when you use your brains you practise something like jiu-jitsu, where you can topple someone far more powerful than yourself. That is really one of the theories of guerilla warfare and also of deception. You manipulate the enemy's psychology to bring him down.'

Like David Sutherland, Michael Calvert also worked at the training school at Lochailort in Scotland. But he was teaching there, all sorts of demolition procedures and sabotage techniques.

'I helped to produce a pamphlet on sabotage which was circulated all over the world. It was printed on rice paper so that you could eat it if the enemy captured you.

'When England was under threat of invasion after Dunkirk, Peter Fleming and I were asked to set up a guerilla force which would operate behind the German lines if and when they got ashore. If they ever had done our job would have been to demolish bridges and other vital points and generally harass the enemy. This "secret army" stretched from the North Kent Coast all the way round the whole of Kent and Sussex. It was constructed on a cell system where no individual group knew their neighbours.

'By September it had become obvious that the invasion threat had receded and so I volunteered for service in Australia, where again I taught techniques of guerilla warfare and sabotage. After a year of that I was brought back to Burma and made Commandant of the British Warfare School, which was the base of Mission 204[2] into China. I was given a file from the War Office to read myself in. At the back of the file there was a signal from Churchill, "Top Secret", and of course I shouldn't have seen it. The signal was to all the Prime Ministers and Commander-in-Chiefs throughout the world. It read something like this: "Britain intends to fight to the bitter end on the islands of Great Britain, but we might go under. In that case plans have been made for the Sovereign and the Royal Navy to be based in Canada. But we must all go on fighting until we can attract powerful allies to meet our common enemy. The purpose is to keep the fighting going by any means until we get these allies on our side.

' "The way to fight will be a form of guerilla warfare and I find that all the expertise in this form of warfare is based on London. In the circumstances this must be absurd, so I am making up missions from these experts to send out to you so that you may use them as you will. I suggest you use them to form internal guerilla defence of your countries or district and also to form sabotage and insurgency units which can enter neighbouring territory, so that you can delay and fight our enemies, (at that time we expected the Japanese to join the Germans and the Italians). Below I have divided the world up into segments. Each of you will fight your designated area. I wish you the best of luck."

'That's my recollection of the substance of Churchill's signal. While I was in Burma the attack on Pearl Harbor occurred and the attack on Singapore and we went on training people for the mission to China. The object of the mission was to raise the standard of efficiency of the Chinese guerillas in order to tie up another 100,000 Japanese. The British policy was to get the Japanese so involved in China that they wouldn't have the strength to go down south. But it didn't make any difference in the end. As a mission it failed.

'At the time the Australians were very worried by the fall of Singapore and Indonesia and wanted their Australian Division back home. Churchill wanted it to go to Burma. I had the idea of simulating a landing by the Australians, using my own Royal Marine group. It was too late to land at Rangoon, which had already fallen, so I pretended that a Brigade had landed further up the coast at a place called Taungup north and west of Rangoon and that we were the advance guard of this Australian Division, which of course wasn't really going to arrive at all. We all wore bush hats and we had a certain number of Australian cap badges. We paddled down the Irrawaddy and blew up one or two railway engines and other things that the retreat had left behind. We left Australian cap badges around and we sent some real Australians to pretend to be drunk in different towns. We had access to an ordnance depot and so we could have any amount of weapons we wanted.

'We got as far as Henzada on the Irrawaddy, and I put in two lay-back positions. I went down there with about four of my men, including Private Medally and I was making a speech through interpreters when a lot of Japanese Burmese "traitor army" people jumped up and said dramatically "Lay down your arms! Lay down your arms! You're surrounded!" Well, my mind froze, but Private Medally, who was much quicker than I was, said "Bollocks!" He was armed with a Thompson sub-machine gun with thirty-eight rounds. He opened fire. We all opened fire and just had time to make a run for it. The first lay-back position gave us covering fire and we escaped back to the second and made it back to our ship. It may have helped that the Royal Marine who was most involved in laying down the covering fire was the Services Vickers Machine Gunner Champion.'

Later Michael Calvert discovered that Japanese documents had been discovered in which their idea of the British order of battle was outlined. Included in that order of battle was his fictional Brigade of Australians. Not very long after this he was to renew his acquaintance with Peter Fleming and to carry on with his deception career.

Since Michael Calvert had worked with him back at home in Kent in the early stages of the war, Peter Fleming had been summoned to the Far East by Wavell himself. At the start of 1942, Wavell was Commander-in-Chief of the Allied Forces in the South West Pacific. In a personal signal to the Chief of the Imperial General Staff he wrote: SHOULD BE GLAD OF PETER FLEMING AS EARLY AS POSSIBLE FOR APPOINTMENT MY STAFF.[3] On his way out to Delhi Fleming had had an opportunity to spend a week in Cairo, working his way through the files of 'A' Force and gaining a good grounding in deception.[4] He arrived in mid March and after a foray into China installed himself in the basement of a building designed by Lutyens, taking over the small section of Wavell's headquarters known as GS1(d), whose role was to devise deception programmes and put them into practice.[5] According to Calvert it was over dinner one evening in Delhi that Wavell expounded at some length on the famous incident of Meinertzhagen's haversack. Meinertzhagen proves that although the Second World War saw the development of deception carried to a degree of complexity and above all strategic coordination that had never existed before, many of the elements for that development had already existed in pockets during the First World War. With such thoughts in mind Calvert remarks that 'It's a pity that more of that kind of thinking did not go into preventing the endless stalemate and slaughter in the trenches.' Soon after he had taken up his command of the Egyptian Expeditionary Force (EEF), General Sir Edmund Allenby approved plans for an offensive in Palestine, which it was hoped would not only ease the pressure of a possible Turkish offensive in Mesopotamia against Baghdad, but also persuade the Turks to abandon the war on the German side once Jaffa and Jerusalem were under British occupation. Before the Third Battle of Gaza came the 'haversack ruse' of Major Richard Meinertzhagen, who was on Allenby's Intelligence staff. It can fairly be said that the success of this ruse was the inspiration for the going map ruse described by Sir David Hunt[6] for possibly the most famous deception of the whole war, Operation Mincemeat[7] and for numerous other attempts to plant a false order of battle on the enemy. While out on a patrol along the Turkish front at Beersheba, Meinertzhagen had contrived to lose a haversack containing carefully prepared documents suggesting that Allenby's main assault was to be on Gaza, whereas in fact it was to be directed at Beersheba. There was also information suggesting that the attack was scheduled later than the actual date of October 31. Here too is another strand of the deception-planners' work which runs through almost every major deception of World War Two, namely persuasive indications that the attack would take place later than planned. This was certainly true for Sidi Barrani, El Alamein and Husky in North Africa, Diadem in Italy and Normandy.[8] In 1917 the Turks had swallowed the bait and had been defeated.

Peter Fleming and Wavell were determined to profit by the lessons learned during Allenby's Palestine campaign and as a result of discussions late into the night, Operation Error was born. At the time, the Allied retreat was proceeding very rapidly and it was decided to prepare a briefcase of documents, supposedly belonging to Wavell himself and abandon them somewhere in front of the advancing Japanese troops. Calvert takes up the story:

'It was April 29 and the Ava Bridge over the Irrawaddy had been prepared by our own boys, for demolition. I'd got my composite battalion across after quite a lot of difficult fighting and I was resting. We were all very tired when Peter Fleming turned up and said: "I've got a job for you." He explained to me that it was a deception plan. Quite apart from the memory of Meinertzhagen and his haversack – and remember that Wavell had served under Allenby – I think that Wavell had only very recently had his memory jogged by a close shave in the Dutch East Indies. He had apparently been motoring up to his aircraft when the Japanese had opened fire on him and he had only just managed to escape. He'd left his attaché case in the car in the heat of the moment. Someone had just managed to run back and get it. Well, Fleming thought that this suggested a way of adapting the Meinertzhagen ruse.

'So they made up an attaché case in which there were genuine letters from Wavell's wife, a photograph of his much loved daughter Pamela and material relating to the strength of the three important things in India: the armour, the Air Force and the aircraft carriers in the Indian Ocean under Admiral Cunningham. I never saw these papers but I understand they gave the order of battle not in so many words but rather by inference. The purpose of the deception was to pretend that we had more armour in India and more aircraft and even aircraft carriers on the way than could possibly be the case and so to try to persuade the Japanese not to attack India.

'This was the plan: Fleming had brought a black Bentley staff car, a very pompous car, just the kind of car that might be on its way to a Dakota waiting on a neighbouring airfield and we were going to drive it across the Ava Bridge before it was blown later that evening. I had a jeep which we hid further north in Saigang near the bridge as a getaway car. Peter Fleming came along with Captain Sandy Reid Scott of the 11th Hussars, Wavell's ADC. I had Private Williams with me, as a spare driver. So, we drove across the river and waited.

'The Gurkhas in the meantime were fighting a rearguard action and we were deliberately stranded, with the bonnet up on the car, as if something was wrong. It was jolly frightening really just sitting there waiting for the Japanese to turn up.

'Now, I'd never crashed a car in my life, but Peter Fleming was sure that I knew how to do so. We had reconnoitred the road and we'd found a place just before a left hand bend. So once the Japanese came after us and we'd had a few shots fired at us, we bundled into the car and made off. I thought I was going very fast. Of course, up until then I'd only driven old bangers. Well, I jammed on the brakes at about sixty miles an hour attempting to skid – well we did skid but came almost to a full stop because the brakes on the Bentley were so damn good. Anyway, I released the brakes so that we plunged over the embankment, about twenty-five feet down and slid over on our side. Fleming, Reid Scott, Private Williams and I scrambled out of the car. I was a bit dazed but they had all the initiative and took a jack handle or something to smash the windscreen. They also had some bottles of blood which was the same group as Wavell's and they left the attaché case in the back of the car. It did look like a crash, I could see the skid mark I'd made. Meanwhile the Japanese were running up behind us. Williams and I ran off to where we'd left the jeep and Fleming and Reid Scott ran off in the other direction. We got away.'

Michael Calvert's account differs in one important detail from Peter Fleming's official report. Fleming does not remember the advancing Japanese breathing down their necks. According to his biographer, he returned to the west bank at first light the following morning, the bridge having been blown at 11.30 p.m. and although he could see enemy shelling bursting some two miles away could see no signs of activity on the other bank. He concluded that that was a good thing as there was a fair chance that the car would remain undisturbed until the Japanese found it.

However successfully the operation may have been carried out and whatever the precise details of timing, the vital question is – did it work? Wavell himself received from Chinese intelligence sources in 1944 a report indicating that the Japanese had captured important documents relating to India's defensive strength. Once you have persuaded the enemy to believe that you are far stronger on the ground than you in fact are, you have to believe that he will act logically, but as Cruickshank goes on to point out, in reference to Michael Calvert's dramatic car crash with 'Wavell':

'The first fake documents ploy came in April 1942 when General Wavell's car was deliberately crashed where the advancing Japanese would find it *and* his abandoned despatch case with documents exaggerating India Command's resources. The papers duly reached the Japanese High Command but had no bearing on their decision not to invade India.'[10] As to whether or not the Japanese saw through the ruse itself, Fleming noted in a typical aside that, 'Sherlock Holmes, had he been promptly on the spot, could without difficulty have deduced from the skidmarks and other indications that there was something fishy about the supposed accident. But it is safe to assume that, long before his Japanese equivalent could have reached the Ava Bridge, large numbers of Dr Watsons had decisively prejudiced all chances of reconstructing the crime.'[11]

Calvert's verdict on the role of deception and on the likely success of the crashed car is an interesting one and illustrates the problem facing Fleming throughout the war against the Japanese: 'I have no idea whether it worked. But the thing about deception is that you have to inject it into the vein. It's no good sticking it in the rump and hoping that something will happen!'

For Fleming and his colleagues it was infuriatingly difficult to find the vein.

CHAPTER 24

THE PILOT'S TALE
Terence O'Brien

Terence O'Brien also found himself drawn into Peter Fleming's schemes in the Far East. Once Fleming had hatched another scheme, the nature of the terrain and the distances involved often required the services of a first-class pilot, with a great deal of nerve. Terence O'Brien flew many missions on behalf of Peter Fleming and has since written two books on his experiences in Burma, *Out of the Blue* and *The Moonlight War*. But long before he could persuade the RAF of his skill as a Special Operations pilot, he really did have to start at the bottom of the pecking order – on a station that only flew balloons, and in a job as far away from flying as conceivable. Terence O'Brien started out his wartime career as a cook.

When war broke out Terence O'Brien was working with a plantation company in the Solomon Islands at Guadalcanal. Guadalcanal was a long way from the war between Britain and Germany and although the Japanese Empire had made little secret of its expansionist intentions, the threat it posed was not an immediate one. Accordingly, he resigned his job and concentrated on getting himself into the European war. He was certainly keen. He returned first to his native Australia and tried to join up there, but he discovered that it was going to take six months to get into the Air Force and sold all his shares in the family company to buy himself an airline ticket and came by flying boat to England. At the time the RAF were inundated with volunteers from overseas. Since they could hardly be sent home, they were allowed to join up and given any odd jobs that could be found. That is how Terence O'Brien came to be a cook on a balloon station: 'Balloon Stations operated in exactly the same way as Air Force stations. You had a

Balloon Unit, a Balloon Flight, a Balloon Squadron and a Balloon Headquarters.

He was officially a Pilot Under Training, PUT, but was not getting any training. Eventually his evident enthusiasm for the fray was recognised and he was moved to Dishforth in Yorkshire, where his flying career began. His training took him all over Britain, most notably to St John's College, Cambridge, where he joined the Initial Training Wing.

His operational career included attacks on Brest harbour to harass and bottle up the German Naval Forces based there and attacks on U-Boats patrolling the Bay of Biscay. He was also involved in the sorties against the formidable German Battleships, *Bismarck* and *Prinz Eugen*.

When Japan entered the war in 1941, O'Brien led a flight of aircraft to Singapore, the first time that the RAF had attempted to take a flight that far. They arrived towards the end of the conflict in Singapore in February 1942 and were soon to lose the entire squadron.

'In the first raid that I led on a Japanese force up in the north we lost four out of the six and on the same day a complete squadron of torpedo aircraft, Wildebeests, were destroyed, 16 of them. I got out of Singapore on the morning the causeway was blown up, February 16. We went down to Sumatra, lasted there about three weeks, and then pulled out to Java. There were about half of us left then. But the rest of the aircraft were lost in Java and I escaped by boat, finishing up in India.'

He made his first contact with the clandestine forces while stationed briefly in Sumatra. He met Spencer Chapman, the representative of the Special Operations Executive, known in the Far East as Force 136. On arrival in India he tried to join Force 136, but they were not yet ready for operation. Instead he was sent to take over the plum job of Station Commander in RAF Bombay. But O'Brien still wanted to be in active operations, so he volunteered for special duty. Just like Michael Calvert, he had to accept a drop in rank to be accepted into this type of service.

He took part in the second Wingate Operation, flown in by glider on the first night of the landing beyond the Irrawaddy in the early months of 1944. By the time he finally emerged from the jungle with the famous Chindits in May of that year, he had spent nearly four months behind enemy lines. When he returned there was no shortage of job offers. He chose to become Flight Commander of 357 Special Duty Squadron which was operating with the Secret forces behind the

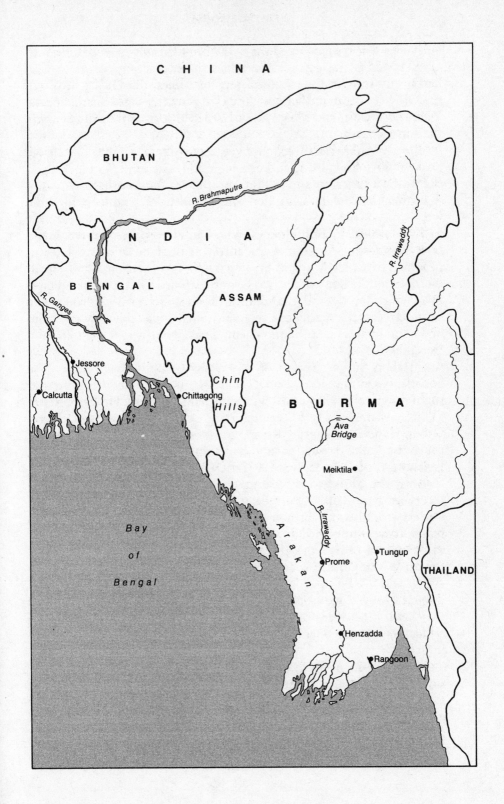

lines. Those forces included the SOE, Peter Fleming's Deception unit GS1(D), 'E' Group, which specialised in evacuating air crews who had been brought down behind Japanese lines, the OSS, which was the Office of Strategic Services, the US Secret Intelligence and Special Operations Unit, and MI6, known in the Far East as the Inter Services Liaison Department.

'Shortly after I had taken over the Dakota Flight, the newly created 357 Squadron, it became a full size unit, comprising a flight of 12 Liberators in addition to the 16 Dakotas I started with. A further flight of 10 Lysanders was planned for landing behind the lines.

'I was joined by Bob Hodges, who had already been in command of a Clandestine Operating Squadron in England and was later to become Air Chief Marshal Sir Lewis Hodges. At Command Headquarters our liaison officer was Group Captain Verity, who had been involved in the Lysander landings in France. So the Squadron was a formidable and experienced team although I was the only one who had actually operated behind enemy lines. That was the situation in December 1944.'

But then, in the Spring of 1945, the Squadron was split. The Squadron Commander, Bob Hodges went off with the Liberator flight down to Ceylon and never returned to Jessore. He left Terence O'Brien with Squadron Headquarters, where there was an elderly Group Captain in charge. 'Group Headquarters seemed to have lost touch. I became Acting CO and had a much closer contact with "D" Division, the SOE people, MI6 (ISLD) and the other clandestines.

'Until the Spring of 1945, my squadron had operated more or less the way any other conventional squadron would have operated. Orders would come through Group Headquarters, Squadron Commanders were informed and they in turn briefed the crews. However, in the nature of its work there was rather more room for individual initiative in my outfit than there would be in a normal RAF Squadron. It was a little more lax than you would normally have been with a squadron. We were a bit closer to the actual source, because we had the clandestine operators on the station with us, so you could make adjustments to the operations without Group actually knowing about it.

'Working on a normal bomber squadron, for instance, they'd say "Your target is Brest. Take off is 23.00 hours, land back at such and such a time." Well, at Jessore, we started on the same principle. Target is this field one hundred miles north of So-and-So and you'll land the four bodies at 0400, live bodies of course, they were our major business but at one stage an awful lot of time was spent working out how to drop a dead body. But when you were dealing with live people, who could talk and you had members of the organisation who had planned the flight actually with you, you had a group which naturally and quite rightly intervened between yourself and the normal RAF chain of command. So, what could happen, even after you'd been briefed, was that you'd look at the photograph of the field where you were supposed to land and you'd say "I don't like this," and he'd say: "I don't like it either!' And, between you, you might decide that some other area on the map looked more promising. It didn't make any difference where you actually dropped them. If they were going to operate in an area, the important thing was to get them down safely, it didn't matter if they were ten miles out or so.

'These adjustments could also happen within the aircraft itself. Once you arrived over the area, you might see some lights that you didn't like. One chap I took one night I refused to drop because I could see some lights on the site. It turned out later that there were Japanese down there. You could have a discussion in the aircraft and you might decide to drop them elsewhere or even to bring them back. It wasn't like a normal operational bomber squadron at all, because of this contact you had with the actual people involved.'

Terence O'Brien had become an expert in clandestine flying and knew all the techniques required to drop an agent or an artefact quietly and efficiently on a specific piece of enemy territory:

'Once the monsoon had started there were two major difficulties. The first problem was getting across the Chin Hills, which separated us at Jessore from the drop zones in Burma away to the east. They went up to ten thousand feet and once the monsoon started it was very, very difficult indeed to make sure you could get under the cloud and over the Chins. You could go right down South a long way behind enemy lines and find a gap, but that was also dangerous. It didn't matter so much for bombers if they had to go up into cloud, because they were probably going to drop their bombs at about fifteen thousand feet. They just hoped that when they got over the area there'd be some sort of break in the cloud and they'd be able to pick up the target. The difficulty for the clandestine pilot was that you had to get under the cloud in the end, which was always very difficult and dangerous if there were hills around. So the only safe way to be sure of dropping on target was to stay under the cloud the whole way.

'The second problem was trying to avoid cumulo-nimbus cloud formations. In the centre of a massive monsoon cloud there would be a cumulo-nimbus, which could tear an aircraft apart. It's a single cumulus of cloud, built up from air currents and it can contain up currents and down currents of eighty to a hundred miles an hour. When flying close to cumulo-nimbus I've had hailstones come out and hit the aircraft like a splash of gravel thrown up by a skidding car.

'Even worse than the cloud and the low flying, you're encountering high, dangerous terrain all around the target area. The worst thing of all perhaps are the high winds that you meet around high ground. You're forced down to a low speed in order to drop parachutists, you'd try to drop them at 100mph or less. Stalling speed was about 80mph with a full load. If you're coming in, say, at 95mph and you have a wind of 25mph on your tail and then, as you come in the valley, the wind veers the other way around, suddenly you're near stalling speed and you can strike disaster.

'I'll give you a parallel: imagine Heathrow Airport and you suddenly move all the buildings in Central London to the end of the runway and each side of the runway and create a valley down the airstrip. Then halve the length of the strip anyway. Then, in addition, you send up giant blowing machines which can create a windforce of seventy or eighty mph for today's aircraft that stall at say 130mph, you'd have aircraft stalling all over the place.

'So what tended to happen was that people would speed up rather more than they should. In the practice grounds at Jessore we'd drop people safely at around 90mph, but once I was in the hills and certainly during the monsoon time I was closer to a hundred than I was to ninety. In fact, once you got down the valley, your airspeed needle would be flickering between stalling speed and over a hundred miles an hour. It was flickering like a watch with a bent mainspring.

'On top of that there was the constant awareness that most aircraft crashes occur in landing and take-off, in other words when the plane is near the ground and we were operating near the ground most of the time, flying in close to all manner of obstacles.'

Not surprisingly, the life expectancy of clandestine pilots was not great. Terence O'Brien received something of a shock when he compared the casualty figures of the agents he was dropping behind enemy lines and his own pilots who were effecting the drops.

'Certainly, by far the safest thing we could have done the first time we went out was to have jumped out with the "bods" we were dropping. Because only two of those "bods" were actually lost in the fighting with the Japanese, whereas we lost over 200 aircrew. The reason for the disparity was partly that you played for a bit more safety when you were dropping bodies. You were conscious that there were real people there behind you in the plane and you had to be careful of their lives. But when you were only carrying packages, you might have thought you could get in in a tighter turn, people took risks. They tried to get it over quickly or duck down under the cloud. They threw the aircraft around and you could throw a Dakota around quite surprisingly. You did it much more violently than you would ever have done when you had people aboard. And, of course, the more violent the turn, the more you increase the speed at which you might stall. If you had wind changes at the same time, then you could be in trouble. You could get these violent downdraughts that could pull an aircraft out of the sky. It might drop a thousand feet in less than seven seconds. I was thrown out of a cumulo-nimbus once, almost on my back. It was just sheer luck that there was blue sky all around me. If I had been thrown out on my back in the middle of a valley somewhere I wouldn't have had much chance at all. Flying out there, going down close to the ground at low speed in violent conditions was a very, very dangerous thing to do.

'It's not surprising that some people found it too much. LMF was the RAF's way of describing those "poor sods" who couldn't face up to this daunting task. They were said to be suffering from "Lack of Moral Fibre". I had a lot of sympathy for them. I can understand the problem. It is far easier in a dangerous situation if you're in control, if you're doing something. The man I always feel sorry for in a dangerous spot is the poor sod who is sitting there and has nothing to do. We didn't have any LMF guys in the Dakotas, but we did in the Liberator flights. They were the navigators and the dispatchers who were sitting there at the time when the aircraft is being thrown around so violently that they thought they were going to bang into a mountain at any moment. Very often they could see trees flashing by above their heads. One passenger I carried one night said to me long afterwards that he and his mate had never been so terrified in all their lives as they sat in my aircraft, simply trying to reach their drop zone. The one thing they wanted to do was get out. They just wanted us to drop them, they didn't care if they were dropped fifty miles away they just wanted out of the aircraft. But I think if you're flying the aircraft and you had reasonable confidence in yourself then fear doesn't enter into it. You're concerned with technical matters the whole time.'

These 'technical matters' were the background to a lot of Peter Fleming's work. Many of his plans relied on the skill and willingness of pilots and operatives like O'Brien. The years 1943–45 had seen Peter Fleming involved in a wide range of deception activities. His new Commander in Chief, Lord Louis Mountbatten, who had taken over from Wavell as Supreme Allied Commander in South East Asia at the end of 1943, was just as supportive of Fleming's activities as his predecessor had been. In March 1944 GS1(D) was formally taken over by Mountbatten's headquarters and renamed 'D' Division. There were many deceptions practised in the months before Terence O'Brien took over and more – simple and ingenious – when he was in command of 357 Squadron. One of the most celebrated was 'The Indian'.

'This one was before I arrived. They wanted to insert an Indian into the Japanese Headquarters, hopefully in the radio set-up there, so then he'd be able to contact "D" Division once he was inserted in the enemy Headquarters. They called for volunteers and selected this Punjabi. He was prepared, with a lot of the training done at Rawalpindi. He was given a false court-martial for theft and the facts were published. He was demoted and moved from his command. From there he was presumed to have volunteered for "D" Division when they asked for people for a dangerous mission. This was simply his cover story. He was in fact given a quite perfunctory training in radio. They reasoned that the Japanese would have their top experts on the job to make sure that the radio worked perfectly well.

'Our job was to take him in one night in a Hudson and drop him. When he went in he told the local Japanese that he'd been dropped in as a spy and that he hated the British and he wanted to work with the Japanese. Well, they beat him up at first, they wouldn't believe the story and they wanted nothing to do with him. But after that the Japanese Military Police, the Kempei Tai took him over and they treated him rather better. They took him down to Rangoon. But the Kempei Tai in Burma were never very bright, not as bright as the people they had down in Malaysia for instance. They didn't utilise him properly. As far as they were concerned he was a rather welcome addition to the Indian National Army they were trying to form.

'They were already trying to get spies out through the Indian National Army behind our lines. They had a Monitoring Group in Rangoon and they thought he'd be marvellous for that. They allowed him to send a message to say that he was there. So that demonstrated clearly that he could set up and maintain contact with the enemy. But then for some astonishing reason, it can only have been ignorance, they didn't try to pursue that or build up the link.

The upshot of it all was that "D" Division lost him. The effect of that whole exercise was simply to provide the Japanese with a very useful member of their Indian National Army, at our expense.

'It's tempting to think that clever deception plans and the laborious build-up of fake backgrounds for spies and double agents must invariably be successful. It's only realistic to point out that many attempts fail. The next big exercise that I came to hear of had its own problems. It was codenamed "Operation Oatmeal" and concerned a Malay who went on to become General Tan Sri Ibrahim Bin Ismael. Ibrahim, at that stage an SOE or "Force 136" Officer, was taken into enemy territory by submarine, in the days before the Liberators could operate down to Malaysia. He was picked up almost immediately and handed over to the Kempei Tai. As I've said the Kempei Tai in Malaysia were pretty bright and they decided that he'd be very useful indeed, particularly because in the long run they knew that the British were going to land back in Malaysia. Also they hoped to find out about our plans throughout the whole of the Far East. They thought he'd be a marvellous man for it. So they nurtured him. Now this was the trick. Every agent who went out had a safety code. The day after you landed you had a check sent out to you. If you didn't follow that check precisely they knew you were in the bag. Well, the first message that Ibrahim had to send out was that he'd arrived. Once we'd received that, the following day, the control sent out a message "Have you met Mariam?" The correct reply was supposed to be: "Two Frenchmen left here two days ago." For some extraordinary reason Ibrahim was actually carrying that correct response with him on a piece of paper! This was quite outside normal practice, it was something that should only have been carried in the head of the agent.

'The day after Ibrahim had said that he wanted very much to work with the Japanese, it was time for this check call. Ibrahim risked a very dangerous double bluff. He told them that the piece of paper they'd found had the false information on it. He said to the Japanese Sergeant: "Do you really think that I would bring with me the real reply for the check knowing full well that when I was picked up the reply would be found by you? Of course not! The real answer is in my head. And the real answer is: 'Yes, I met her yesterday.' "

'The Japanese believed him. So he sent out the message, "Yes, I met her yesterday" whereupon we knew he was in the bag. Now at that time, Force 136 got in touch with "D" Division and said we've got someone here you can start utilising. Once he was in the bag he was out of the scope of SOE, Force 136, activity so they handed him over to "D" Division, who gladly took him over and began to send him chunks of false information. They did it very thoroughly too. We did one false drop to him as well. As far as the rest of our forces were concerned we were carrying on as if Ibrahim were still free and still operating. Therefore, when he called for a drop, we said, yes, yes, yes, of course. We just altered the procedure a bit, so as not to give away any plans. I think we asked him to make a "C" of fires on the ground, rather than "T", which was the correct procedure. We did do a drop. We dropped him a radio if I recall.

'Basically, "D" Division spent a lot of time and trouble building him up, so that when the time came for the landing he would be the one who'd give a false place of landing and a false time. In the meantime he was establishing very good credibility with the Japanese. A certain amount of true information was being sent to him – nothing that would compromise any of the other agents who were going in. But in the end he was never utilised in the landing, because no landing was ever made. The atomic bomb was dropped instead.'

The Japanese let Ibrahim Bin Ismael go. They gave him money and offered to help him escape to Siam. He contrived to avoid their offers and contacted the British Forces instead. He subsequently became a General and Head of the Independent Malaysian Army. He published a book in Malaysia about his extraordinary experiences called: *Have You Met Mariam?*[1]

'On another occasion, I don't know whether Peter Fleming was inspired by the European version of "The Man Who Never Was" or not, but he certainly came up with a Far East version for us to carry out. The background was this: Force 136 had already considered an attempt at "the corpse ploy" to take pressure off one of their agents that the Japanese were desperately trying to find. His name was Lieutenant Colonel Hugh Seagrim and he had been left behind enemy lines at the fall of Burma. Although he was safely hidden he had no radio, so various attempts were made to drop one to him. In late 1944 my squadron dropped in two agents who were meant to deliver a radio to Seagrim. Both the agents were captured by the Japanese. It was a blunder because the Burmese alerted the Japanese and they moved in on the dropping zone in force. As a result the enemy found out about Seagrim, whom they'd been trying to track down for some considerable time. The Japanese were so desperate to find out where he was hiding that they were killing villagers to try to force the local people, the Karens, to tell them. But Seagrim had befriended the villagers and helped them so they wouldn't betray him. During the intense hunt for Seagrim, while the Karens were suffering so much, one of them suggested that the British should drop the body of a European in the hills and then the local people could produce this body for the Japanese. The suggestion came back to Force 136 through the enemy lines. But this imaginative, if macabre, scheme was called off.

'It was never carried out apparently because Seagrim himself was a very devout Christian and he had very strong views about death and about how human bodies should be treated. He thought this was an outrageous suggestion and would have nothing to do with it. In the end Seagrim himself couldn't stand it, and he gave himself up to the Japanese on the basis that they would stop killing the Karen villagers if they had Seagrim. Despite a promise from the Japanese that he would not be harmed, they killed him.

'The idea of a deception involving a corpse was now firmly established in the mind of Peter Fleming. He knew about the potential for confusion that could be created if you could place the right dead body in the right place at the right time. In mid 1944 he decided to try to mislead the enemy with a fake agent. It should appear that he had died when his parachute failed and that he had crashed into enemy territory carrying documents designed to convey a totally false impression of Allied plans. But first of all the right body had to be found and in Calcutta in the hot season this was a difficult and uncomfortable process. There were all sorts of technical problems. Number one is the technical problem of finding the body. It's all very well to say there are thousands of people dying in Calcutta, but you can't drop someone who's starved to death, because clearly he's not the kind of person who'd be an SOE agent. Then it was decided that he had to be a Muslim and there's the problem that Muslims are circumcised and Hindus aren't. Bengal of course had a Hindu majority and it's only North of Bengal that the Muslims are to be found. Therefore to get a good healthy Muslim about 30 years of age, at a time of famine, was extremely difficult.'

According to one of Terence O'Brien's Force 136 contacts, the man who was in charge of Operation Corpse (Hiccups), Gordon Rennie, finally found a body from the General Military Hospital. 'D' Division had already arranged for a safe house near the Golf Club in the suburb of Tooligunj where they could go to work on it:

'The corpse underwent a full manicure. It was shaved, its finger-nails and toenails were cut, it had to be fitted with a special uniform, had to have the right size of boots, proper identity cards and all that sort of thing. It had to have a radio to go with it, because the Japanese were going to use the radio afterwards and use it for identity. That was not all, there was another, rather critical "technical" problem. It was the height of the hot season and the body had to be photographed for the identity cards and for fingerprinting. Clearly none of this could be done with the body fully frozen. Similarly the body had to be dressed and you couldn't dress the freezing thing. So it had to be allowed to warm up, but not too much.

'It was in the hot sun at the aerodrome in Calcutta for most of the day, being prepared and set up at the back of the aircraft. The aircraft in those days in the hot season was rather like an oven. You got temperatures of 150, 160 degrees. I fried an egg on the entrance to the aircraft door one day. I dropped an egg and it settled quite quickly, in about four minutes it was quite hard. So you can understand that a body going into that could start to deteriorate quite rapidly. They eventually spread carbolic all around it to try to minimise the smell and the possibility of infection. The man who was flying the mission that night was called Churchill. I have spoken to him since then and the main thing that he remembers about the flight was the moment when he actually entered the aircraft:

'There was this shape with a white sheet over it at the back of the plane. He shut the door on entry, looked back at his "cargo", and the first thing he saw as the aircraft shook was an arm which flopped out and dangled down. He said he went forward to the cockpit and, like the Ancient Mariner, "turned no more his head that night". He knew what he was carrying by then!

'The other technical problem that we had to resolve was nothing like as gory. If the enemy were going to believe that this body had fallen from a British aircraft, then there had to be some convincing evidence of parachute failure. The Major in charge of parachutes at Jessore, Bob Thornton, decided that the best way to suggest a convincing parachute failure was to fracture the metal clip which attached the parachute to its static line. If the body were found on the ground with an unopened parachute and a length of static line attached to it with a broken clip at the end then that would be self-explanatory. By the time he came to this conclusion he'd tried everything he could think of. They'd tried abrading the lines of the parachute, they'd tried dipping it in water, they'd tried sending it out with torn panels. Then purely by chance, while training some learners one day, he was telling them how careful they had to be that the static line was sound. Suddenly, he realised that if he could contrive that the clip holding it to the plane should break, ostensibly from metal fatigue, then this would be the most plausible explanation of the lot.

'It's difficult to convince anybody about parachute failure. Let's face it, ever since the parachute was invented, there have been a number of failures and every single failure has been investigated so thoroughly that parachutes are generally considered to be intrinsically safe. In fact, as I've already mentioned, if you went up in an aircraft at the beginning of the war by far the best and safest way statistically to come down to the ground again was to get in your parachute and jump. They were a lot safer than the aircraft themselves.

'The Static Line must stay with the aircraft. It's rather like an arm attached to it. The normal procedure is that the parachutist attaches the static line by a clip to a strong point in the aircraft and then jumps. The static line stretches out taut, snaps the twine at the end of the parachute, opening it out and allowing the man to float to the ground. You have a clatter of static lines against the aircraft as a string of two or three jump out. Obviously, if the clip breaks, as could possibly happen through metal fatigue or a faulty piece of metal, then the static line goes out with the man, and there's nothing to pull the parachute open. The parachutist can't get at the thing on his back. There's no time at six hundred feet. If he's jumping at 20,000 feet then he can probably do it, but not at 600 feet.

'Churchill dropped the radio package first and then the body. He could see the body quite clearly on the ground, near to a Japanese camp. It was pretty certain he'd be found and, just as importantly, that the Japanese would know about it. It would be unlikely that the villagers would snitch what valuables there were and then run away and deny all knowledge of the dead parachutist. After the body had been dropped amid a flurry of Pintails and their Very lights, all "D" Division could do after their meticulous preparations was to sit back and wait for the Japanese to start sending them messages, pretending to be the agent. Because, of course, we'd sent him down with all the correct call codes and the correct challenge. Nothing happened. "O" Division waited for about a week, then they thought that maybe the radio had broken on landing, so they asked us if we could drop a second one. We did drop another radio and they continued to wait. It was five or six weeks before they had to admit that their "corpse" ploy had not worked. The Japanese had either been too foolish to capitalise on the imitation of a foreign agent or too clever to be taken in by the "gift" of an agent complete with radio and handy code books. As usual with deception, you could never be sure.

'Fortunately this happened at the same time as the SOE agent Ibrahim was picked up by the Japanese down in Malaysia. So SOE, or Force 136, offered him to "D" Division, who were only too glad to accept Ibrahim and abandon their own unsuccessful corpse.'

The records of The Joint Chiefs of Staff later concluded that the corpse plan was 'too boldly conceived to appeal to the timid and bungling Japanese'.[2]

The first deception job which Terence O'Brien experienced at first hand for 'D' Division had honourable antecedents, for both Meinertzhagen and Wavell had tried similar ploys.[3] It involved dropping the kind of mapcase or satchel that brigadiers of the time habitually carried. In this pre-plastic age, such satchels were covered in a mica-like transparency called 'talc'.

'A junior officer came up to me one day in the Mess. He said he knew that I was doing a sortie in northern Burma and asked if I could take this satchel with me. It was a mapcase with a pouch at the back in which he had pyjamas and toothpaste and slippers and things like that and a Brigadier's cap, which was the important thing. It was a rather tatty cap. He was proud of the fact that it was tatty, very proud of the squeezed toothpaste, and that the toothbrush was rather grotty. The "talc" itself was scratched as if from long use, making the map details difficult to see. It was all very carefully prepared. There were some papers in it, of course carrying false military information. The idea was inspired by Peter Fleming, because he had actually seen a brigadier produce a satchel at a meeting in Delhi and it occurred to him that it would be a very nice thing to drop to the Japanese.

'I took the satchel out that night and I dropped it on an open road, near a little Burmese temple. It was a matter of getting down low, it wasn't attached to a parachute, obviously, so you went down to about twenty or thirty feet and you made sure you dropped it right in the centre of the road. I knew the road was used, because I saw two trucks moving along it the same night. So no doubt it was picked up.

In this calculating world of deception nothing was sacred. A simple, affecting love letter from a soldier's girl to his unit could provide enough misleading information. Peter Fleming had a girl in his office who used to write a whole series of love letters, purporting to come from all the girls left behind. Terence O'Brien dropped a whole sackful of these billets doux near a crashed aircraft. The idea was that any of them could have been carrying important papers and, if it was going anywhere near the front line, it could well be carrying a sack of mail. In this case the contents of the love letters were not at all important. What mattered were the addresses. The letters would be grouped in units, so that any Japanese Intelligence Officer who saw them would guess where certain units were deployed. Effectively they revealed a false order of battle.

'We did a number of these drops. They had a store of suitable love letters. They also had a store of love letters sent out from England, airmail lettergrams which they used for the same deceptive purpose. Some of them were done in different handwriting, some were typed, they even used different typewriters in case the enemy got suspicious and checked on the typefaces. At one time we dropped a load of mail with a set of Force 136 rations. It was dropped on a road, south of Mandalay. We dropped other things too. Live homing pigeons were an unglamorous but very practical weapon for the secret agent. They were totally inconspicuous and usually completely reliable in a way that a secret radio message could never be. In any case, an agent dropped with a wireless set could well discover that it had been badly damaged in the drop. The American OSS always travelled with a homing pigeon, so that they could release it on arrival and confirm in the quietest of ways that they had reached the correct drop zone.

' "D" Division and Peter Fleming did their usual piece of lateral thinking. If live pigeons were known to be part of the agent's armoury, then a dead pigeon, fallen from the sky with a false message attached would have some relevance for the enemy Intelligence. It was a particularly happy piece of deception, since a genuinely dead pigeon actually would fall from the sky and a dead pigeon manipulated by the clandestine forces could be dropped from an aircraft in the sky. The best of forensic detectives would no doubt find it hard to distinguish between the two. We dropped a number of dead pigeons with messages attached – I don't know what the messages said, but obviously it's one way of getting false information to the enemy. We would try to reduce the odds of failure a little by taking care to drop them where we knew there was a Japanese camp, or if we saw some traffic on a road at night we'd try to drop them near that road. But I doubt if people would stop a truck just to pick up a dead pigeon. I have to admit that I often wondered myself about the efficacy of dropping dead birds from airplanes. I would have thought that the reaction of a normal Burmese on finding a dead pigeon on the road would be to take it home, pluck it and eat it. If it had a message attached, so what?'

'D' Division's main means of transmitting information to the Japanese was through a small network of agents, most of whom were double agents. Like its much bigger sister organisations, 'A' Force and the LCS through the XX Committee, Fleming's 'D' Division made use of a number of men, hired first by the Germans or the Japanese, who were then either forced or persuaded to work for the Allies. It is Terence O'Brien's understanding that by the time he came

225

into the picture every single agent that the Japanese and the Germans had sent into India had been picked up or identified and was being worked by 'D' Division. They kept them working the whole time and supplied them with information. Most of the agents knew they were identified and had no choice but to connive at false messages. Some, though, were unaware that they were being manipulated and passed misleading information fed to them by 'D' Division. Maybe the most impressive of the double agents was a Hindu codenamed Silver, whose real name was Bhagat Ram. He was so trusted by his Axis controllers that he was awarded the German Iron Cross. Silver's main allegiance was to Russia however and it was only because the British were allies of the Russians that he was prepared to lead his double life. A fine story is told about Silver in action in the field. At one stage, his credentials with the Germans were running very high indeed. They had gone so far as to provide him with a transmitter powerful enough to communicate directly with his controllers in Berlin. His cover was almost blown when he was spotted in Delhi by an Afghan, who knew him well, in the company of British service personnel. Ignoring the advice of the British not to return to Kabul, he accepted an invitation to dinner from the Afghan and promptly poisoned his host by slipping a portion of chopped up tiger whiskers into his curry.[4]

Alongside running the double agents in the hope of being able to build sufficient credibility to pass misinformation; alongside the continuing attempts to confuse the Japanese about the orders of battle, ran another major problem for the deception-planners of 'D' Division. From time to time their own strategic thinking came dangerously near the truth. They knew, of course, what the basic battle-plan would be, but it was almost impossible for them to know what all the contingency planning contained. Terence O'Brien remembers a specific instance.

'On one occasion we dropped some documents which suggested that the Army was going to make a landing on the coast and push inland towards Prome, when, in point of fact, the main drive was going to be down the Irrawaddy valley. The Army only heard about this at a very late stage and told "D" Division to stop it at once, because it was in fact a *genuine* contingency plan. Peter Fleming was not easily put off by such awkward coincidences and he was certainly never short of imagination. Once he had posters printed saying that Bob Hope, Bing Crosby and Dorothy Lamour were giving a big concert. He had a list of the formations down the Arakan, the Bengal Coast, south of Chittagong, who were going to attend this concert.

Just inland from the coast there was a gap in the hills where they could possibly break through into the plain. The plan was to drop the documents and the poster advertising this big concert in that area. It was abundantly clear which divisions would be in attendance. The concert was due to go on for two or three nights, so the impression was given that there was a very large army indeed in that area, which was planning to drive through this gap in the hills. Again, the Army only found out about this deception at the last minute. In this case it seems that they suddenly realised that breaking through this particular gap in the hills might be a very sound piece of military planning. Then, to their horror, they discovered that "D" Division were about to try to attract a large Japanese force to the very area they were now seriously considering invading. "D" Division was once more told to stop.'

Strategic deception in the Far East never achieved the levels of sophistication that were possible in the other main theatres of war. The kind of confusion whereby Allied Command suddenly discovered a deception plan, which ran the risk of jeopardising genuine operations, was precisely the kind of confusion that the LCS back in London was designed to avoid. Tactical deception on the other hand worked as well here as anywhere else, and in the later stages of the Burmese Campaign, it made a significant contribution to what was perhaps the major strategic success for 'D' Division of the entire war, Operation Cloak.

'D' Force was a field deception unit, whose equipment was provided by the Inter-services Technical Bureau under the Directorship of Lieutenant Colonel Bicat, another peacetime artist. 'D' Force employed sonic deception, everything from covering troop movements with croaking frogs and cicadas, to the Bicat 'Sausages', which were little strips of explosive designed to simulate rifle fire.[5] One of the weapons in the armoury of tactical deception, the Pintail, was invented by Fleming himself. It was a bomb which stuck nose up in the air and after a short period of time would start to send up Very lights. Parafexes simulated rifle fire and grenades exploding while Aquaskits and Aquatails provided various effects on the water. The dummy parachutists, Paragons, were also put to good use and were particularly suited to the confusions of jungle warfare.

Terence O'Brien and his squadron were very closely involved with Operation Cloak, which put much of this tactical know how to good effect. The main drive in February 1945 was the attack on Rangoon down the valley. It was critically important to get into Rangoon before the monsoon broke, otherwise the British would find themselves fighting at the end of a 600 mile supply line, which would by then consist of flooded rivers and impassable roads. The Japanese, by comparison, would have their main supply base almost at their backs, only ten or fifteen miles away. This meant that they would be able to hold the British up during the monsoon, or quite conceivably drive them on to the retreat, so it was vital that once the British had committed themselves to the main drive down the valley they should get right through to Rangoon, quickly. The main obstacle was the Irrawaddy river, which in places could be four or five miles across.

The British plan was to make a frontal assault across the Irrawaddy near Mandalay. But at the same time a Division of men would loop around about 200 miles south and make a rapid crossing of the Irrawaddy by night. There was a flat plain from there to the valley road. The plan was to cut the valley road behind the Japanese, who were protecting Mandalay. This was at Meiktila, where there were also three important airfields. So there was to be a feint attack on Mandalay and the real attack was going to be the loop south, driving across the plain and cutting the Japanese lines of communication, grabbing three airfields and clearing the way through to Rangoon. The attack was a vital part of the whole campaign and Operation Cloak, the deception plan, was a major part of it. O'Brien remembers the part that he played: 'Near the Irrawaddy we dropped broken bits of aeroplane with an explosive charge attached. Included in the debris was a satchel of papers. We were trying to give the impression that an aircraft had exploded in mid-air. The papers of course gave a strong indication that a group of military units was operating in that area. In addition "D" Division sent messages to a spurious agent on the Japanese side of the river, giving the name of the person to whom he should report after the landings. "D" Division arranged that there should be daily flights opposite the false landing place of small aircraft which would raise a lot of dust taking off and landing. They had a real tank as well, which also spent its time in that area raising a lot of dust.

'The night before they carried out the fake attack, they sent out six aircraft full of fake battle devices, like Parafexes, Paragons and Pintails. It must have been a convincing display since the enemy retaliated and the squadron lost one of its aircraft. It was all designed to convince the Japanese that the false location, where the British wanted them to concentrate their forces, was already the scene of a major battle. It was of course the wrong section of the river and 4 Corps were able to make their crossing at the chosen spot without any opposition whatsoever. They took one and a half Divisions across complete with tanks without a single shot being fired. The following evening they had reached and captured Meiktila and cut the Japanese lines of communication. Four days later, against a Japanese army of 200,000, they succeeded in making the crossing to Mandalay. The Japanese by then were in total confusion, realising that their lines of supply and communication had been so comprehensively interrupted. I think that may have been the most important contribution that Fleming made to the whole of the campaign.

'I have to confess I was never very impressed by the deception thing. I thought it was a bit of a game. I could see the point of Operation Cloak, for instance, because it was a neat operation and it was good tactics. I could see a purpose before it started, I could believe in it and I'm pretty sure it did achieve something. But all the rest of the business, the dead pigeons, the brigadier's satchel and the rest of it struck me as rather drunken capers. As though someone thought, "Oh! what a good idea, we'll do this, Charlie!" The very complicated ones with the documents I could admire but I was never convinced that they would work.

'The presumption was that the Japanese were as intelligent and as astute as the Germans and had as lively an Intelligence Service and that the ploys would reach the really bright people in the Japanese army. I think basically that both assumptions were false.'

EPILOGUE

In the course of our many interviews with the men and women involved in deception one story has cropped up again and again. It runs like this: after elaborate efforts to construct a fake airfield, the real airfield nearby is badly bombed. As the enemy bombers leave, they divert across the newly constructed false aerodrome and drop a wooden bomb in the middle of the runway. The Germans are supposed to have done it to the Allies, the British to the Germans. It happened in Kent, it happened in North Africa, it happened in Italy. There are variations. It was not a dummy airfield but wooden guns on the South Coast of England during the invasion scare of autumn 1940 which drew the wooden bomb, or there was no genuine air raid, simply a single enemy plane on a mission to tease. Each time we heard the story it was relayed to us as a first-hand experience or if not first-hand then at least something that happened to a best friend 'stationed out in Alexandria'. Something like it presumably happened somewhere, but it seems unlikely that there were dozens of witty bomber crews acting independently of each other all over the world. Maybe the story is apochryphal but it illustrates well the power of rumour and misinformation. It also reveals how difficult it is to disentangle the stratagems of the deceivers with confidence all these years after the events described in this book.

Four decades after the end of the Second World War there is still a substantial body of relevant sources that is denied to historians. There is also the suspicion that a great deal of what would have been important to an understanding of the history of deception during the Second World War was never committed to the archives in the first place. This book has been able to draw on some important primary sources but has, by choice, relied heavily on memory. As nearly all our contributors have cautioned, memory is a capricious thing particularly at a distance of almost 50 years. One interviewee pointed out to us that he had been retelling certain stories down through the years with considerable conviction, only to discover, when certain records finally became available in the Public Records Office at Kew, that documents with his initials on them flatly contradicted what he had long believed to be the truth.

In 1945 Cyril Connolly wrote that: 'Truth is a river that is always splitting up into arms that reunite. Islanded between the arms the inhabitants argue for a lifetime as to which is the main river.' Historians have the luxury of a lifetime to argue about which is the main river. In war there is less time for the protagonists to make up their minds and they have an added burden. They have to commit themselves to a course of action. Resources will always be limited and the military commander has to take decisions about how the men and materiel at his disposal will be deployed to maximum effect. The deceiver seeks to undermine the basis on which his enemy makes those decisions and in so doing he uses information as both a sword and a shield. With these weapons he fights to make his enemy do what he wants him to do. Ruminations around a Staff Conference table are not enough.

Dudley Clarke, developing a theatrical image in a letter to an American colleague written in 1946[1] emphasised that the General's audience is the enemy and that 'he alone must decide what he wants them to do – to advance? to withdraw? to thin out or to reinforce? Whatever he chooses, the main point is that his "object" must be to make the enemy do something. It matters nothing what the enemy *thinks*, it is only what he *does* that can affect the battle.'[2]

Is it possible to draw up a balance sheet of success and failure for deception during the Second World War? Can we detect enough occasions when the enemy did what an Allied commander wanted him to do? Is it always possible to be sure that when the enemy acted in a way which accorded with Allied wishes it was because he had been deceived? An old German proverb observes: 'He who will not be deceived must have as many eyes as hairs on his head.' Despite the emergence of a revisionist school of thought about the impact of deception on German strategic thinking,[3] it still seems clear that at certain crucial moments during the war the German High Command *did* do what the Allies wanted them to do, that the result of their action or inaction *was* disadvantageous to their cause and that they acted in full possession of information which

231

had been passed to them through a variety of channels manipulated by the Allied deception-planners. What an isolated commander may or may not have suspected about Allied intentions, or what other elements influenced the decision to dispose force in one way rather than another, simply illustrates how difficult it is to separate any one piece of tactical deception from its strategic context and then to seek to determine its worth. It is far beyond the scope of this book to attempt a thorough analysis of the efficacy of deception during the war. Indeed Sir Roger Hesketh, chronicling from his first-hand experience the history of Fortitude, whose significance for the outcome of Overlord few would question, chooses a quotation from Francis Bacon, which illustrates the scale of the task confronting anyone seeking to attempt such an analysis. He places the quotation at the top of his Preface where it acts as a gentle reminder to the reader to beware overemphasising the importance of deception: 'It was prettily devised of Aesop: "The fly sat upon the axle-tree of the chariot wheel and said, 'What a dust do I raise!' " So there are vain persons that, whatsoever goeth alone or moveth upon great means if they have never so little hand in it, they think it is they that carry it.'

He goes on to say that 'it is always tempting for those who set out to deceive and who see their objects fulfilled, to claim the credit for their attainment when, in fact, the motive force lay in another quarter.'[4] When Michael Howard's official history of deception during the Second World War is finally published it may well prove to have been the case that Sir Roger Hesketh was being over modest. Despite his caveat, he himself in his conclusion to the report writes that 'when all is said and done, one is left with a sense of astonishment that men in such responsible positions as were those who controlled the destinies of Germany during the late war, could have been so fatally misled. The short answer must be that the German High Command could only act on the evidence in its possession and ... practically all the information that it did acquire from this side of the English Channel was supplied by the Controlled Agents.'[5]

Without dismissing the other channels that were used to deceive the Germans before D-Day, Hesketh places the greatest emphasis on the double cross agent as 'the only method which combines the precision, certainty and speed necessary for the conduct of strategic deception at long range over an extended period'.[6] After the war Sir Roger Hesketh had the opportunity to interview senior German Officers, among them Field Marshal von Rundstedt and his Chief of General Staff General Guenther Blumentritt and these interviews confirmed his views. Field Marshals Keitel and Jodl were seen by Sir Roger Hesketh's brother and he returned from his visit to Germany convinced that it was Garbo's message, sent at such length to his controller on the evening of June 9, that changed the course of the battle of Normandy. Keitel is quoted by Hesketh as being of the opinion that it was 99% certain that Garbo's message was the immediate cause of the order to halt the First Panzer Division and cancel Case Three. The vital division was ordered from Turnhout in Belgium to Ghent not to the Normandy beachheads. Masterman echoes the importance of the controlled agents Garbo and Brutus: 'In all some seven offensive German divisions which were expected to be sent to the Cherbourg area were retained in the Pas de Calais area for a fortnight after D-Day.'[7]

Masterman's book, *The Double Cross System*,[8] was published before the significance of Ultra became public knowledge. Without Ultra the enormous strategic deceptions of the Second World War could never have been devised. Masterman himself refers obliquely to Ultra when he writes that the final confirmation of the belief that MI5, through its special subsection B.1a, controlled the German espionage system in the United Kingdom, had come gradually from a study of 'secret sources'. Had his book been published after 1972 he would have named his 'secret sources' as Ultra.

Ultra Intelligence was of vital importance and many books have been written since the early seventies about its application on the battlefield. In *Ultra Goes to War*[9] Ronald Lewin singles out Terence Airey, 'Bill' Williams, Joe Ewart and Sir David Hunt as representatives of the kind of donnish talent that was mobilised during the war to handle Ultra:

These unusual men are worth attention because, with others of similar calibre like Enoch Powell, they set in the field a standard of intellectual ability and freedom from the mental conventions of the Regular Army which matched the qualities of their brilliant contemporaries at Bletchley Park. They could understand what Ultra was about. With minds trained in evaluation, they saw that this special intelligence was not a form of esoteric magic but simply another tool, valuable, demanding a sceptical respect – but above all to be handled with imagination . . . men like Williams and Hunt were not only battle-tested: they were also, fortunately, no more inhibited about Ultra than about any other kind of intelligence – for as scholars the weighing of evidence was their normal trade.[10]

233

Back at home others, equally able, were involved in processing Abwehr Intelligence after it had been deciphered. They included Sir Denys Page, who went on to be Regius Professor of Greek at Cambridge and Master of Jesus College, L. R. Palmer, Professor of Comparative Philology at Oxford and Hugh Trevor Roper, a Professor of Modern History at Oxford and later Master of Peterhouse at Cambridge. Page and Palmer worked at Bletchley, dealing with the evaluation of decrypts on the premises while Trevor Roper became a sort of clearing house and point of reference on Abwehr intelligence.[11] Much of this information was passed on to Colonel Bevan at Storey's Gate, where the precious information was available only to a few of his colleagues in the LCS.

Ultra performed two vital functions for the deceivers at LCS, and their counterparts at the XX Committee and Ops B at SHAEF. It gave them a fair indication of how their stratagems were being assessed by various German intelligence agencies. The decrypts also provided them with information about the disposition of the enemy forces, whose movements they sought to influence. Hitler's continuing delusions about the importance of Norway from 1940 onwards illustrate how important it was for the deception-planners to know the German Order of Battle. Until the Ardennes offensive in December 1944, when Bletchley provided evidence of increasing shipping activity between Oslofjord and Denmark, Bevan and his colleagues were able to see the value of continued threats to Norway through Ultra decrypts of 'German strength returns or personnel appointments, weapon states and so on'.[12] Throughout the war Ultra, supported by 'Y' service radio traffic analysis, enabled the deceivers to gauge the strength of Hitler's commitment to protecting his Northern flank and to continue to feed his delusion with their stratagems. This was equally true of the Balkans, where 'A' Force was at work with its own double agents, immeasurably strengthened by Ultra.

This combination of intelligence and deception was at its most potent during the re-entry to Europe. The risks taken in continuing to build up the ability of the controlled agents to tell 'the big lie' required an insurance policy. Physical deception, which had played its part since the beginning of the War in North Africa, provided the insurance before D-Day. Hesketh suggests that:

Although Fortitude would in the event have worked just as well if there had been no physical deception at all, it would be unwise to assume that such devices can be dispensed with in the strategic field. The majority of them should however be regarded less as instruments of deception than as security measures to be taken at those points where there is a danger of the enemy breaking through the security ring, so that if he does he will find nothing to contradict and if possible (something) to confirm the story which is being told by the controlled agents. It is a matter of insurance and in this as in all cases where risks are run, one is not necessarily justified in allowing a policy to lapse because no claim has been made.[13]

In other theatres of war and in other circumstances it may have been the physical misrepresentation on the ground placed there for the enemy reconnaissance plane or the hostile spy that tipped the balance. General Sir Charles Richardson's tale suggests that physical deception had a crucial role to play before El Alamein where 'on the battlefield a group of dummy guns, or the simulated noise of a mechanised column may well draw the enemy to the wrong flank'.[14]

Physical deception undoubtedly played its part through the North African Campaigns and continued to do so as Alexander fought his way through Italy. The lessons that had been learned by Dudley Clarke and the exchange of personnel that took place between 'A' Force and the deception-planners back in England, of whom David Strangeways is a good example, meant a continuity of thought and experience which stretched from Sidi Barrani to D-Day. This experience was important to the deception-planners as they considered how best to operate the FUSAG deception before and after the Normandy landings.

FUSAG had been activated on October 18, 1943 and by May 1944 it comprised the genuine Third United States Army, with nine divisions, and the First Canadian Army. British Sigint showed that the Germans were well aware of the presence of these troops and of General Patton's arrival to take command. Hinsley suggests that this information led directly to the devising of Fortitude South, the extension of Fortitude, which sought to persuade the enemy that the *schwerpunkt* would come in the Pas de Calais, and that even when the invasion of Normandy had begun the enemy should believe that it was only a feint.[15] There were numerous deceptions employed to support the lie. Codenamed Quicksilver I to VI, they involved radio deception, the display of landing craft, the bombing of the Pas de Calais beaches and of lines of communication in the region and the creation of fake lighting displays.

The creation of FUSAG under the command of Patton was a remarkable achievement. Even if Garbo's message of June 9 can be isolated as a single deception of supreme importance, its credibility in the eyes of the Germans would surely have been far less assured had there not been, underwriting it, the comprehensive insurance policy that FUSAG provided. Garbo's message was delivered at a time when intelligence reports provided by Ultra were revealing an alarming risk to the beachheads at Normandy. It was the moment when the careful husbandry of many years could be drawn on to give immediate aid, but Hesketh points out that 'it is generally more correct to regard it [deception] as a method which achieves its results by a slow and gradual process rather than by lightning strokes'.[16]

In his memoirs, General Omar Bradley, Commander of the United States First Army, has no doubt how vital that slow and gradual deception proved to be for the men on the Normandy beachhead:

> While the enemy's 7th Army, over-worked and under strength, struggled to pin us down on the beachhead, the German High Command declined to reinforce it with troops from the Pas de Calais. There, for seven decisive weeks, the 15th Army waited for an invasion that never came, convinced beyond all reasonable doubt that Patton would lead the main Allied assault across the narrow neck of the Channel. Thus the enemy mobilized 19 Divisions and played directly into our hands in the biggest single hoax of the War.[17]

This testimony has added significance coming as it does from an American source. The Americans had been slow to put their faith in the value of strategic deception. Colonel W. A. Harris had been a particularly harsh critic. He arrived in England in the wake of the resounding failure of the deception operations Starkey, Wadham and Tindall, part of Operation Cockade. Cockade was the plan to put pressure on the Germans throughout the summer of 1943 and to make them believe in the possibility of major cross-Channel operations. Starkey was an amphibious feint across the Channel, Tindall was a plan to tie up German forces in Normandy and Wadham suggested a large scale American landing in Brittany. Cockade was the moment when deception, at the behest of its operational masters, significantly overreached itself. The Germans barely noticed all the activity that the plans generated. It is not surprising that with the smell of Cockade's failure still in the air an American sent to evaluate the possibilities of strategic deception should have required more than a little convincing. By the end of the war his attitude had been profoundly changed: 'The success of the Fortitude plans is a monolithic fact in any appreciation of the effectiveness of Cover and Deception . . . credit for the basic conceptions of operations which led to this victory must go to the British who built on several years' experience in the Middle East to achieve an organization of trained and imaginative personnel, and who worked out the command and control relationships which made it effective.'[18]

Here is testimony to the work which had been started by Wavell and Dudley Clarke in North Africa and which had culminated in Fortitude. Ultra, the 'Y' Service, day to day intelligence work, the efforts of a small number of genuinely significant controlled agents and their case officers, supported by the immense practical achievements of physical misrepresentation, were the mainstays of the successful deceptions of the Second World War. The glue that held all this together was the recognition quite early in the war that strategic deception should become the focus of formally organised staff work. On the battlefield, deception plans had to be closely co-ordinated between Staff and Operations. The movement of dummy forces had to reflect carefully the movement of real troops. On a wider scale the complexity of strategic deception demanded rigorous control over who was telling which lies to whom and when. In 1943–4 co-ordination was required between the deceivers in London and 'A' Force and, to a lesser extent, 'D' Division as operations continued in Northwest Europe, the Western and Central Mediterranean and South East Asia. A failure to co-ordinate might have allowed a collaboration between German and Japanese intelligence to reveal the same division, genuine or bogus, in two different areas. This might expose the whole deception effort and could jeopardise the entire intelligence system on which it was based, the double cross system and Ultra. The role of the LCS was of immense importance and through a combination of good luck, efficient co-ordination and the failings of German strategic intelligence, the Allies were able to persuade the Germans consistently to overestimate their strength in Northwestern Europe, the Mediterranean and the Far East.

The war was thus a contest of information as well as a contest of arms. The more conflicting, confusing and troublesome information that could land on the enemy's decision-makers, the thicker the fog of war would be. But the deception-planners had to be careful to allow the enemy the opportunity to make out the shapes that would suggest to them the actions that the planners wanted them to take. How much effect the myriad small 'shapes', ruses and deception schemes had on the enemy is difficult to say, yet it is the bold and slightly tortuous plans like Mincemeat and Copperhead involving dead bodies, dead of night sorties in submarines and actors impersonating Generals that have, not surprisingly, most caught the public's imagination.

Without belittling the contribution made by Mincemeat and Copperhead, two less well known stories sum up the fantastical, far-fetched aspects of deception. It was allegedly a spy in Geneva, one of the main centres of espionage during the war, who decided to spend his day going shopping. What did he buy? The Michelin European Map No. 51, not one but every single copy he could find in the whole of Geneva. It was the map of the Pas de Calais region and it was his small contribution to Fortitude. The other story involves a 'sib'. Sibs were rumours, from the Latin sibilare, to whisper. Throughout the war they were manufactured in London and at Woburn, the home of the Political Warfare Executive. They were distributed through the press, through casual conversations and through the staff in British embassies all over the world. One such 'sib' was placed simultaneously in Stockholm, Lisbon and Geneva. It stated that a shipment of sardine tins bound for England from Portugal had ended up in Germany and that the British were mightily upset about it. The sardine cans, it was whispered, contained much needed platinum for the British war effort. Platinum was valuable for the Germans too, so it was hoped that when the Germans discovered this potentially valuable haul a patriotic call would go out to the *Hausfraus* of Germany to return their sardine cans and that valuable manpower would be tied up trying to collect the platinum – all a very long way from the importance of the message that Garbo sent.

Much of the physical deception recalled by our deceivers has the same rough and ready feel to it; the enormous, unwieldy fake landing craft, floating on top of the water and simulating an invasion fleet, recalled by Peter Tooley; Mrs Hodgkin's awe as she and her girls saw the fruits of their labours, line upon line of rubber lorries; Stan Perkins, the electrician, describing his collection of rags and cisterns; Terence O'Brien dropping dead pigeons on the Japanese and David Strangeways diverting enemy divisions to his tiny group of deceivers in the middle of the North African desert and not being sure whether to be terrified or delighted.

As almost everybody who has written on deception has pointed out, deception is as old as warfare itself. The military advisers to the Chou Emperors wrote over three thousand years ago:

> When able to attack we must seem unable; when using our forces, we must seem inactive; when we are near, we must make the enemy believe that we are far away; when far away we must make him believe we are near.
> Hold out the bait: entice the enemy.
> Feign disorder and crush him.

Every one of those ancient tenets was adhered to by the deceivers thousands of years later, as they prepared to take Europe back from Adolf Hitler. They were able to attack on June 6 1944, Hitler believed they were unable to; as they moved their forces across the Channel, they seemed inactive, the enemy Commander, Rommel, was on leave back in Germany. All the techniques of camouflage, fake material and sonic deception were designed to confuse the enemy about how near or far the Allied forces were. Did they 'hold out the bait: entice the enemy'? Colonel David Strangeways had his own version of that maxim: 'It's a bit like fly-fishing, I suppose.'

Nearly all the deceivers we talked to asked us to stress one more point: that thousands of lives were saved by the intelligent use of deception. The determination to use clever deception methods arose out of Britain's vulnerability in the early part of the war and was strengthened by memories of the carnage of the First World War where military strategy dug itself into a muddy impasse in the trenches. The men who had experienced the heartless lack of imagination that caused such destruction – and Winston Churchill was among them – resolved that there must be better ways of organising military strategy. One of those ways was the construction of clever deceptions and the elevation of deceptive strategy itself into a fully fledged institution of war.

Maybe the most appropriate epitaph for deception during the Second World War, at its zenith during the liberation of Europe in the summer of 1944, is provided by Charles Caleb Colton, who in the nineteenth century claimed that: 'There are some frauds so well conducted that it would be stupidity not to be deceived by them.'

GLOSSARY OF MILITARY TERMS

ADEE: Air defence experimental establishment.

A Force: Dudley Clarke's deception organisation in the Mediterranean and the Middle East.

ATS: Auxiliary Territorial Service, which would become the Women's Royal Army Corps after the war.

B1A: The section of MI5 which controlled German spies in Britain.

CAM: Catapult Aircraft Merchantman.

COSSAC: Chief of Staff, Supreme Allied Commander.

CSM: Committee for Special Means, the department in SHAEF dealing with deception. This was also called Ops.B.

DEMS: Defensively Equipped Merchant Ship.

D Force, Far East: Peter Fleming's deception organisation in the Far East Theatre.

DMI: Director Military Intelligence.

EEF: Egyptian Expeditionary Force in the First World War.

E Group: organisation for evacuating air crew from behind Japanese lines.

Force 136: SOE in the Far East.

FUSAG: First United States Army Group.

GOR: Gunnery Operations Room.

GSIA: General Staff Intelligence Army.

GSI (d): the section of General Staff Intelligence which became D Division in March 1944.

GSO: General Staff Officer.

ISLD: Inter Service Liaison Department.

ISSB: Inter Services Security Board.

JPS: Joint Planning Staff.

JSC: the American Joint Security Council.

Kempei Tai: Japanese Military Police.

K sites: simple decoy airfields, developed by Colonel Turner's department.

LCS: London Controlling Section.

LCT: Landing Craft, Tank.

LCVP: small assault craft.

LMF: RAF term for lack of moral fibre in shell-shocked troops.

LST: Landing Ship Tank.

MI5: the British counter-intelligence and security organisation.

MI6: the British espionage service.

MI10: a department of Military Intelligence responsible for collection of technical information relating to enemy equipment etc.

MO4: sabotage and deception department in Cairo.

OCTU: Officer Cadet Training Unit.

Ops.B, Shaef: See CSM, the department in SHAEF dealing with deception.

OSS: Office of Strategic Services, the American department of intelligence and secret operations.

OWI: the American Office of War Information, dealing with political warfare.

PUT: Pilot under Training.

PWE: the British Political Warfare Executive.

Q sites: elaborate decoy airfields situated between 1800 and 3000 yards away from the real airfield.

RAST: Royal Army Supplies and Transport.

REME: Royal Electrical and Mechanical Engineers.

RE: Royal Engineers.

R Force: the deception organisation at Montgomery's headquarters in the months before D Day and beyond.

RMA: Royal Military Academy.

RTC: Royal Tank Company.

SAS: Special Air Service.

SBS: Special Boat Service.

SHAEF: Supreme Headquarters, Allied Expeditionary Force.

Sigint: Signals Intelligence.

SIME: Security Intelligence, Middle East.

SLU: Special Liaison Units, formed to co-operate with Ultra Intelligence and to protect it.

SOE: Special Operations Executive, also known as Force 136 in the Far East.

TAC R: Tactical reconnaissance.

Ultra: codename for the decrypts of German wireless traffic, enciphered by the German Enigma system.

XX Committee: the Twenty or Double Cross Committee responsible for overall policy in connection with employment of double agents.

Y: The interception and analysis of enemy wireless traffic in low and medium grade codes and cyphers.

NOTES

PROLOGUE

1   *The Brutal Friendship*. Sir W. Deakin. Weidenfeld and Nicolson, pp. 350–6, cited in 'Intelligence and National Security', Vol. 3, January 1988, No. 7.

2   *The Great War*. Winston Churchill. George Newnes, Vol. 1, p.498. (N.B. Churchill is writing here about the First World War.)

3   *The Camouflage Story*. Geoffrey Barkas. Cassell 1952, p.216.

4   Cited in *On the Psychology of Military Incompetence*. Norman F. Dixon. Jonathan Cape, p.17.

5   Ibid.

6   *Hitler's Table Talk*. Edited by Hugh Trevor Roper. OUP Paperback, p.93.

7   *Strategic and Operational Deception in the Second World War*. Edited by Michael Handel. Frank Cass 1987, p.31.

8   *Bodyguard of Lies*. Anthony Cave Brown. W.H. Allen Paperback 1986, p.46.

9   *The Deception Planners*. Dennis Wheatley. Hutchinson 1980, pp.19–20.

10   Quoted in *Master of Deception*. David Mure. William Kimber 1980, p.83, from a letter written by Dudley Clarke himself to Peter Fleming.

11   *Deception in the Second World War*. Charles Cruickshank. Enlarged OUP edition 1981, p.19.

12   Cruickshank, op.cit. p.46.

13   Ibid. p.33.

14   Handel, op.cit. p.2.
15   By far the best description of this is Christopher Andrew's *Secret Service, The Making of the British Intelligence Community*. Heinemann 1985.
16   Quoted in *Fortitude: A History of Deception in North Western Europe, April 1943 to May 1945*. The so-called Hesketh Report — Preface. Unpublished.
17   Wheatley, op.cit. p.57.
18   Cited in Wheatley, op.cit. p.221, from a copy of a minute dated 11 October 1944 from the Secretary, Chiefs of Staff Committee to London Controlling Officer.
19   Ibid. p.58.
20   Ibid. p.189.
21   Cave Brown, op.cit. p.273.
22   *Ultra Goes to War*. Ronald Lewin. Hutchinson 1978, p.301.
23   Mure Papers, Imperial War Museum.
24   Lewin, op.cit. p.20.
25   Ibid. p.17.
26   *The Double Cross System*. J. C. Masterman. Yale University Press, p.xii.
27   Handel, op. cit. p.22.
28   Masterman, op.cit.
29   Mure, op.cit. p.274.
30   *The Fall of Fortress Europe, 1943–1945*. Albert Seaton. B. T. Batsford 1981, *passim*.
31   See the Agents' Tale p.183.
32   Cruickshank, op.cit. p.60.
33   *British Intelligence in the Second World War*. F. H. Hinsley, E. E. Thomas, C. A. G. Simkins, C. F. G. Ransom. HMSO 1988, Vol. 3, Part 2, p.46.
34   Ibid. p.48.
35   Hesketh, op.cit. Preface.
36   Masterman, op. cit. pp. 157–8.
37   Cave Brown, op. cit. p.687.

CHAPTER 1
1   Handel, op. cit. *passim*.
2   Wheatley, op.cit. p.85.
3   Ibid. p.86. There is a small discrepancy here between Wheatley and Strangeways. Wheatley remembers the book as having been planted to be discovered in Gibraltar. Strangeways stayed with Gort in Gibraltar and thinks that it was more likely that the plan

was intended for the hotels in Cairo.

4   Cruickshank, op.cit. p.19.

5   See the Tank Builder's Tale p.103.

6   General Richardson who also fought in North Africa and was closely involved in planning the deception for El Alamein tells his story on p.68.

7   Wheatley, op.cit. p.87.

8   See Prologue p.3–4.

9   Hinsley et al., op.cit. pp.46–7.

10   See the Sound Men's Tales p.87.

11   See Stan Perkins' interview and others p.122f for descriptions of night lighting and decoy work.

12   David Strangeways did later become head of the Rhine Intelligence Liaison Section after R Force and G(R) folded up.

13   See the Scriptwriter's Tale p.98.

14   See the Sailor's Tale p.108.

15   See the Intelligence Colonel's Tale p.53.

16   See the Neighbour's Tale p.49.

CHAPTER 3

1   Handel et al., op.cit., quoting T. L. Cubbage, an Intelligence analyst in the Pentagon after the Vietnam War.

2   Lewin, op.cit. p.125.

3   Ibid. p.138.

4   Ibid. p.140.

5   Handel, op.cit. p.66.

6   Maunsell Papers, Imperial War Museum.

7   See Prologue p.24.

8   Lewin, op.cit. p.288.

9   Ibid.

CHAPTER 4

1   *The Memoirs of Field Marshal Montgomery.* Collins 1958, pp.121, 122.

CHAPTER 6

1   See Prologue p.4.

2   Barkas. Most Secret paper. WO 201/2649.

3   Clarke paper. WO 201/2649 87237.

4   See the Historian's Tale p.75.

5   Leopold Canal; Elst; crossing the Rhine.

CHAPTER 7
1   See the Canon's Tale p.33.

CHAPTER 8
1   From General Wavell's Introduction in Dudley Clarke's book, *Seven Assignments*. Jonathan Cape 1948, p.7.
2   *Masquerade*. Seymour Reit. Hawthorn Books, New York, 1948, pp.135–6.
3   See the Canon's Tale *passim*.
4   See the Seamstress's Tale p.146.

CHAPTER 9
1   See The Canon's Tale p.33.

CHAPTER 11
1   Reit, op. cit. p.52
2   See the Illusionists' Tales p.122.
3   Reit, op.cit. p.59.
4   *Encyclopaedia Brittanica*, Vol. 4, p.709.

CHAPTER 15
1   See pp.11–12 for description of Dudley Clarke.

CHAPTER 16
1   See double-agent John Moe's recollection of a similar incident p.194.

CHAPTER 19
1   See Prologue p.15.
2   Lewin, op.cit. p.301.
3   See the Brigadier's Tale p.204, the Pilot's Tale p.211 and Prologue pp.21–25.
4   See Prologue about Michael Howard's Official History, p.2.

CHAPTER 21
1   Lewin, op.cit. p.351.
2   See the Historian's Tale p.75 and the Actor's Tale p.165.
3   See the Pilot's Tale p.211.

CHAPTER 22
1   See the Plasterer's Tale, p.117.
2   Hinsley et al., op.cit. p. 289.

CHAPTER 23
1 *Peter Fleming*. Duff Hart Davies. OUP Paperback, p.258.
2 Ibid. p. 263.
3 Ibid. p.265.
4 Handel, op.cit. p.6.
5 See the Intelligence Colonel's Tale p.53.
6 Handel, op.cit. p.8.
7 Cruickshank, op.cit. p.216.
8 Hart Davies, op.cit. p. 269.

CHAPTER 24
1 *Have you met Mariam?* Tan Sri Ibrahim Bin Ismael. Johor Bahru, Malaysia, 1984.
2 Cruickshank, op.cit. p.217.
3 See the Brigadier's Tale p.204.
4 Hart Davies, op.cit. p.280.
5 Cruickshank, op.cit. p.218.

EPILOGUE
1 Cited in Handel et al., op.cit. p.88, from a letter written to Major General Lowell Brooks.
2 Ibid. p.89.
3 Professor Klaus Jurgen Muller in Handel et al., op.cit., in *A German Perception on Allied Deception Operations in World War Two*, pp.301–326.
4 Hesketh, op.cit. Preface.
5 Ibid. p.176.
6 Ibid. p.171.
7 Masterman, op.cit. p.158.
8 Ibid. *passim.*
9 *Ultra Goes to War*. Ronald Lewin.
10 Lewin, op.cit. p.182.
11 Ibid. p.307.
12 Ibid. p.310.
13 Hesketh, op.cit. p.172.
14 Ibid. p.177.
15 Hinsley et. al., op.cit. p.49.
16 Hesketh, op.cit. p.176.
17 Reit, op. cit. p.47, quoting Omar Bradley, *A Soldier's Story*, Henry Holt, New York 1951, p.344.
18 Cited in Cruickshank, op.cit. p.244, from RG 319 Records of the Army Staff G-3 Cover and Deception: Folder 1.

SELECT BIBLIOGRAPHY

Andrew, Christopher: *Secret Service: The Making of the British Intelligence Community*. Heinemann, 1985.

Arnold Foster, Mark: *The World at War*. Collins, 1973.

Barkas, Geoffrey: *The Camouflage Story*. Cassell, 1952.

Barnett, Corelli: *The Audit of War*. Macmillan London, 1987.

Calvocoressi, Peter: *Top Secret Ultra*. Cassell, 1980.

Cave Brown, Anthony: *Bodyguard of Lies*. W. H. Allen & Co., 1976.

Charmley, John: *Duff Cooper, The Authorised Biography*. Weidenfeld & Nicholson, 1986.

Churchill, Winston: *The Great War*. 3 volumes, George Newnes, 1933.

Clarke, Dudley: *Seven Assignments*. Jonathan Cape, 1948. London.

Cooper, Duff: *Operation Heartbreak*. 1950 Publisher?

Cruickshank, Charles: *Deception in World War Two*. OUP, 1979.

Deakin, Sir W: *The Brutal Friendship, Mussolini's Last Years*. Weidenfeld & Nicholson, 1962.

Delmer, Sefton: *Black Boomerang*. Viking, 1962. *The Counterfeit Spy*. Harper and Row, 1971.

Dixon, Norman F: *On the Psychology of Military Incompetence*. Jonathan Cape, 1976.

Handel, Michael: Editor, *Strategic and Operational Deception in World War Two*. Frank Cass, 1987.

Hart Davies, Duff: *Peter Fleming*. OUP Paperback, 1987.

Hesketh, Roger F: *Fortitude: A History of Strategic Deception in North Western Europe April 1943 to May 1945*. Unpublished.

Hinsley, F. H. et al: *British Intelligence in the Second World War*. Volumes 1–3, parts 1 & 2. HMSO.

Howard, Michael: *Clausewitz*. Oxford University Press paperback, 1983.

Ibrahim Bin Ismael, Tan Sri: *Have you met Mariam?* Johor Bahru, Malaysia, 1984.

Ismay: *The Memoirs of Lord*. Heinemann 1960.

James, Clifton: *I Was Monty's Double*. Rider, 1954.

Jones, R. V: *Most Secret War, British Scientific Intelligence, 1939–45*. Hamish Hamilton Ltd., 1978.

Lewin, Ronald: *Ultra Goes to War*. Hutchinson, 1978.

Masterman, J. C: *The Double Cross System in the War 1939–45*, Yale University Press, 1972.

Maunsell Papers: Imperial War Museum.

Moen, Jan; *John Moe: Double Agent*. Mainstream Publishing 1986.

Montagu, Ewan: *The Man Who Never Was*. Evans, 1966.

 Beyond Top Secret Ultra. Peter Davies, 1977.

 Montgomery, The Memoirs of Field Marshal. Collins, 1958.

Mure, David: *The Deception Planners*. William Kimber & Co., 1977.

 Practice To Deceive. William Kimber, 1980.

O'Brien, Terence: *Out of the Blue*. Collins, 1984.

The Moonlight War, Collins, 1987.

Seaton, Albert: *The Fall of Fortress Europe, 1943–1945*. B. T. Batsford, 1981.

Trevor-Roper, Hugh: *Hitler's Table Talk*: Hitler's conversations recorded by Martin Bormann. OUP paperback, 1988.

West, Nigel: *GCHQ: The Secret Wireless War, 1900–1986*. Weidenfeld & Nicholson, 1986.

Wheatley, Denis: *The Deception Planners*. Hutchinson & Co. London, 1980.

Winterbotham, F. W: *The Ultra Secret*. Harper & Row, 1974.

INDEX

251